Ulrich Flegel   Danilo Bruschi (I

T0237952

Detection of Intrusions and Malware, and Vulnerability Assessment

6th International Conference, DIMVA 2009
Como, Italy, July 9-10, 2009
Proceedings

 Springer

Volume Editors

Ulrich Flegel
SAP Research Center Karlsruhe
Karlsruhe, Germany
E-mail: ulrich.flegel@sap.com

Danilo Bruschi
Università degli Studi di Milano
Dipartimento di Informatica e Comunicazione
Milano, Italy
E-mail: bruschi@dico.unimi.it

Library of Congress Control Number: Applied for

CR Subject Classification (1998): E.3, K.6.5, K.4, C.2, D.4.6

LNCS Sublibrary: SL 4 – Security and Cryptology

ISSN   0302-9743
ISBN-10   3-642-02917-5 Springer Berlin Heidelberg New York
ISBN-13   978-3-642-02917-2 Springer Berlin Heidelberg New York

springer.com

© Springer-Verlag Berlin Heidelberg 2009
Printed in Germany

Typesetting: Camera-ready by author, data conversion by Scientific Publishing Services, Chennai, India
Printed on acid-free paper   SPIN: 12716173   06/3180   5 4 3 2 1 0

Lecture Notes in Computer Science 5587

Commenced Publication in 1973
Founding and Former Series Editors:
Gerhard Goos, Juris Hartmanis, and Jan van Leeuwen

Preface

On behalf of the Program Committee, it is our pleasure to present the proceedings of the 6th GI International Conference on Detection of Intrusions and Malware, and Vulnerability Assessment (DIMVA).

Since 2004, DIMVA annually brings together leading researchers and practitioners from academia, government and industry to present and discuss novel security research. DIMVA is organized by the Special Interest Group *Security—Intrusion Detection and Response* (SIDAR)—of the German Informatics Society (GI).

The DIMVA 2009 Program Committee received 44 submissions from industrial and academic organizations from 17 different countries. Each submission was carefully reviewed by at least three Program Committee members or external experts. The submissions were evaluated on the basis of scientific novelty, importance to the field and technical quality. The final selection took place at the Program Committee meeting held on March 23, 2009, in Brussels, Belgium. Ten full papers and three extended abstracts were selected for presentation and publication in the conference proceedings.

The conference took place during July 9–10, 2009, at Villa Gallia, Lake Como, Italy, with the program grouped into five sessions. Two keynote speeches were presented by Richard A. Kemmerer (University of California, Santa Barbara) and Henry Stern (Ironport / Cisco). The conference program was complemented by the Capture-the-Flag contest CIPHER (Challenges in Informatics: Programming, Hosting and ExploRing) organized by Lexi Pimenidis (iDev GmbH) and a rump session organized by Sven Dietrich (Stevens Institute of Technology).

A successful conference is the result of the joint effort of many people. In particular, we would like to thank all the authors who submitted contributions. We also thank the Program Committee members and the additional reviewers for their hard work and diligent evaluation of the submissions. In addition we thank Thorsten Holz (University of Mannheim) for sponsor arrangements and Sebastian Schmerl (Technical University of Cottbus) for advertising the conference.

July 2009

Ulrich Flegel
Danilo Bruschi

Organization

DIMVA was organized by the Special Interest Group *Security – Intrusion Detection and Response* (SIDAR)—of the German Informatics Society (GI).

Organizing Committee

General Chair	Danilo M. Bruschi, Università degli Studi di Milano, Italy
Program Chair	Ulrich Flegel, SAP Research
Rump Session Chair	Sven Dietrich, Stevens Institute of Technology, USA
Sponsorship Chair	Thorsten Holz, University of Mannheim, Germany
Publicity Chair	Sebastian Schmerl, Technical University of Cottbus, Germany

Program Committee

Thomas Biege	Novell, Germany
Gunter Bitz	SAP AG, Germany
Herbert Bos	Vrije Universiteit Amsterdam, The Netherlands
Danilo Bruschi	Università degli Studi di Milano, Italy
Roland Büschkes	RWE IT, Germany
Marc Dacier	Symantec Research Labs Europe, France
Hervé Debar	France Télécom R&D, France
Sven Dietrich	Stevens Institute of Technology, USA
Toralv Dirro	McAfee Avert Labs, Germany
Thomas Dullien	Zynamics, Germany
Bernhard Hämmerli	Acris GmbH and HSLU Lucerne, Switzerland
Marc Heuse	Baseline Security Consulting, Germany
Thorsten Holz	University of Mannheim, Germany
Erland Jonsson	Chalmers University of Technology, Sweden
Klaus Julisch	IBM Zurich Research Laboratory, Switzerland
Engin Kirda	Eurecom, France
Christian Kreibich	International Computer Science Institute, USA
Christopher Kruegel	UC Santa Barbara, USA
Pavel Laskov	University of Tuebingen, Germany
Wenke Lee	Georgia Institute of Technology, USA
Javier Lopez	University of Malaga, Spain

John McHugh	UNC and Dalhousie University, Canada
Michael Meier	Technical University of Dortmund, Germany
George Mohay	Queensland University of Technology, Australia
Martin Rehák	Czech Technical University in Prague, Czech Republic
Konrad Rieck	Berlin Institute of Technology, Germany
Sebastian Schmerl	BTU-Cottbus, Germany
Robin Sommer	ICSI/LBNL, USA
Salvatore Stolfo	Columbia University, USA
Peter Szor	Symantec Corporation, USA
Bernhard Thurm	SAP Research, Germany
Al Valdes	SRI International, USA

Additional Reviewers

Martin Apel	Christian Gehl	Lorenzo Martignoni
Marco Balduzzi	Cristian Grozea	Tomas Olovsson
Ulrich Bayer	Grégoire Jacob	Emanuele Passerini
Armin Büscher	Wolfgang John	Pratap Prabhu
Patrick Duessel	Matthias Kohler	Guido Schwenk
Manuel Egele	Tammo Krueger	Asia Slowinska

Steering Committee

Chairs	Ulrich Flegel, SAP Research
	Michael Meier, Technical University of Dortmund, Germany
Members	Roland Büschkes, RWE IT
	Hervé Debar, France Télécom R & D, France
	Bernhard Hämmerli, Acris GmbH and HSLU Lucerne, Switzerland
	Marc Heuse, Baseline Security Consulting
	Klaus Julisch, IBM Zurich Research Lab, Switzerland
	Christopher Kruegel, UC Santa Barbara, USA
	Pavel Laskov, University of Tuebingen, Germany
	Robin Sommer, ICSI/LBNL
	Diego Zamboni, IBM Zurich Research Lab, Switzerland

Table of Contents

Anomaly Detection

A Case Study on Asprox Infection Dynamics

Youngsang Shin[1], Steven Myers[2], and Minaxi Gupta[1]

[1] Computer Science Department,
Indiana University,
Bloomington, Indiana
{shiny,minaxi}@cs.indiana.edu
[2] School of Informatics,
Indiana University,
Bloomington, Indiana
samyers@indiana.edu

Abstract. The Asprox infection weaves a complex chain of dependencies involving bots that perform SQL injections on vulnerable web servers, and visitors whose machines get compromised simply by visiting infected websites. Using real-world data sets, we study Asprox bots, infected web servers, and the malicious infrastructure behind Asprox propagation. We find that the malware-propagation infrastructure in Asprox is aggressively provisioned to resist take-down efforts. This, combined with the easy availability of vulnerable user machines and web servers whose administrators are probably constrained in time and resources necessary to fix the problem, indicates that cleaning up Asprox infections is not going to be easy.

Keywords: Asprox, Malware, SQL Injection, Security.

1 Introduction

The Asprox botnet has been around since 2007. It was initially used exclusively for sending phishing emails. Around May 2008, a new update was pushed to Asprox bots in an attempt to grow the size of the botnet [1]. This update added an SQL injection vector. The updated bots could attack legitimate websites and inject scripts that redirected the browsers of visitors to these sites to infrastructure that cause the drive-by-download of malware. This malware is normally the Asprox botnet itself, but other payloads have been observed. Since the SQL injection vector was added, a significant number of web servers have been attacked and their unsuspecting visitor machines turned into Asprox bots [2] [3].

The Asprox botnet has a multi-step life-cycle, shown in Figure 1. The bots begin by using a search engine, such as Google, to find vulnerable web servers. Specifically, they search for servers that use asp, aspx, or php scripts to dynamically generate web pages from SQL databases. Next, the bots attempt an SQL injection attack on each server. If successful, the injection inserts malicious JavaScripts that invisibly redirects the browsers of visiting machines to malicious infrastructure. The infrastructure is also typically comprised of Asprox bots. Any visitor that browses an SQL-injected web server is at the risk of being infected

U. Flegel and D. Bruschi (Eds.): DIMVA 2009, LNCS 5587, pp. 1–20, 2009.

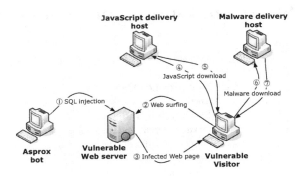

Fig. 1. Components of a typical Asprox infection. 1) A bot performs a successful SQL injection attack on a vulnerable web server. 2) A user visits the attacked server and views infected web pages, causing the download and execution of JavaScript code with `<script>` tags. 3-4) The (hidden) JavaScript invisibly directs the user's browser to a malicious host by exploiting `<iframe>` tags. 5) JavaScript of the malicious host scans the visitor's machine for vulnerabilities in the browser and OS, and redirects accordingly to potentially yet another final malicious site. 6-7) The final malicious site launches a drive-by-download that takes specific advantage of the vulnerability discovered in Step 5.

with Asprox malware, with infection ultimately depending on whether or not the visitor's system is vulnerable to the attacks targeted by the drive-by-download. If the drive-by-download is successful, the typical payload includes—at the very least—the Asprox bot code. The life-cycle is complete, and ready to repeat.

As with all botnets, there are many types of harm and fraud that can be committed with Asprox. We have directly observed it being used to commit fraud through traditional phishing activities and fake virus protection scams. However, what makes Asprox interesting to study is both the multi-stage infection techniques it uses to spread, and the counter-countermeasures it uses to defend itself from take-down and detection attempts. Examples of such techniques include fast flux and JavaScript obfuscation.

Goals of the Study: In this paper, we analyze Asprox from three perspectives. First, we study the beginning of Asprox life-cycle by looking at the bots that were attempting to perform SQL injection on the web servers at Indiana University. Second, we study the extent to which the SQL injection attack is successful on a global population of web servers, and how long the infection persists by directly searching for infected servers on the Web. Finally, we study the defensive posture of the infrastructure responsible for scanning for vulnerabilities and delivering malicious content to machines whose browsers are redirected due to successful SQL injections. We also consider how it is provisioned to resist take-down attempts. Our study offers a unique perspective on the Asprox infection, a perspective that would not be possible through passive data collections techniques, such as honeypots.

Key Observations: We make several observations about the Asprox infection from our data: Though Asprox is a global phenomenon, over one third of the Asprox bots that were detected injecting SQL into vulnerable web servers were physically located in China. Yet only 5% of the SQL-injected web servers we found were located in China. Additionally, the the majority of the infrastructure that hosted the malicious JavaScripts and drive-by-downloads was located in the USA. This suggests that the botmasters are actively partitioning their infrastructure along technical, geographic or jurisdictional boundaries.

The Asprox bots exhibited activity patterns that strongly suggested that many of them were residential machines. Miscreants also seemed to rotate the bots, we hypothesize this is to prevent them from being sterilized by blacklisting of the bots. Our data did not contain any popular web servers (as defined by the Alexa data set [4]), indicating that those are either better secured or are quickly cleaned when SQL injections are found. A number of high-profile sites that garnered media attention when they were found to be infected suggest that it might be the latter case, more than the former. Unfortunately, we measured that over 1/4 of the infected web servers in our data set continued to host SQL-injected pages for over 100 days, and many of them are likely still hosting the injection! The remaining 3/4 of the sites were cleaned, but 60% of these took over a month to be cleaned. This clearly points to the need for either better awareness and/or resources for the operators of these servers. We note we cannot definitively say if the sites remain uncleaned for so long because the administrators are not aware of the injection, or if it is because they lack the tools to easily clean their databases.

Finally, we found that 58% of the hosts that delivered malicious JavaScripts were provisioned using *fast flux* to actively resist take-down efforts.

Roadmap: The remainder is organized as follows: Section 2 describes the data collection; Section 3 presents our analysis of Asprox infection dynamics; related work is discussed in Section 4; and Section 5 concludes the paper.

2   Data Collection and Overview

We collected three types of data for analysis. The first data set contains a network log of the Asprox bots that tried to launch numerous SQL injection attacks on various Indiana University web servers in August of 2008. The second data set contains the URLs of the infrastructure that delivered the malicious JavaScript. The last data set contains information gathered about infected web servers, and how quickly they were cleaned, if at all. Although the first two data sets play different roles in the Asprox infection process, we believe that they are in the same Asprox botnet. This is because even though we gathered the two data sets over different time periods and from different sources, we actually saw 8 common IP addresses in those two data sets. This is a small overlap, but it implies that infected machines can act as either SQL injection attackers, or as JavaScript/drive-by-download hosts. In the following subsections we describe them and their collection method in a detail.

2.1   Data on Asprox Bots

The first data set contains the IP addresses and time stamps of the Asprox bots
that launched SQL injection attacks on various Indiana University web servers
in August 2008. The attacks were filtered via a router's firewall by looking for
an Asprox SQL injection-specific string [5]. The attacks peaked in August 2008
causing massive amounts of unwanted traffic for the university. Table 1 shows
the overview of this data set.

Table 1. Asprox bots and their targets

Collection period	8/9/2008 - 8/25/2008
Unique IP addresses of attacking bots	57,419
Autonomous systems attackers belonged to	1,847
Web servers targeted	581

Figure 2 depicts the geographical distribution of the IP addresses of the Asprox bots in our data. Though most of the bots belonged to North America,
Europe, or East Asia, they cover much of the globe. *China had the largest number of Asprox bots; accounting for 36.68% of the attackers.* No other country
accounted for more than 8% of the bots.

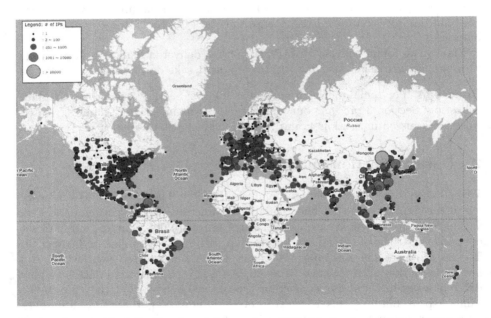

Fig. 2. Geographical distribution of Asprox bots (IP addresses) performing SQL injection attacks on Indiana University web servers (August 2008). Icon size is proportional
to the number of attackers (IP addresses) in that location.

2.2   Data on JavaScript-Delivery Hosts

The second data set consists of URLs of the malicious infrastructure that delivered the malicious JavaScript and drive-by-downloads, and meta information about servers provisioning the domains related to such URLs. We refer to the hosts of theses URLs as *JavaScript-delivery hosts* throughout this paper. These URLs were collected from [6], which has been tracking such URLs since the 5th of May, 2008.[1] On average, the site posted two new URLs each day. From October 2008 to the end of January 2009, we monitored all of the URLs that had previously appeared on [6], or that were newly added. (The attack continues but [6] stopped reporting new URLs on 11/26/08.)

Table 2. Overview of JavaScript-delivery URLs and host names

Collection period	10/26/2008 - 1/31/2009
Number of URLs	373
TLDs	13
gTLDs	5 (.com, .mobi, .net, .org, .name)
ccTLDs	8 (.ru, .cn, .jp, .cc, .tk, .kz, .eu, .me)
Unique host names	324
with gTLDs	151 (.com: 105, .name: 28, .mobi: 11, .net: 4, .org: 3)
with ccTLDs	173 (.ru: 127, .cn: 34, .jp: 4, .cc: 4, .tk: 1, .kz: 1, .eu: 1, .me: 1)

Table 2 breaks down the 373 URLs that were observed into different top level domains (TLDs), both generic (gTLD) and country-code TLD (ccTLD). The most popular TLDs for JavaScript-delivery hosts are .com and .ru.

To learn about how the JavaScript-delivery were provisioned, we collected metadata on the URLs. Specifically, DNS lookups were performed to obtain the IP address(es) of each host. We also periodically looked up the DNS servers used by these hosts in each level of the DNS hierarchy. For each of the IP addresses corresponding to the host name discovered in the A records[2] and each of their DNS servers (on all levels) we looked up their geographic location using the IP2Location software [7]. The lookups were performed every 15 minutes, until the host was no longer alive. We chose the 15-minute granularity to strike a balance between the validity of retrieved DNS records, which is typically no more than 5 minutes, and the overhead on our institution's DNS resolver.

Table 3 provides an overview of the data obtained from our DNS resolutions and geolocation for the JavaScript-delivery hosts. Of the 324 hosts that delivered malicious JavaScripts, we could resolve only 55. This is because when we began data collection in October 2008, many of the older URLs posted on [6] were already inactive. The 55 resolved names yielded 2,214 unique IP addresses over

---

[1] We initially were collecting such data ourselves, but were forced to abandon this direction due to University requirement that we disconnect our infected bots.

[2] An A record is a DNS resource record used for storing an IP address associated with a domain name.

Table 3. Data collected through DNS resolutions of JavaScript-delivery hosts

(a)   JavaScript-delivery hosts

Resolved host names	55
IP addresses	2,214
Autonomous systems	308
BGP prefixes	898
Countries	64

(b) DNS servers for JavaScript-delivery hosts

Resolved DNS server names	619
IP addresses	147
Autonomous systems	67
BGP prefixes	115
Countries	11

our entire monitoring period for the DNS resolutions. *Interestingly, while more than 1/3 of the Asprox bots were located in China, 2/3 of the JavaScript-delivery hosts were located in the US.* Similar findings that say that the primary malware-serving infrastructure is located in the US have been reported in other botnet studies as well [8]. Our data set has fewer IP addresses than DNS server host names. This is because several DNS server host names resolve to the same IP address. Although a relatively small number of IP addresses are used to host DNS servers, they are distributed over different networks according to their ASN, BGP prefix, and country information, to make detection and take-down difficult.

2.3   Data on Infected Web Servers

Our third data set gathers information about web servers that were affected by the SQL injection attacks. To collect this data set we searched for web pages that contained the URLs pointing to the malicious JavaScript hosts listed in the second data set. We automated this search by using the Google AJAX Web Search API [9] and Yahoo! Web Search API [10]. Both APIs are limited: i) The Google API returns at most 64 results per query; and ii) The Yahoo! API limits each querier's IP address to 1000 queries per day, but, unlike Google, there is no limit on the number of returned results per query. We invoked both of types of search APIs, using the malicious URLs as query keywords, and merged the returned results.

The result of these searches was a set of URLs from potentially-SQL injected[3] web servers around the world. For each URL, we first extracted the cached pages from both Google and Yahoo!, and the date the cache was made. Next, we visited the URLs. Each visit could *fail or succeed*. A *failure* result could be due to either the unavailability of the web server or the page. Specifically, a page may be

---

[3] Some web sites introduce Asprox and provide some of the URLs as an example, not as actual JavaScript embedding. Furthermore, Google or Yahoo search presents a few false positives that do not actually have URLs which we specify as keywords. Thus, we need to verify the infection of the web servers returned from Google or Yahoo search.

unavailable because the page was dynamically generated and is no longer valid. In contrast, *success* denotes that the requested page was returned.

If a page's cache has the SQL injection, but our subsequent visit to the URL results in a failure, we cannot be sure if the server is still infected. Therefore, we classify such servers as *infected but unreachable*. For cases in which the visit succeeds, the retrieved page may be clean or infected (i.e., it does or does not respectively contain an SQL-injection of the given URL). When clean, we cannot be certain that the server or page was ever infected. To verify, we again turn to the cached page and only if the cached page confirms the presence of an infection do we consider the server to be infected. In this case we can deduce that the server was cleaned some time before our data collection, but after the page was cached. This case is labeled *infected, reachable, but undecidable* in Table 4. Finally, only in cases when the visit succeeds and the retrieved page contains the offending URL can we determine the duration for which the infection persisted with a high degree of accuracy. This case represents 56% of all the servers we examined. They are labeled *infected, reachable, and identifiable* in Table 4.

Table 4. Web servers infected by Asprox for a data collection period between 11/01/2008 - 01/31/2009

Class	# of Servers	% of Servers
Total number of infected web servers	8926	100%
Infected but unreachable	2751	30.82%
Infected, reachable, but undecidable	1141	12.78%
Infected, reachable, and identifiable	5034	56.40%

2.4   Limitations of Our Data Sets

There are a few limitations to our data sets. The first is our inability to comment on how many and which bots compromised which web servers. The Asprox bots in our first data set are not necessarily the ones that compromised the web servers we studied. Getting data from servers that knew they were under attack is difficult due to either an unwillingness to share the data, or a lack of data from the organization that ran these servers – they may not be collecting at the time of the attack, or they may be unaware that they were being attacked. Our second limitation is that our data on Asprox bots performing SQL injection attacks is only for the massive August 2008 attack on Indiana University web servers. This precludes studying attacker evolution. The third limitation stems from the inability to guarantee that there may have been other JavaScript-delivery hosts during our data collection period that were not reported by [6]. The fourth limitation is that we do not have data to understand how and when the JavaScript-delivery hosts redirected visitors to malware-delivery sites. Doing so would have required us to execute the malicious JavaScript and visit the malware-delivery infrastructure. Unfortunately, this limitation is a direct result of our University's policy preventing us from knowingly installing malware and then doing the traversals necessary to collect this data set. Finally, our data on infected web servers is limited by the Google and Yahoo! Web search APIs that only permitted us to collect a subset of the highest ranked search results. And those results were only in the English-dominated regions of the Web.[4] **In spite of all the limitations, we believe our data allows us to gain important insights into the Asprox infection.**

3   Analysis of Asprox Infection Dynamics

We now analyze each data set described in Section 2 to understand the dynamics of Asprox infections.

3.1   Analysis of Asprox Bots

Figure 3 shows the numbers of unique SQL-injection attackers and the web servers they target on each day for which we have data (August 2009). One trend is clear: *The number of attacking bots is lesser on weekdays than weekends.* This comes as no surprise as this has been previously observed in other botnets, and is an artifact of the fact that many bots are residential machines which are likely to be available for longer on the weekends than weekdays. Correspondingly, the total number of attacks launched on the weekends are also higher than those on the weekdays. Further, the number of web servers attacked is also higher on the weekends than weekdays, as expected.

Next, we look at bot reuse. Figure 4 shows how many new attacking bots are observed each day and how they compare with those seen the day before or even prior. *Clearly, new bots are added to the pool as the week progresses, with peaks on Saturdays. Furthermore, some modest number of bots (up to 3000) are being reused. The change in the number of daily reused ones also follows that of new ones. This explains why more bots are observed on the weekends.*

To study in detail the differential between the behavior of Asprox bots on weekends versus weekdays, we picked a representative day from each. Figure 5 shows the number of attacks on these representative days broken down for every hour. (We normalized the time of attack in our data based on *attacker's time zone (based on IP address)* in this figure, and not the time zone of the attacked.) *On the weekday, the attacks peak at three times, 10am, 5pm, and 8:30pm.* These peaks roughly correspond to the start and end of the work day, and an early evening period after dinner. On weekends there is a more uniform distribution of attack times corroborating the lack of synchronization among users' schedules outside of the work week.

We also looked at the active lifetime of attacking bots. Figure 6a shows both how many days of the SQL injection attack at Indiana University a specific attacker was seen, and for how long a given Indiana University web server was

---

[4] We did not attempt to increase the probability that web pages based on other language were returned in our searches by explicitly choosing a language other than English as a search selection option in the Google or Yahoo search API.

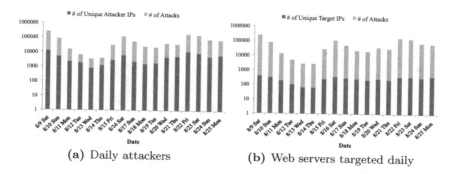

(a) Daily attackers   (b) Web servers targeted daily

Fig. 3. Attackers' and targets' daily numbers

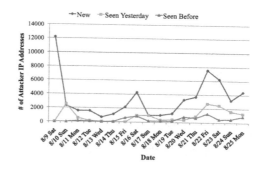

Fig. 4. New and old Asprox bots observed on a daily basis

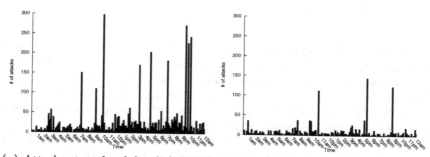

(a) Attacks at weekend day (8/9/2008)   (b) Attacks at weekday (8/20/2008)

Fig. 5. Peak attack times on a weekend and a weekday. Times are normalized based on attacker's time zone.

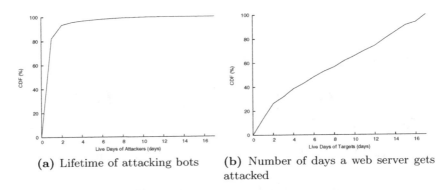

(a) Lifetime of attacking bots   **(b)** Number of days a web server gets attacked

Fig. 6. Attacker lifetime and the duration for which web servers face attacks

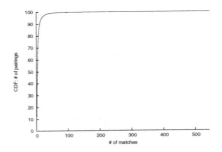

Fig. 7. Repeat attacks on Indiana University web servers by Asprox bots. The number of matches indicates how many times the same attacker attacks the same target. The number of pairings represents how many such a pair of an attacker and a target with the specific number of occurrences exists.

attacked. *Roughly 95% of attacking bots were observed for less than 2 days.* We hypothesize that this is to avoid any IP blacklisting. On the other hand, over 50% of web servers were continuously attacked for over 8 days. This seems to imply that the attackers are not systematic about avoiding repeat attacks on web servers – as they replace bots, the newer bots continue to attack servers that proved to be not vulnerable in the past.

Finally, we looked at the number of times an attacker repeatedly attacked any given target in Figure 7. *We find that 90% of the bots attacked the same web server about 10 times. In fact, in some cases one attacker hit the same target over 500 times.* Clearly, the Asprox bots are not synchronizing among themselves in choosing who they attack, nor keeping any individual state information on whom they have already attacked. This suggests that the bots independently search for web servers serving `asp`, `aspx`, and `php` pages and blindly attack the returned list. We cannot definitively say if the same machines that perform the web-searches are those that launch the SQL injection attacks, or if one set of bots queries and passes lists off to another set of attackers. However, given the apparent lack of coordinate we hypothesize that they are the same. This would then explain the high frequency of attacks on some web servers. Additionally and/or alternately, since search engines are likely to index many pages from the same web server, the server gets targeted again and again.

3.2   Analysis of Infected Web Servers

An SQL injection attack is successful only if people visit the websites with infected pages. To see how often popular web servers get infected, we cross-referenced our list of infected web servers with the list of popular web servers reported by the Alexa [4]. There were no matches, confirming that the popular web servers are either better secured or quickly cleaned when successfully attacked. This certainly does not imply that the attackers do not target popular web servers. For example, there are confirmed attacks against Sony's Playstation website [11]. Further, when looking at which web servers were targeted most often in our Asprox-bot data, we found that the two most popular web servers at Indiana University were those most frequently targeted in the attack. This, of course, also makes sense when we remember the targets are chosen based on the results of search engine queries, which generally put some emphasis in ordering based on popularity of the site.

Recall from Section 2.3, that of the 8,926 web servers we confirmed to have been infected at some point of time, 31% were unreachable. Another 13% were reachable and had been cleaned but not enough information was available to precisely lower-bound when they were cleaned up. For the rest of the 56% of the infected servers that were also reachable, we had sufficient data to estimate *lower bounds* on how long the servers stayed infected. Table 5 shows the TLDs these 56% web servers belonged to. As expected, .com was the TLD with most of the infected servers, claiming almost half of the positions. Other TLDs with more than a hundred infected web servers include: .pl (Poland), .net, .org, .cn (China), .kr (Korea) and .uk (United Kingdom). The infected servers belong to 6 other gTLDs and 87 other ccTLDs, confirming that the Asprox infection is truly a global epidemic.

The 5,034 web servers reported in Table 5 were all victim to SQL injection because when we first retrieved their URLs found through Google and Yahoo! web searches, the URL inserted by SQL injection was still present in those pages. To determine how long the servers would remain SQL-injected, we both retrieved the same pages from Google and Yahoo! caches and retrieved them actively every day throughout our data collection process. When the page's cache date was not available in the cache, which was the case for 54% of the servers, we considered only the infection duration from our active measurements. In either case, both are lower bounds for how long web servers stayed infected, and thus are conservative bounds.

Figure 8 shows the CDF of the servers that were cleaned up. Figure 9 shows the CDF of servers that still contained SQL-injections at the end of our data

Table 5. TLDs of infected web servers that were reachable and whose infection dates could be estimated

TLD	Number of web servers
.com	2307
.pl	341
.net	313
.org	294
.cn	242
.kr	201
.uk	125
Other gTLDs	105
Other ccTLDs	1070
No server name, just IP address	36
Total # of web servers	5034

collection. *Overall, 77% of the servers were cleaned and the rest stayed infected. In fact, it took over a month for 60% of the web servers to be cleaned. Of those, 55% stayed infected for over 100 days!* These observations reveal that the SQL injection component of Asprox is effective for the attackers and damaging to the visitors of these web servers. Because there are no usage statistics on any of the sites, we could not estimate how many browsers might have visited the sites over such a time period.

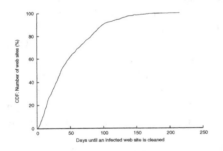

Fig. 8. Duration of infection for web servers whose infection was cleaned within our data collection

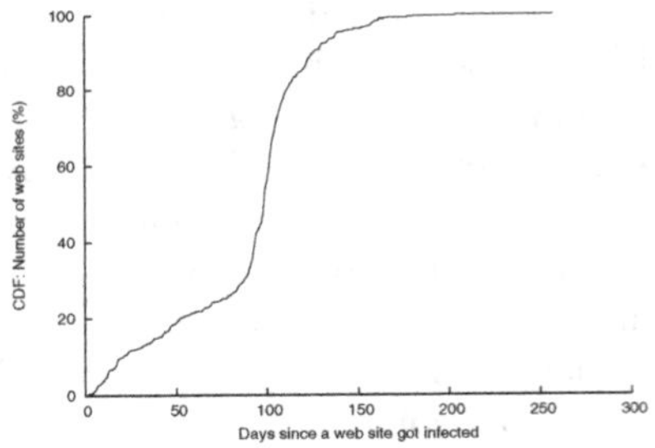

Fig. 9. Status of web servers whose infection persisted till the end of our data collection

3.3   Analysis of JavaScript-Delivery Hosts

We now analyze the infrastructure that serves malicious JavaScripts (and potentially drive-by-downloads) to the unsuspecting visitors of infected web servers. Recall that our data contains the DNS resolutions for JavaScript-delivery hosts that were *live*, including the DNS servers and their IP addresses, and for each level of the DNS hierarchy.

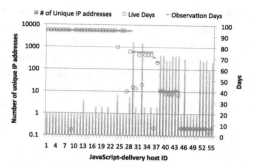

Fig. 10. Number of unique IP addresses and live days for each JavaScript-delivery host. *Live days* is defined as the days when we succeed to do DNS resolution for a host. *Observation days* is the period for which we tried to do a DNS resolution for a host.

We focus on Asprox's use of *fast flux* to provision the infrastructure used to deliver the malicious JavaScript. Fast flux is a recent technique used by attackers to keep their phishing and malware campaigns afloat for longer, and its goal is to prevent take-down and blacklisting. The key idea involved in fast flux is to have the attacker rapidly change the DNS bindings between the host name and its IP address. Two key indicators that fast flux is being used is that in the DNS resolutions of hosts are: 1) Host names resolve to a large number of IP addresses, generally scattered across many domains; and 2) each IP address has a short validity. The large number of IP addresses ensure availability under take-down attempts. The short validity ensures that any subsequent queries for the host name gives the attacker an opportunity to revise the list of IP addresses, should an IP address be taken down, blacklisted, or the supporting bot is shutoff. It is not known if IP addresses are spread across many administrative domains simply due to an artifact of a random subset of the botnet population, or if it results from an active attempt to prevent too many IP addresses under the same domains from coming down.

Fast flux comes in two flavors, which can be used independently or concurrently. The first is when the host itself fluxes. The second is when the DNS servers used to resolve the host name themselves flux. To distinguish the two cases we will term the former as fast flux and the latter as *DNS flux*. When both types of flux are used, we term the case as double flux. The Asprox botnet uses double flux.

Recall, as discussed in Sec. 2.2, that we collected data on the live JavaScript-delivery hosts, including information about their DNS servers. For each host observed, Figure 10 presents the number of unique IP addresses it resolved to through our observations, as well as the number of days each host was up. While phishing servers are often known to be taken down within a few days [12], the Asprox JavaScript-delivery hosts seem to survive for a surprisingly long time.

We note that hosts 1 trough 28 were reported by [6] before we started collecting data. Thus, the fact that most of these hosts had only one IP address over the data collection period suggests that it may be in an artifact of data collection.

In particular, the botnet masters may have given up on using them, due to their detection. We do note that all of these hosts except one are currently blacklisted by Google, as we verified with a Firefox browser. In an attempt to validate the above hypothesis we verified the `whois` information for domains 1 through 28. It was returned for only 7 of them. Two of the seven seem to have been bought by a domain management company. Another two have been created and maintained by two organizations; one of them has even been removed from the blacklists. The remaining 3 hosts had very poor quality `whois` information, which is a common feature for attacker-controlled domains, and so these are likely to be still under the control of Asprox's bot masters. One might question why the Asprox botnet masters would even want to maintain control of these domains, if they do not seem to be used, and they are blacklisted. We hypothesize that they are no longer in use precisely because they are blacklisted, but the masters keep control of the domain in case they are removed from the blacklists. It should of course be noted that any web server that has an SQL injection which points to an inactive host is safe for its legitimate users to visit. Hosts 29 through 55 in Figure 10 were part of the JavaScript-delivery infrastructure during our data collection period. 58% *of these hosts appear to be actively fluxing*. We examine this in more detail next.

To examine the details of fast flux, we use the three *fluxiness* metrics proposed by Holz et al in [13]:

$$F_A = N_A / n_{A\_average\_single} \tag{1}$$

$$F_{NS} = N_{NS} / n_{NS\_average\_single} \tag{2}$$

$$f_{NS_A} = N_{NS_A} / n_{NS_A\_average\_single} \tag{3}$$

$$F_{NS_A} = (\Sigma f_{NS_A}) / N_{NS} \tag{4}$$

Here, F_A represents the degree of fast flux for each JavaScript-delivery host. N_A is the number of unique A records, that is, IP addresses returned in all DNS resolutions for a host. The value, $n_{A\_average\_single}$ is the average number of A records returned for a single DNS resolution. [13] uses n_{single} which is the number of A records for a single lookup. However, as we observe the returned A records, the number are periodically changed. Thus, we use an average value for it instead. Host 29 and 32 give the highest value for it. Another fast fluxing hosts present a similar degree of fast flux. The others do not show fast flux at all. For double flux, F_{NS}, and F_{NS_A} describe the degree of DNS flux for the DNS servers of the JavaScript-delivery hosts. N_{NS} is the number of unique NS records, that is, DNS servers returned in all DNS resolutions for a host. $n_{NS\_average\_single}$ is the average number of NS records returned for a single DNS resolution. N_{NS_A} is the number of unique A records, that is, IP addresses returned in all DNS resolutions for a DNS server. $n_{NS_A\_average\_single}$ the average number of A records for a DNS server, which is returned for a single DNS resolution. Thus, f_{NS_A} is *fluxiness* for each DNS server. F_{NS_A} is the average of f_{NS_A}. F_{NS} shows that in the double fluxing hosts, the returned NS records for them are changed although its degree is low. F_{NS_A} shows that each DNS server also does fast flux and its degree is higher than F_{NS}.

Figure 11 shows all types of flux for each host. Although F_{NS_A} seems to be comparable to F_A for each host except those for Host 29 and 32, N_{NS} is much smaller than $n_{A\_average\_single}$. *The small number of IP addresses for the DNS servers implies that taking the DNS servers down is a fruitful avenue to fight the Asprox malware-serving infrastructure.*

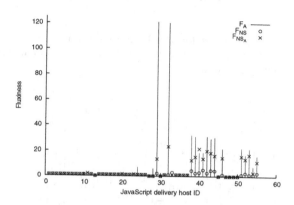

Fig. 11. Fluxiness: F_A, F_{NS}, and F_{NS_A}

Hosts 29 and 32 are `www.81dns.ru` and `www.berjke.ru` exhibiting the highest degree of fast flux. They are active for over 40 days and resolve to 1669 and 1542 unique IP addresses respectively. We now examine them in detail. First, we see if they share IP addresses. Surprisingly, they shared 1397 (over 82%) IP addresses. Since these hosts are very similarly provisioned, we examine `www.berjke.ru` in more detail.

Figure 12 shows the number of A records returned by DNS resolution for the host name, `www.berjke.ru`. *On average, most of resolutions for www. berjke. ru have 14 A records.* Around 4 A records are changed each resolution with a standard deviation of 4. However, for most of the 4th week of observation they resolved into 7 fixed A records. We hypothesize that this may be the result of a bug on their part, which they fixed over the period of a week. In addition to seeing listed A records, we checked to ensure they are reachable by connecting to the IP address via port 80 (the JavaScript URL is over the HTTP protocol whose default port number is 80). On average, over 90% of IP addresses were reachable. Thus, they were highly available. Although modern web browsers understand round robin DNS and try another IP address when the chosen IP address is not reachable, this high availability makes the infection less detectable.

Figure 13 depicts the geolocational distribution of IP addresses returned in our DNS lookups for `www.berjke.ru`. *The IP addresses for www. berjke. ru is geographically spread throughout 60 countries, representing over 25% of country*

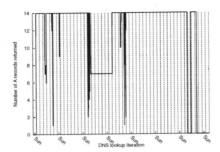

Fig. 12. Number of IP addresses for the DNS resolution of `www.berjke.ru`. Each vertical line indicates a separation of a day. DNS lookup iteration means one DNS resolution, repeated every 15 minutes.

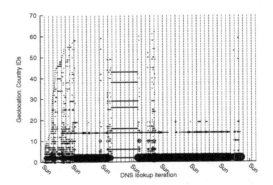

Fig. 13. Change in geolocational distribution of IP addresses for `www.berjke.ru`. The size of each point is proportional to the number of IP addresses observed in the given country. Each vertical line indicates a separation of day. Each iteration means one DNS resolution and is repeated every 15 minutes.

codes. This indicates that the bots in Asprox botnet are geographically well distributed even though the number of its observed TLDs are small.

Figure 14 illustrates the geographical distribution of the IP addresses of the JavaScript-delivery hosts in our data. Unlike the geographical distribution of Asprox bots in Figure 2, most of the bots belonged only to North America or Europe. *While China had only 2.67% of he JavaScript-delivery hosts, the United States had the largest number, which was 65.90% of them.* Potentially related, at one point during our observations we found that the malicious JavaScript-delivery hosts would check to see if the default language on the visiting browser was Chinese, and not attempt to infect the browser if it was. No other country accounted for more than 4% of the hosts.

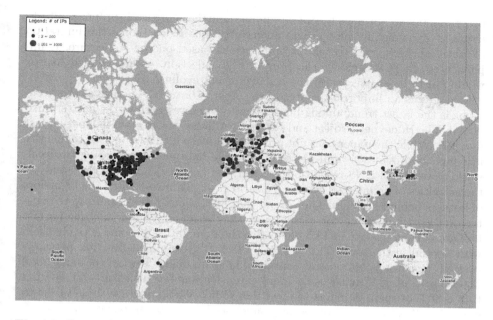

Fig. 14. Geographical distribution of IP addresses of JavaScript-delivery hosts. The size of icons for each point is proportional to the number of IP addresses for that location.

4 Related Work

Various case studies have been done to understand worms. These studies share a flavor similar to ours. A recent such study traced the Blaster worm for an extensive period and showed that it persisted in spite of significant mitigation effort [14]. Botnets have been studied extensively, particularly in the context of spam and phishing [15] [8] [16] [17] [18]. The Asprox botnet shares many of the features reported by these studies, particularly as they relate to the use of residential machines. Recently, Brown presented the anatomy of the Asprox in [19]. It presents Asprox's history and comprehensive infection process, and infected machine's behaviors with various examples. It also introduces the case where Asprox botnet is used by Rock Phish hosts [20]. However, it does not investigate and quantify the detail infrastructural provisioning for Asprox botnet. Furthermore, it does not trace the web severs infected by Asprox SQL injection attack.

SQL injection is central to the Asprox infection discussed in this paper. It is a well known attack on web servers with back-end databases. Consequently, various approaches have been proposed for detection and prevention of SQL injection. They can be categorized into three types [21]: coding practices with defensive mechanisms, vulnerability detection by static analysis, and defense techniques preventing vulnerabilities as well as detecting them. The defensive techniques transform programs to prevent SQL injection attack so that the programmers do not have to validate inputs. Furthermore, [21] proposes a technique to dynamically infer programmer intentions to overcome the limitation of static analysis, and transform applications based on the conjecture. If implemented, these techniques can prevent SQL injection, without which Asprox would fail to be as effective without a significant evolution.

Fast flux is an important aspect of the Asprox botnets. The use of this technique is the latest trend among botnets and several research works have studied it well. The Honeynet Project and Research Alliance wrote a whitepaper on fast flux [22]. While the paper does not provide a model which can be used to identify fast flux, it provides several pieces of valuable information including two real-world examples of DNS resolutions for fast flux host names, and a case study of the activities of an infected system. Nazario *et al.* [23] investigated the behaviors of botnets behind fast flux. They found that 80% of fast flux domains were registered at least a month before actual use. They also found a long lifetime for fast flux domains, a median of 18.5 days after the domain has become actively used, with several lasting over 50 days. Holz *et al.* [13] examined fast flux networks through resolutions of domains contained in spam mails. Toward the same goal, Passerini *et al.* [24] make use a more extensive number of features. They find that 8-30% of spam domains use fast flux today. We simply use these works to study fast flux among hosts serving malicious JavaScripts in our data.

5   Concluding Remarks

The Asprox botnet continues to grow and infect web servers around the world. With extensive use of fast flux, it is well provisioned to resist take-down attempts. Honeypots, while useful for detecting individual phases of the attack, are insufficient to understand the attack in its entirety or to detect changes or modifications to the final vulnerabilities used to attack users machines, or the malware payload delivered. Therefore, an active monitoring—and thus more costly—approach will be necessary to monitor changes to this botnet. Due to the use of JavaScript obfuscation, multi-layer fast flux, and redirects, a take-down of the JavaScript-delivery hosts and malware-delivery hosts seems unlikely to succeed, unless better mitigation techniques are developed in the community for specifically these problems. Thus, there is an urgent need to ensure that users use anti-virus software and keep their operating systems patched.

While there are a number of web servers that have fallen prey to the SQL injection attack, halting this portion of the life-cycle seems unlikely as well. The ability to patch a large number of improper SQL-accessing scripts to perform proper input validation or use SQL bind parameters on different web servers can only be effectively done through a long education cycle that is unlikely to yield results any time soon. Positively and as expected, we did not find any of the popular sites injected with Asprox. Note that this is not due to a lack of attacks, but rather because these servers are secured better and/or restored quickly. Unfortunately, this is not true of a large portion of the Web, for many web severs are small, and are unlikely to be updated (or fixed) frequently or in a timely manner.

The most vulnerable part of the Asprox life-cycle that we could discern was the specific URLs that are injected as part of the SQL injection segment of the life-cycle. These URLs point to the JavaScript-delivery hosts and can be blacklisted, if identified quickly. In fact, Google is currently blacklisting many of the them already, so Firefox and other modern browsers that use their blacklisting services, are protected if the blacklists are properly updated.

Acknowledgments

We would like to thank Matthew Rainey and Andrew Korty for providing data on Asprox bots that attacked Indiana University web servers. We also thank Bob Cameron of the FBI for discussions on the Asprox botnet, and for URLs to cross-reference against our own. IP2Location [7] provided their geolocation software for our use, for which we are grateful. Finally, we would like to thank Rob Henderson for his help in guarding our data collection when we were accidentally mistaken for being miscreants ourselves.

References

1. Stewart, J.: Danmec/Asprox SQL Injection Attack Tool Analysis, http://www.secureworks.com/research/threats/danmecasprox
2. The Times: Asprox computer virus infects key government and consumer websites, http://technology.timesonline.co.uk/tol/news/tech_and_web/the_web/article4381034.ece
3. CyberInsecure.com: Asprox botnet mass attack hits governmental, healthcare, and top business websites, http://cyberinsecure.com/asprox-botnet-mass-attack-hits-governmental-healthcare-and-top-business-websites/
4. Amazon.com, Inc.: Alexa web information service, AWIS (2008), http://aws.amazon.com/awis
5. Cisco News: ASPROX SQL Injection Attacks - Block them using a Cisco router (July 2008), http://cisconews.co.uk/2008/07/09/asprox-sql-injection-attacks-block-them-using-a-cisco-router
6. Zino, M.: ASCII Encoded/Binary string automated SQL injection attack, http://www.bloombit.com/Articles/2008/05/ASCII-Encoded-Binary-String-Automated-SQL-Injection.aspx
7. Hexasoft Development Sdn. Bhd.: IP2Location geolocation service (February 2008), http://www.ip2location.com/
8. Anderson, D.S., Fleizach, C., Savage, S., Voelker, G.M.: Spamscatter: Characterizing internet scam hosting infrastructure. In: USENIX Security (2007)
9. Google: Google AJAX Search API, http://code.google.com/apis/ajaxsearch/
10. Yahoo: Web Search APIs from Yahoo! Search, http://developer.yahoo.com/search/web/
11. Danchev, D.: Sony PlayStation's site SQL injected, redirecting to rogue security software (July 2008), http://blogs.zdnet.com/security/?p=1394

12. McGrath, D.K., Gupta, M.: Behind Phishing: An Examination of the Phisher Modi Operandi. In: USENIX Workshop on Large-Scale Exploits and Emergent Threats (2008)
13. Holz, T., Gorecki, C., Rieck, K., Freiling, F.C.: Measuring and Detecting Fast-Flux Service Networks. In: NDSS (2008)
14. Bailey, M., Cooke, E., Jahanian, F., Watson, D.: The Blaster Worm: Then and Now. In: IEEE Security and Privacy (2005)
15. Xie, Y., Yu, F., Achan, K., Panigrahy, R., Hulten, G., Osipkov, I.: Spamming Botnets: Signatures and Characteristics. In: ACM SIGCOMM (2008)
16. Rajab, M.A., Zarfoss, J., Monrose, F., Terzis, A.: A Multifaced Approach to Understanding the Botnet Phenomenon. In: ACM IMC (2006)
17. Zhuang, L., Dunagan, J., Simon, D.R., Wang, H.J., Tygar, J.D.: Characterizing Botnets from Email Spam Records. In: USENIX Workshop on Large-Scale Exploits and Emergent Threats (2008)
18. Holz, T., Steiner, M., Dahl, F., Biersack, E., Freiling, F.: Measurements and Mitigation of Peer-to-Peer-based botnets: A Case Study on Storm Worm. In: USENIX Workshop on Large-Scale Exploits and Emergent Threats, LEET (2008)
19. Brown, D.: Anatomy of the Asprox Bonet. ToorCon X - San Diego (September 2008)
20. McMillan, R.: 'Rock Phish' blamed for surge in phishing (December 2006), http://www.infoworld.com/article/06/12/12/HNrockphish_1.html
21. Bandhakavi, S., Bisht, P., Madhusudan, P., Venkatakrishnan, V.N.: CANDID: Preventing SQL Injection Attacks using Dynamic Candidate Evaluations. In: CCS (2007)
22. The Honeynet Project: Know Your Enemy: Fast-Flux Service Networks (July 2007), http://www.honeynet.org/papers/ff/
23. Nazario, J., Holz, T.: As the net churns: Fast-flux botnet observations. In: International Conference on Malicious and Unwanted Software, MALWARE (2008)
24. Passerini, E., Paleari, R., Martignoni, L., Bruschi, D.: Fluxor: detecting and monitoring fast-flux service networks. In: Zamboni, D. (ed.) DIMVA 2008. LNCS, vol. 5137, pp. 186–206. Springer, Heidelberg (2008)

How Good Are Malware Detectors at Remediating Infected Systems?

Emanuele Passerini[1], Roberto Paleari[1], and Lorenzo Martignoni[2]

[1] Università degli Studi di Milano
[2] Università degli Studi di Udine
{ema,roberto,lorenzo}@security.dico.unimi.it

Abstract. Malware detectors are applications that attempt to identify and block malicious programs. Unfortunately, malware detectors might not always be able to preemptively block a malicious program from infecting the system (e.g., when the signatures database is not promptly updated). In these situations, the only way to eradicate the infection without having to reinstall the entire system is to rely on the remediation capabilities of the detectors. Therefore, it is essential to evaluate the efficacy and accuracy of anti-malware software in such situations. This paper presents a testing methodology to assess the quality (completeness) of the *remediation procedures* used by malware detectors to revert the effect of an infection from a compromised system. To evaluate the efficacy of our testing methodology, we developed a prototype and used it to test six of the top-rated commercial malware detectors currently available on the market. The results of our evaluation witness that in many situations the tested malware detectors fail to completely remove the effects of an infection.

Keywords: Malware, malware detection, software testing.

1 Introduction

One of the biggest problems the Internet community has to face today is the widespread diffusion of *malware*, malicious programs written with the explicit intent to damage users and to use compromised systems for various types of frauds. The second half of 2007 witnessed a drastic increase (about 135%) of the number of threats related to malware [1]. This can be ascribed to a number of different root causes, but the main reason is probably the easy financial gain malware authors obtain by selling their creations in the underground market [2]. Besides the rapid spread of malware, we are observing a parallel advance in the techniques for protecting end-users against malicious code. In order to face the growing complexity in the techniques employed by malware writers to evade detection, traditional signature-based anti-malware solutions are now being supported by behavioural, semantics-aware, approaches [3,4], that mainstream commercial products are starting to include [5,6,7].

To defend against malicious programs, users typically rely on malware detectors, which try to detect and prevent threats before the system is damaged.

U. Flegel and D. Bruschi (Eds.): DIMVA 2009, LNCS 5587, pp. 21–37, 2009.

Unfortunately, in many cases detection and prevention are not possible. Imagine for example a user that is not running a malware detector or a user that is running a malware detector but who gets infected before the appropriate detection signature is released. In such a situation, post-infection remediation remains the only solution to get rid of a malware and of the damages it may have caused to the system, other than reinstalling the entire system. However, the experience has taught us that sometimes automatic remediation procedures could cause more problems than they would solve [8,9].

As any kind of software application, malware detectors require thorough testing. Users do not only need a stable application, but also a product capable of detecting threats with low false-negative and false-positive rates, and capable of remediating their system from a damage caused by a malicious program that was not detected in time. For these reasons, the testing and the evaluation of a malware detector require particular attentions, to the point that the leading industries and researchers in the field have recently defined common guidelines to test this particular class of software [10]. Although these guidelines describe what should be evaluated, they do not describe any precise methodology to do that.

In this paper we address the problem of evaluating the remediation capabilities of a malware detector and we propose a fully automated testing methodology to evaluate this characteristic. The proposed methodology is dynamic. We run a malicious program in a victim system and we monitor the execution to detect what modifications are made to the environment. Subsequently, we trigger the remediation procedure of the tested malware detector to clean up the victim system. Finally, we analyse the state of the environment to verify which of the modifications previously caused by the malicious program have been successfully reverted. We have implemented the proposed methodology in a prototype and evaluated six of the most rated malware detectors on the marked. Our evaluation testifies the effectiveness of our tests and shows that the remediation procedures of the tested detectors suffers incompleteness. For example, we have empirically observed that only about 80% of the untrusted executables dropped by malicious programs on infected systems are properly removed by malware detectors.

To summarise, the paper makes the following contributions:

- a fully automated testing methodology to evaluate the completeness of remediation procedures in commercial malware detectors;
- a prototype implementation of our testing methodology;
- an empirical evaluation of six malware detectors currently available on the market, with about 100 malware samples each.

The paper is organised as follows. Section 2 motivates the importance of complete post-infection remediation. Section 3 presents the requirements of the ideal remediation procedure and sketches an overview of our testing methodology. Section 4 discusses the implementation of the infrastructure we have developed. Section 5 discusses the results of our experimental evaluation. Section 6 presents the related work. Finally, Section 7 concludes the paper.

2 The Importance of Remediation

To comprehend why remediation is a key issue in defeating malware, let us consider a sample malicious program. Fig. 1 shows a fragment of an execution trace of the sample malware, reporting the most important modifications to the system performed by the application. The malicious program replicates itself into a new executable (c:\windows\poq.exe), creates a registry key to configure the system to start the new executable automatically at boot, and tampers the configuration of the resolver (writing into c:\windows\system32\drivers\etc\hosts) to hijack network traffic, directed to www.google.com and www.citi.com, to a malicious web site. Moreover, let us imagine a user whose system gets infected by this malware and that, at the time of infection, his system was not properly protected (e.g., the infection took place before a signature for detecting the malware was released). Only after a while, when the appropriate signature becomes available, the malware detector can detect the presence of the malware on the system and can remediate the damages.

What the user expects from the detector is that it is able to remediate completely the system. That is, the malware detector has to revert *all* the modifications made to the system by the malicious program. In the case of the example, that means that the original malicious executable (malware.exe), the executable created (c:\windows\poq.exe), and the registry key (\HKLM\Software\Microsoft\Windows\CurrentVersion\Run\v) have to be removed from the system. Similarly the process started has to be killed, and the malicious entries added to the configuration of the resolver removed (c:\windows\system32\drivers\etc\hosts).

If the remediation procedure is not complete, the system can be left in an unsafe state. Imagine for example that the malware detector reverts all the actions performed by the malicious program, but that it is not able to restore the proper configuration of the resolver (i.e., to remove the malicious entries added to the file c:\windows\system32\drivers\etc\hosts). Even though all the malicious executables dropped by the malware are removed from the system, the security of the user is still compromised because part of the network traffic is hijacked to a malicious web site. This site can be used to steal sensitive information or to deliver new malware to the user.

```
WriteFile("c:\windows\poq.exe", "malicious code")
CreateProcess("c:\windows\poq.exe")
QueryKeyValue("\HKLM\...\CurrentVersion\Run", "v")  →  ""
CreateKeyValue("\HKLM\...\CurrentVersion\Run", "v", "c:\windows\poq.exe")
ReadFile("c:\...\drivers\etc\hosts")  →  "Copyri... 127.0.0.1 localhost"
WriteFile("c:\...\drivers\etc\hosts", "67.23.124.83 www.google.com\n
          67.23.124.85 www.citi.com\n")
DeleteFile("c:\malware.exe")
```

Fig. 1. High-level execution trace of a sample malicious program (malware.exe)

3   Testing Methodology

This section defines the ideal remediation procedure (Section 3.1) and presents the testing methodology we have developed to verify whether the remediation procedures available in a malware detector resemble the ideal one or not (Section 3.2).

3.1   The Ideal Remediation Procedure

For the purpose of defining the ideal remediation procedure, we can think the execution of a malicious program as characterised only by interactions with the environment, where each interaction corresponds to the invocation of a particular OS routine (or system call). Let $S = \langle s_0, s_1, \ldots, s_n \rangle$ be the execution trace of our malware sample. The system calls in S can be classified in two classes: those that modify the state of the environment and those that do not. For example, to replicate itself into a system folder, a malicious program has to create a file and to copy its code into the file. Similarly, to install itself at boot, the program has to create a particular registry key. Both activities involve a modification of the state of the environment. On the other hand, a program that reads and parses the content of a file does not alter the state of the environment. For our purpose, it is sufficient to consider only a subset of all the system calls executed by the malicious program, including only the ones that modify the state of the local environment: $S' = \langle s_j \in S : s_j$ contributes to modify the state of the local system$\rangle$.

To achieve a particular high-level goal, the malicious program has to execute multiple system calls. As an example, to replicate itself, the program has to create a file and then to write its payload into the file (typically in multiple passes). Nevertheless, for remediating a system from a malware infection, it is not important to know which system calls the malicious program executed to modify the system, but instead what modifications were made to the local system by the program. For this reason, we can abstract the sequence of system calls S' executed by the malicious program to infect the system through a set of *high-level system state transitions* T. Each transition $t \in T$ represents the effect on the local system produced by the execution of a sequence of related system calls. Let us consider again our sample malicious behaviour of Fig. 1 and the corresponding system calls trace shown in Fig. 2, where each high-level behaviour is associated with the sequence of system calls executed by the malware and that produces a particular state transition. In the figure, irrelevant system calls (i.e., the system calls that do not modify the state of the system) are reported in gray. As an example, to create a file on the file system (which consists in a copy of the malicious program) the following system calls are executed: `NtCreateFile`, `NtWriteFile`, and `NtClose`. The high-level state transition associated with this sequence of system calls is the creation of a new file on the system.

The set of high-level system state transitions T can be divided in multiple classes, each of which represents a state transition involving a particular class of OS resource. For example, for a Microsoft Windows system we have $T = F \cup R \cup P \cup S$ where: F represents the state transitions involving files, R the state

System call trace (S)	High-level behaviour (T)
NtCreateFile("...\poq.exe") → f NtWriteFile(f, "malicious code") NtWriteFile(f, "other malicious code") NtClose(f) ...	WriteFile("...\poq.exe", "malicious ...")
NtOpenFile("...\poq.exe") → f NtCreateSection(...) → s NtMapViewOfSection(h, s) NtCreateProcess(h) → p NtCreateThread(p) → t ...	CreateProcess("...\poq.exe")
NtOpenKey("...\Run") → r NtQueryValueKey(r, "v") → FAILURE NtSetValueKey(r, "v", "...\poq.exe") NtClose(r) ...	CreateKeyValue("...\Run", "v", "...\poq.exe")
NtOpenFile("...\etc\hosts") → f NtReadFile(f, 1024) → "Cop..." NtWriteFile(f, "67... www.google...") NtWriteFile(f, "67... www.citi...") NtClose(f) ...	WriteFile("...\hosts", "67... www.citi.com\n")
NtDeleteFile("c:\malware.exe")	DeleteFile("c:\malware.exe")

Fig. 2. System call trace of our sample malicious program (`malware.exe`) and corresponding high-level execution trace

transitions involving registry keys, P those involving processes, and S those involving system services. This separation is important because each class of state transition requires a specific mechanisms for remediation. It is worth pointing out that, in our context, we are interested only in the state transitions that modify the local system, as no remediation could be accomplished for transitions that affect remote hosts. Furthermore, we do not consider system state transitions caused by other benign processes that might be running in the test environment.

A remediation procedure $\mathcal{P}$ is *complete* if it is able to revert all the effects (i.e., the high-level state transitions) of the execution of the malware: $\forall t \in \mathcal{T}$, t is reverted by $\mathcal{P}$. The ideal remediation procedure is the one that is complete. Reverting a particular state-transition means to bring the state of the system back to that preceding the transition. Practically speaking, if a malicious program creates a file we expect the malware detector to remove the file; if the malicious program reconfigures the resolver, we expect the malware detector to adjust the configuration of the resolver.

3.2　Testing the Completeness of a Remediation Procedure

Testing scenarios. The following paragraphs present two real-world scenarios that resemble the one we use to perform the testing of a malware detector. The first scenario involves a system protected by a conventional malware detector, while the second one involves a system protected by a behaviour-based detector.

Scenario 1 – Conventional malware detector. A user's system gets infected by a malicious program because the conventional (signature based) malware detector running on the system is not able to promptly detect and to prevent the infection (e.g., because the appropriate signature has not been published yet). Only later, the malware detector detects the presence of the malicious program on the system and cleans the system to get rid of the threat.

Scenario 2 – Behaviour-based malware detector. A user is running a behaviour-based malware detector on his system. The system is infected by a malicious program but the detector does not detect it until any malicious activity is observed. For example, consider malicious program that creates some files on the system and then tries to infect a running process. As the initial activity is legitimate, the malicious program is blocked only when it tries to infect other processes (or after the infection has taken place). The malware detector, after having detected the malicious behaviour, repairs the system to rollback all the potentially dangerous activities performed before the detection.

Overview of the testing methodology. Our goal is to measure remediation capabilities of the detector in any of the aforementioned scenarios. To accomplish this goal, we select a set of sample malware and we use each of these programs to infect a test system, we let to the detector to remediate the damages caused to the system by each infection, and finally we check the state of the system to see if the detector was able to revert the state to that prior to the infection. In other words, by infecting our test system with a malicious program we identify the set of system state transitions which are direct consequences of the infection and then we use these information to measure the completeness of the remediation procedure.

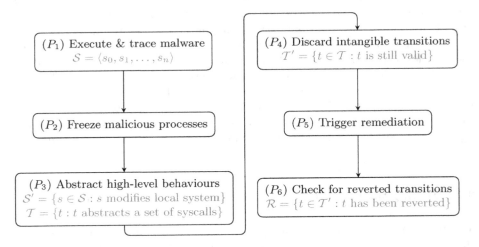

Fig. 3. Overview of our testing methodology. In gray we report the outcome of each phase.

A generalisation of our testing methodology is outlined in Fig. 3 and is summarised in the following paragraphs.

(P_1) – *Execute and trace the malicious sample.* We select a malicious program we know in advance is detected by the malware detector under testing, and we run it in the test system. To simulate the scenario involving a conventional malware detector it is sufficient to disable the detector temporarily. On the other hand, to simulate the scenario involving a behaviour-based detector the malicious program is run with the detector enabled. The execution is stopped when a timeout is reached or when the behaviour-based malware detector detects a malicious behaviour. As the execution of the malicious program is monitored by an external monitor, at the end of the execution we obtain $\mathcal{S}$, the complete trace of the system calls invoked by the program during the execution.

(P_2) – *Freeze malicious processes.* We freeze the state of the malicious program to prevent it from further altering the state of the system. Subsequent steps of the analysis will refer to that state.

(P_3) – *Abstract high-level behaviours.* We analyse the recorded execution trace $\mathcal{S}$ to extract $\mathcal{S}'$, by excluding all the system calls that do not alter the state of the system (e.g., those used to open a file in read-only mode, or to read a registry key). Then, we analyse the resulting trace to infer the high-level behaviours of the program and the corresponding set $\mathcal{T}$ of high-level system state transitions.

It is worth noting that we analyse only the behaviour of the malicious process, and its children, and we do not consider high-level state-transitions associated with other processes running concurrently on the system. Thus, some of the high-level state transitions we analyse could conflict with those associated with other processes. To mitigate this problem without increasing the complexity of the analysis, we trace the malicious program in highly passive environments, with a minimal number of potentially conflicting processes and with no user interaction at all.

(P_4) – *Discard intangible transitions.* Not all the observed high-level program behaviours lead to tangible system state transitions. As an example imagine our sample malicious programs that deletes the original executable after it has replicated. It is important to preemptively detect intangible state transitions because otherwise one might think that the transitions is reverted by the remediation procedure. For this reason, we identify such transitions and filter them out. The next phases of the testing will target only tangible transitions: $\mathcal{T}' = \{t \in \mathcal{T} : t \text{ is tangible on the test system}\}$.

(P_5) – *Trigger remediation.* Having collected all the information necessary to test the completeness of the remediation procedure, we can now trigger the malware detector to remediate the infection and to cleanup the system. In the case of a conventional detector we have to launch a full-system scan, which includes the scanning of all files and running processes. In the case of a behaviour-based detector we have to authorise the detector to quarantine the malicious program; recall the behaviour-based detector has been active since the beginning of the execution of the malicious program and it has already blocked the execution of the program.

(P_6) – *Check for reverted transitions.* Once the malware detector has completed the remediation, we have to check whether each of the high-level state transitions $t \in \mathcal{T}'$ has been properly reverted. Practically speaking, that means that we have to compare the state of the system prior to the infection with the state after the infection and the remediation, to detect any mismatch that can be ascribed to the malicious program. It is worth pointing out that we cannot expect the conventional malware detector to revert state transitions that caused data loss. On the other hand, it is legitimate to expect that from the behaviour-based malware detector, as it has observed the whole execution of the malicious program since the beginning. At the end of this phase, we obtain a set $\mathcal{R} \subseteq \mathcal{T}'$ of abstract transitions that have been reverted by the malware detector. If the remediation procedure is complete, then $\mathcal{R} = \mathcal{T}'$; instead, if $\mathcal{R} \subset \mathcal{T}'$, then every transition $t \in \mathcal{T}' \setminus \mathcal{R}$ testifies the incompleteness of the remediation procedure for the malicious program used for the testing. It is worth noting that $\mathcal{R}$ could also include some state transitions that are not in $\mathcal{T}$. This happens when the malware detector incorrectly attributes a spurious action to the malicious program [8]. However, as our analysis is driven by the observed behaviours, we do not handle this situation.

4   Implementation

We have developed a prototype that implements the testing methodology discussed in the previous section, specific for testing malware detectors for Microsoft Windows. In this section, we discuss the technical details regarding the implementation of our testing infrastructure. The methodology described previously can be used to test the completeness of remediation procedures of both conventional and behaviour-based malware detectors. In the following, we describe in detail only the implementation specific for the testing of conventional detectors. Nevertheless, the implementation for behaviour-based detectors only differs in the fact the detector is active when the malicious program is executed and traced.

Fig. 4 depicts our testing infrastructure. The main components of our architecture are the victim test system, where the malware sample and the detector are located, and the analysis environment, where execution traces are analysed. The malicious sample is uploaded into the test machine and its execution is monitored. Syscall traces are subsequently analysed in the analysis environment, and further abstracted into high-level state transitions that are then verified. Finally, the malware detector is allowed to scan the whole system, and then the state of the system is checked to detect the set of transitions that have been reverted.

4.1   Tracing the Malware Sample

The malware sample is executed and traced in the test system (steps 1–3 in Fig. 4). For the tracing we relay on our home made system call tracer, codenamed

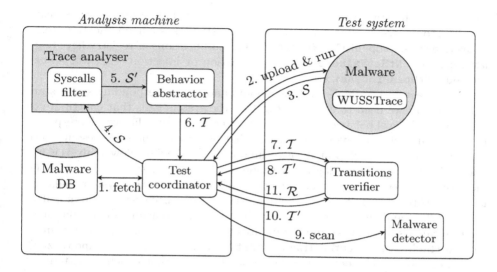

Fig. 4. Architecture of the testing infrastructure

WUSSTrace [11], a user-space system call tracer for Windows. WUSSTrace parses the majority of the arguments of system calls, thus allowing a subsequent fine-grained analysis of the behaviour of the program. Each intercepted system call is logged into an easy-to-parse XML trace, together with its input and output arguments. If the monitored process creates other processes or threads, these are monitored recursively. We are aware that user-space tracing can be easily circumvented by a nasty malware and that safer solutions exist (e.g., hooking from kernel space or through virtual machine introspection). However, we made this decision only to ease the development of our prototype.

We set a timeout on the execution of the malicious program and the other processes it creates. If a monitored process does not terminate spontaneously before the timeout expires, we freeze the process, by suspending the execution of all its threads. By freezing the malicious process instead of terminating it, we allow the malware detector to operate in a "best-case scenario", where it can apply in-memory scanning techniques to analyse the memory image of the processes and to apply all the available heuristics.

4.2   Analysis of the System Call Trace

In order to analyse the system calls issued by the monitored malware sample, we developed a trace analysis tool that off-line performs the abstractions needed to infer the high-level program behaviours and the corresponding system state transitions. In our current implementation, we focus on the identification of the files, registry keys, processes, and system services that have been created or tampered by the malicious sample or by any of its child processes. For this reason, starting from a trace $\mathcal{S}$, we obtain (steps 4 and 5 in Fig. 4) the set of system calls that modify the state of the environment (S') by including only those syscalls that lead to the system state transitions of interest: file-system modifications (e.g., NtCreateFile, NtOpenFile, NtWriteFile), modifications of registry keys (e.g., NtCreateKey, NtSetValueKey), process creation or infection (e.g., NtCreate-Process, NtOpenProcess), *etc.*

To abstract S' into high-level behaviours and the corresponding set of state transitions T, we need to correlate together the system calls that contribute to the same high-level behaviour (step 6). In order to identify the syscalls responsible for a particular behaviour (i.e., those that operate on the same resource) we employ standard data-flow analysis techniques [12]. The data-flow analysis is not fine-grained, as we do not log every single machine instruction executed by the monitored processes. Thus, dependency relationships between system calls are identified through handles (i.e., Windows resources identifiers): if system call s_2 uses handle h and the system call s_1 is the (dynamic) reaching definition for h, then we can assume that s_1 and s_2 operate on the same resource. As an example, when we find in the execution trace a NtSetValueKey(r, "v", "...\poq.exe") system call we need to determine the name of the key that is being written; for this purpose, we compute the dynamic backward slice for the key handle r and we analyse the arguments of the system call that originally defined it [13]. Similarly, in order to compute the name of the files that are actually modified by the malware, we calculate the dynamic reaching definition for the file handle f used by the system call NtWriteFile(f, "..."); this reaching definition will correspond to a NtCreateFile or NtOpenFile, and through the analysis of its input arguments we can infer the name of the file being written.

4.3   Filtering of Intangible High-Level Transitions

Having built the set T of high-level state transitions that represent the modification of the system caused by the malicious program, it is important to ensure that each transition $t \in T$ is valid (i.e., it represent an actual modification of the state of the environment, that is tangible after the malicious program has terminated or it has been frozen). Indeed, any spurious state transition must be discarded, as it could negatively affect the accuracy of the evaluation of the remediation procedure.

As an example consider again our sample malicious program, whose high-level behaviour is summarised in Fig. 1. The program replicates its payload and then deletes the original executable. When the execution of the program in the test system terminates (or is frozen) the executable no longer exists on the system. If we do not test whether the file still exists on the system prior to the invocation of the malware detector we might erroneously praise the malware detector for something it has not done. On the other hand we want to be sure that system state-transition, even if not annihilated by the malicious program itself, are effectively tangible. The assumption that each write access to a resource of the system produces a modification of the system state might be too broad. For example, several malware often overwrite registry keys with the actual content of the keys; thus, despite the keys are overwritten, the system state does not mutate (this is probably a side effect caused by the use of some high-level libraries). A similar situation might occur with memory mapped files, because these files are written without invoking system calls and thus we have to conservatively assume that a file mapped with write permission is eventually modified.

We identify intangible state transitions by querying directly the test system in the exact same way we query it to detect if a transitions has been reverted by the malware detector (steps 7 and 8). Only tangible transitions $T' \subseteq T$ are targeted by the remaining phases of the testing. We detect registry keys or files that are effectively modified by comparing their actual content with their content preceding the infection. To do that we maintain a database of hashes of the content of all files and registry keys of the test-system before the infection. We discard all the behaviours that preserve the content of these resources. Similarly we also discard all the behaviours that involve the creation of files, registry keys, and processes that cannot be found on the test system at the end of the execution of the malicious program. Further details about how the test system is queried are given in the next paragraphs.

4.4   Execution and Evaluation of the Remediation Procedure

At this point it is possible to trigger the malware detector to analyse the system and clean it from the infection. We invoke it to perform a full-scan of the file system, of the registry, and of the image of running processes (step 9 in Fig. 4). We also enable all the heuristics supported to improve the detection and remediation rate. When the detector terminates the analysis of the system, we verify which of the state transitions associated with the execution of the malicious program have been reverted (step 10 and 11). Recall that the system state transitions T' can be divided in multiple classes according to the type of resource affected by a transition. That is, $T' = F \cup R \cup P \cup S$, where F, R, P, and S are the classes of transitions involving respectively files, registry keys, processes, and system services. Each class of transitions requires a particular procedure to verify whether the transition has been reverted or not. A transition $t \in T'$ is considered to be reverted by the malware detector when one of the following conditions is satisfied:

- if $t \in F$, the file subject of the transition is deleted or modified by the malware detector;
- if $t \in R$, the registry key subject of the transition is removed or modified by the malware detector;
- if $t \in P$, the process spawned by the malicious program is terminated;
- if $t \in S$, the system service created by the malicious program is disabled.

Note that we optimistically assume that any modification made by the remediation procedure to a resource manipulated by the malicious program successfully restores the initial state of the resource.

To test the aforementioned conditions, we leverage a small helper program we run in the test system, that allows us to query the state of a particular resource. For example, if we have observed the malicious program to create a registry key, we query the helper to check whether the key still exists on the system and, if so, to retrieve its contents and perform the appropriate comparisons.

5   Experimental Results

This section presents the results of the testing of six of the top-rated commercial malware detectors. The goal of our experimental evaluation was to prove the effectiveness of the proposed testing methodology and not to compare the tested malware detectors to tell which was the best and which was the worst. The experiments witnessed the effectiveness of our testing methodology. Indeed, they highlighted that none of the tested malware detector has complete remediation procedures. Furthermore, the experiments showed that the type and percentage of system state transitions reverted varies substantially among detectors.

5.1   Experimental Setup

We tested the following malware detectors: Avast Professional 4.8, Kaspersky Anti-virus 2009, McAfee VirusScan Enterprise 8.5.0, Nod32 Anti-virus 3.0, Panda Anti-virus 9.0.5 and Sophos Anti-virus 7.6. We selected the malware detectors that facilitated the most the batch analysis, that is, those invokable directly from the command line and with the ability to cleanup the system automatically. We assumed that the detection capabilities of the command line version (with the proper arguments) and the GUI version corresponded. The virus definitions of each product were last updated on 15 January 2009. To discourage any direct comparison among the malware detectors, they were tested using different sets of about 100 malware samples, chosen randomly from a corpus composed by several thousand samples collected in the last quarter of 2008. All the samples tested were detected by the six detectors.

We performed the evaluation of our testing methodology using as test systems multiple VirtualBox virtual machines, each one running a different malware detector. To prevent other processes to alter the state of the system resources affected by the malicious programs used for the testing, we stripped down the virtual environments used for the analysis: we stopped all unnecessary services and processes and we did not interact at all with the environments. We traced the execution of the selected malicious program for five minutes and we performed all the steps of the analysis without restarting the test system. After each test, we restored the original clean state of the virtual machine.

5.2   Evaluation of State-of-the-Art Malware Detectors

Fig. 5 presents the overall results of our experiments. The names of the malware detectors have been anonymised to discourage comparisons. For each malware detector, we report the average percentage of system state transitions that were reverted. The average is computed on the total number of malware used to test each detector. The transitions are separated in two groups, according to their security impact on the system: primary and ancillary. Primary transitions are those that have a high impact on the system, while ancillary transitions have a minor impact. A user should expect all primary transitions to be reverted by the malware detector, while he could tolerate if some ancillary transitions were not reverted. The

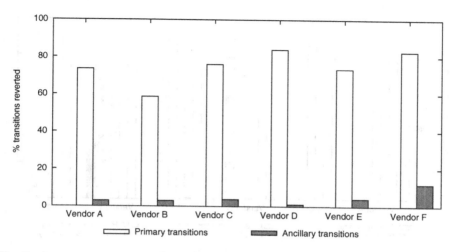

Fig. 5. Average percentage of system state transitions reverted by each malware detector

partitioning of transitions in the two groups has a certain degree of subjectivity. We divided each of the transitions classes F, R, P, and S in primary and ancillary as follows:

- F (files): we consider as primary transitions all those that involve executable files (e.g., .exe, .dll, .bat, .pif, .scr), while as ancillary those involving the remaining types of files.
- R (registry keys): we consider primary transitions those that involve registry keys that can be used to start programs automatically and ancillary all the remaining ones.
- P (processes): we consider primary the transitions that create processes where the executed files match any of the files dropped on the system by the malicious program; the remaining processes started by the malware but executing programs already present on the system are instead considered ancillary.
- S (services): for simplicity we treat system services as normal processes.

The graph in Fig. 5 clearly shows the effectiveness of our testing methodology at evaluating the completeness of remediation procedures. None of the tested malware detectors turned out to be complete, even if only primary transitions are taken into account: about 75% of the total primary transitions and only 4% of the total ancillary transitions were reverted.

A more detailed overview of the average distribution of primary and ancillary system state transitions reverted, for each transition class, is reported in Fig. 6 (product names have been anonymised). While all malware detectors reverted the majority of primary transitions involving files, some of them (e.g., Vendor C and Vendor F) did not revert transitions involving registry keys at all. Other detectors instead (e.g., Vendor A and Vendor B) did not seem to terminate malicious processes, although we did not check the state of the system after a reboot.

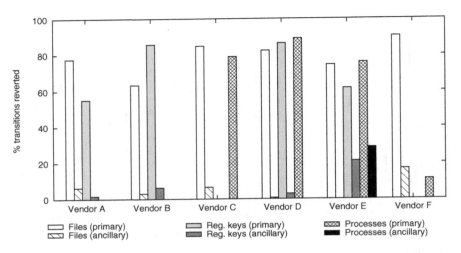

Fig. 6. Average percentage of primary and ancillary state transitions, partitioned by the system resources involved, reverted by each malware detector

We did not test interactively whether the system continued to work properly after infection and remediation. Indeed, there could exist situations in which an incomplete or improper remediation might render the system unusable. For example, imagine a malicious program that creates a registry key pointing to an executable, and that the existence of the key mandates the existence of the file (e.g., in Windows XP, the `Image File Execution Options` registry key). If the executable were removed, but the key were not, the system would stop working. We plan to address this problem in the future.

6   Related Work

In this section we briefly review the work done by the research community on malware detection and analysis. We also present some recent results that focus on execution of untrusted applications without any risk for the system and on the problem of testing malware detectors.

6.1   Malware Detection and Analysis

The traditional approach for the detection of malicious code is based on signature matching of various complexity [14]. A signature can be a sequence of bytes that identifies pieces of data or code of the malicious program, but even very complex algorithms that test whether a particular program satisfies certain properties. The advantage of using sophisticated detection methods is that signatures become more generic and thus a single signature can be used to detect multiple variants derived from the same family. On the other hand, from the remediation point of view, excessively generic signatures do not allow to distinguish variants. If single variants cannot be told apart, the remediation procedure cannot take variant-specific behaviours into account and cannot perform a complete cleanup.

Purely signature-based approaches have demonstrated their weaknesses when packed, polymorphic and metamorphic malware appeared. The research community started to move toward behaviour-based solutions. Behaviour-based detection [3,4] and analysis [15,16,17,18] approaches do not focus on the syntactic structure of the analysed program, but try to consider its semantics. Because these solutions work by observing a concrete execution of the malicious sample, they could provide much more accurate remediation procedures.

6.2 Execution of Untrusted Applications

In [19], Hsu et al. present a framework to automatically remove a malicious program from the system and also to repair any damage it could have done. The safe state of the system is restored by using the logs of the execution and by reverting each logged operation. An alternative approach is proposed by Liang et al. [20]. Untrusted programs are executed in a sandbox and the changes made to the "virtual" system are committed to the real one at the end of the execution, only if the program can be considered innocuous.

In the operating systems and self-healing communities, a number of different works investigate the problem of automatically reverting the modifications made by an unwanted program. As an example, in [21] the authors present Speculator, a modified Linux kernel that allows speculative execution of user-space processes. Speculator avoids blocking user processes during slow I/O operations (such as remote I/O operations): the system predicts the operation's result, checkpoints the process and allows it to continue; later, if the prediction is found to be incorrect, the process is reverted to the checkpointed state.

6.3 Evaluation of State-of-the-Art Malware Detectors

The need for automatic testing methodologies targeting anti-malware products has been clearly stated by the Anti-Malware Testing Standards Organisation (AMTSO) [10]. However, little research work focuses on the evaluation of malware detection and remediation solutions. One of the few examples is represented by [22]; in this paper, Christodorescu et al. present a technique for generating test-cases to stress malware detectors. They use program obfuscation techniques to evaluate the resilience of malware detectors to various transformations of the malicious code. The goal of our paper instead is to estimate the completeness of remediation procedures. For this reason, the testing infrastructure described in our paper could complement their work, in order to produce more comprehensive testing methodologies.

Other researchers highlighted the importance cleaning infected systems and the importance of testing such functionality [23,24]. Motivated by the same convictions, this paper contributes to address this problem by proposing a fully automated testing methodology and an extensive evaluation of several state-of-the-art commercial products.

7   Conclusions

Malware detectors are essential components for preserving the security of computer systems. They allow to detect and prevent malicious software and, when malware cannot be stopped from infecting a system, they allow to recover from the infection. In this paper we presented an automated testing methodology to assess the completeness of remediation procedures used by malware detector to clean up compromised systems. We used this methodology to test six of the most rated malware detectors on the market and found out that the dangerous effects of an infection are seldom completely removed. In the future we plan to investigate automatic techniques for generating more complete remediation procedures.

References

1. Symantec Inc.: Symantec internet security threat report: vol. XIII. Technical report, Symantec Inc. (April 2008)
2. Franklin, J., Perrig, A., Paxson, V., Savage, S.: An inquiry into the nature and causes of the wealth of internet miscreants. In: Proceedings of the 14th ACM conference on Computer and communications security (CCS 2007), pp. 375–388. ACM, New York (2007)
3. Christodorescu, M., Jha, S., Seshia, S.A., Song, D., Bryant, R.E.: Semantics-aware malware detection. In: Proceedings of the 2005 IEEE Symposium on Security and Privacy (Oakland 2005), pp. 32–46. ACM Press, Oakland (2005)
4. Martignoni, L., Stinson, E., Fredrikson, M., Jha, S., Mitchell, J.C.: A Layered Architecture for Detecting Malicious Behaviors. In: Lippmann, R., Kirda, E., Trachtenberg, A. (eds.) RAID 2008. LNCS, vol. 5230, pp. 78–97. Springer, Heidelberg (2008)
5. NovaShield Inc.: NovaShield Anti-Malware, http://www.novashield.com/
6. Sana Security: Primary Response SafeConnect, http://www.sanasecurity.com/
7. PC Tools: ThreatFire AntiVirus – Behavioral Virus and Spyware Protection, http://www.threatfire.com/
8. Slashdot: AVG virus scanner removes critical Windows file, http://tech.slashdot.org/article.pl?sid=08/11/10/2319209
9. Heise Media: Bitdefender and GData delete winlogon system file, http://www.h-online.com/security/Bitdefender-and-GData-delete-winlogon-system-file--/news/112652
10. AMTSO: Fundamental principles of testing, http://www.amtso.org/documents/doc_download/6-amtso-fundamental-principles-of-testing.html
11. Martignoni, L., Paleari, R.: WUSSTrace – a user-space syscall tracer for Microsoft Windows, http://security.dico.unimi.it/projects.shtml
12. Nielson, F., Nielson, H.R., Hankin, C.L.: Principles of Program Analysis. Springer, Heidelberg (1999)
13. Agrawal, H., Horgan, J.R.: Dynamic Program Slicing. In: Proceedings of the ACM SIGPLAN 1990 Conference on Programming Language Design and Implementation, White Plains, NY, USA, June 1990, pp. 246–256 (1990)
14. Szor, P.: The Art of Computer Virus Research and Defense. Addison-Wesley Professional, Reading (2005)

15. Bayer, U., Kruegel, C., Kirda, E.: TTAnalyze: A Tool for Analyzing Malware. In: 15th Annual Conference of the European Institute for Computer Antivirus Research, EICAR (2006)
16. Willems, C., Holz, T., Freiling, F.: Toward automated dynamic malware analysis using CWSandbox. IEEE Security & Privacy 5(2), 32–39 (2007)
17. Moser, A., Kruegel, C., Kirda, E.: Exploring Multiple Execution Paths for Malware Analysis. In: Proceeding of the 2007 IEEE Symposium on Security and Privacy, pp. 231–245. IEEE Computer Society Press, Oakland (2007)
18. Yin, H., Song, D., Egele, M., Kirda, E., Kruegel, C.: Panorama: Capturing System-wide Information Flow for Malware Detection and Analysis. In: Proceedings of the 14th ACM Conference on Computer and Communications Security, CCS. ACM, Alexandria (2007)
19. Hsu, F., Chen, H., Ristenpart, T., Li, J., Su, Z.: Back to the Future: A Framework for Automatic Malware Removal and System Repair. In: ACSAC 2006, pp. 257–268. IEEE Computer Society, Los Alamitos (2006)
20. Liang, Z., Venkatakrishnan, V.N., Sekar, R.: Isolated Program Execution: An Application Transparent Approach for Executing Untrusted Programs. In: Proceedings of the 19th Annual Computer Security Applications Conference (ACSAC 2003), pp. 182–191. IEEE Computer Society, Los Alamitos (2003)
21. Nightingale, E.B., Chen, P.M., Flinn, J.: Speculative execution in a distributed file system. In: Proceedings of the twentieth ACM symposium on Operating systems principles, pp. 191–205. ACM, New York (2005)
22. Christodorescu, M., Jha, S.: Testing malware detectors. SIGSOFT Software Engineering Notes 29(4), 34–44 (2004)
23. Bruce, J.: The Challenge of Detecting and Removing Installed Threats. In: Virus Bulletin Conference (October 2006)
24. Morgenstern, M., Marx, A.: System Cleaning: Getting Rid of Malware from Infected PCs. In: Virus Bulletin Conference (June 2008)

Towards Proactive Spam Filtering
(Extended Abstract)

Jan Göbel, Thorsten Holz, and Philipp Trinius

Laboratory for Dependable Distributed Systems
University of Mannheim, Germany
{goebel,holz,trinius}@informatik.uni-mannheim.de

Abstract. With increasing security measures in network services, remote exploitation is getting harder. As a result, attackers concentrate on
more reliable attack vectors like email: victims are infected using either
malicious attachments or links leading to malicious websites. Therefore
efficient filtering and blocking methods for spam messages are needed.
Unfortunately, most spam filtering solutions proposed so far are *reactive*, they require a large amount of both ham and spam messages to
efficiently generate rules to differentiate between both. In this paper, we
introduce a more *proactive* approach that allows us to directly collect
spam message by interacting with the spam botnet controllers. We are
able to observe *current* spam runs and obtain a copy of latest spam messages in a fast and efficient way. Based on the collected information we
are able to generate *templates* that represent a concise summary of a
spam run. The collected data can then be used to improve current spam
filtering techniques and develop new venues to efficiently filter mails.

1   Introduction

In the recent years, we observe a shift how attackers proceed to compromise
system on a larger scale: instead of using random scanning and remote exploits
against common Windows network services, more and more attacks use email
messages as propagation vector. These spam messages either contain a malicious
attachment or a link to a malicious web page to compromise victims by exploiting
client side applications, like the victim's browser [8,11,18].

Current approaches to deal with email spam have the problem that they are
commonly *reactive*: Given a large collection of email messages collected at end-
user mailboxes or dedicated mailboxes (so called *spamtraps*), the algorithms
extract features of all messages that can be used to distinguish spam from ham
messages, for example by using a Bayesian model [2,14] or other machine learning techniques [3]. A complementary approach is to generate a blacklist of IP
addresses that are known to be related to spam. Such blacklists can for example be constructed by extracting frequently appearing sender IP addresses from
spam email headers [6]. Another example are URIBLs (*Uniform Resource Identifier Blacklists*) that list domain names that appear in URIs such as web sites

U. Flegel and D. Bruschi (Eds.): DIMVA 2009, LNCS 5587, pp. 38–47, 2009.

mentioned in messages more than a given threshold of times [7]. All these approaches have the drawback that they need a larger collection of email messages in order to generate precise rules, to distinguish ham and spam emails.

In this paper, we present an approach to deal with spam in a more *proactive* way: instead of waiting at the end-user's mailboxes or spamtraps for spam to arrive and decide whether or not this is spam, we directly *interact* with the servers that are used to send spam. The basic idea is that we execute *spambots*, i.e., malicious software dedicated to sending spam emails, in a controlled environment and collect all email messages sent by the bots. This enables us to directly interfere with botnet control servers to collect *current* spam messages sent by a specific botnet. Based on the collected information, we can generate models of how spam messages look like (so called *spam templates*), identify unique spam runs, and extract information that can be used to enhance spam filtering techniques. Current research shows that the actual number of unique spam botnets out there is not very large (in the order of hundreds or thousands [5,15,16]), and thus it may be feasible to continuously collect information about a significant number of spam botnets in the wild with only a limited amount of resources.

The contributions of this paper are threefold. First, we propose a proactive approach to filter email messages. With the help of controlled spambot executions, we are able to collect spam messages in the very early phases of a spam run and can continuously observe different kinds of bots. Second, we show how the collected information allows us to generate filter rules which can be used to detect spam messages, or to generate blacklists to efficiently block spam, way ahead of current techniques to mitigate spam. Third, we implemented the system and present first results of running the system for a limited amount of time.

2   Related Work

Concurrent with our work, Xie et al. [20] and John et al. [5] introduced similar techniques to study current spambots. The basic idea of all three projects is to execute spambots in a controlled environment and collect current spam messages by observing the behavior of the bots. In contrast to the other two projects, our focus is on generating spam templates that can then be used to filter incoming spam. We use the complete email text and not only embedded URLs to be able to detect a wider range of spam. For example, image-based spam or spam messages that contain links to popular websites can potentially not be handled correctly by the other two projects.

Venkataraman et al. introduced a method to use the network structure for proactive spam mitigation [17]. Their approach is orthogonal to ours and could be combined: we use information about the actual spam sources and the spam messages sent, whereas their approach focusses on filtering known bad IP netblocks. Ramachandran et al. studied DNSBLs and the techniques used by spammers in detail [13,12]. These techniques also complement our work, since we focus on directly interacting with the spam botnets to extract information about new spam runs as early as possible.

The effectiveness of blacklists was studied by Jung et al. [6]. Since spammers behave very dynamic and change their tactics frequently, it is questionable whether or not the results from 2004 still hold. Especially due to the spammer's move to (reverse) SOCKS proxies and template-based spamming, the effectiveness of blacklists is limited. Kreibich et al. studied Storm Worm in great detail and provide more information about template-based spamming [8], one of the most popular techniques used by spammers.

3   Overview of Current Spamming Techniques

Traditional Spamming Techniques. The traditional technique for sending spam is *direct spamming*: a spammer uses a set of machines under his control to send spam mails to the intended recipients directly. This specific behavior can easily be detected by an ISP (e.g., a large amount of outgoing SMTP connections or many complaints about a specific IP address), who then shuts down the spammer's account or blocks further SMTP requests from the specific IP addresses.

As a result, spammers started to use *open email relays* to send out spam mails [6]. The basic idea is that misconfigured mail servers can be easily abused to send out large amounts of spam: a spammer has to scan the network for such open mail relays and then send all his spam emails using this server. This technique was mainly used by spammers several years ago, thus efficient techniques exist to block spam sent via open relays, e.g., blacklists as explained in Section 4. *Proxy pots* (i.e, honeypots that act as open relays [1,10]) can be used to study spammers that still use open relays and provide additional input to spam detection filters.

A similar technique to send out spam emails is based on *open proxies*: the spammer scans the network for open proxies (typically either SOCKS protocol version 4 or 5). Once he has found an open proxy, he uses this machine to relay SMTP commands to the recipient's mail server via the proxy. The open proxies thus acts as a intermediary between the spammer and the mail server, efficiently hiding the spammer's true identity. Nevertheless, there exist several blacklists which contain IP addresses of current open proxies.

(Reverse) SOCKS Proxy-based Spamming. To counter the success of blacklists, spammers use compromised machines as proxies: the attacker installs a SOCKS proxy on the compromised machine and then uses these proxies to send SMTP commands to the mail server (see Figure 1(a) for an illustration). Since the IP address of the bots changes frequently — for example due to reboots of the infected machine or other DHCP effects — blacklists have a hard time to keep up with the dynamic changes. In order to be more efficient, the attackers invented the concept of *reverse proxy-based spamming* [4]. The bot connects in the first phase to the controller and establishes a reverse SOCKS proxy connection. All SMTP commands are then relayed through this tunnel from the controller to the actual mail server. The basic concept is the same, the main advantage is that the bots announce to the controller once they are available and can then immediately be used for spamming purposes. Furthermore, the approach also has the fundamental advantage that bots behind a NAT gateway can be used by

the spammer as well: these machines are typically not directly reachable and can thus not be used for proxy-based spamming. However, if they use a reverse proxy approach, also these machines, which are typically end-user machines running behind a DSL router, can be used for spamming purposes. Again, due to the dynamic nature of these machines, blacklists are often not able to accurately list these machines. Therefore, reverse proxy-based spamming is an interesting method from an attacker's point of view to send out spam emails.

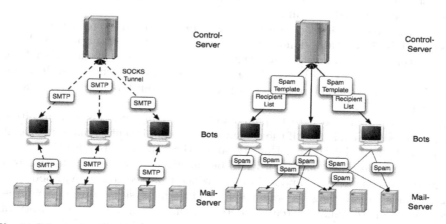

Fig. 1. Schematic overview of (a) SOCKS proxy-based spamming (b) template-based spamming, two common spamming techniques nowadays

Template-based Spamming. Another modern technique used by spammers is *template-based spamming*, as illustrated in Figure 1(b). Instead of relaying the SMTP commands through the compromised machines, the attacker sends the bots a *spam template* that describes the structure of the spam message to be sent. Furthermore, the attacker sends meta-data like recipient list, subject list, and a list of URLs that are used to fill in variables in the template. The bots then construct an email based on the template and the meta-data, and send this email to the targets. As a result, the actual work of handling the SMTP communication is moved from the control server to the bots. Nowadays this technique is used by most large spam botnets, like Storm Worm, Bobax, Rustock, and a lot of the other major spam botnets [15,16].

One indication that this technique is widely used by spammers can be seen by the huge drop in spam emails after the web hosting service provider McColo was shutdown in November 2008 [9]. This provider is suspected to have supported spammers by hosting many control servers used in template-based spamming [16]. When the provider McColo was disconnected on Tuesday, November 11, 2008, the average number of detected spam mails dropped more than half on many networks [9].

4   Towards Proactive Spam Filtering

In this section we discuss a few of the current techniques to filter spam mails. A *DNS blacklist* (*DNSBL*) contains a list of IP addresses that mail servers should block and not accept mail from. A DNSBL can be queried with the help of the DNS system and allows an efficient way to perform lookups. DNSBLs typically list either open mail relays or open proxies. However, there exist also DNSBLs that list other suspicious hosts, e.g., machines running within specific networks or supposedly infected machines.

Closely related to DNSBLs are URIBLs (*Uniform Resource Identifier Blacklists*). An URIBL contains domain names and IP addresses that appear in URIs such as web sites mentioned in message bodies more than a given threshold of times. In contrast to DNSBLs, which are used to check the sender's address, an URIBL checks the *content* of mail messages for suspicious links and complements the DNSBL check.

Another approach to detect spam mail are *hashing systems*: the intuition behind this approach is that if the same message body is sent to many people, it is bulk and should be filtered. Unfortunately, these systems require that many people receive the same mail in order to be effective. This can be defeated by a spammer with the help of random content which is added to the mail body.

Bayesian spam filtering [14] and rule-based filtering systems such as SpamAssassin focus on the mail content to detect spam. Given a large repository of both spam and ham messages, these approaches extract features of all messages that can be used to distinguish spam from ham messages, e.g., via a Bayesian model [2,14] or other machine learning techniques [3].

An orthogonal approach to prevent spam messages is *greylisting*: a mail server does not accept an incoming messages from an unknown sender and responds with a temporarily reject message (often SMTP return code 450 or 451). A legitimate mail server will typically re-send the message after a short timeout, whereas current bots commonly try to send a message only once. Therefore, messages sent via bots are effectively blocked. Unfortunately, this approach only works since bots do not try to re-send messages. Once enough mail servers use greylisting, the spammers will presumably adopt and also re-send messages.

4.1   Infrastructure for Proactive Spam Collection

Most approaches to filter mail as discussed in the previous section require a corpus of both spam and ham messages. Based on these two sets, filtering rules are extracted. These rules can for example be either a model how spam messages look like (Bayesian or rule-based filtering) or a threshold-based approach to classify a given message as spam if it contains certain URIs. To be more efficient, it is desirable to obtain spam messages as accurately and early as possible when the bots start spamming. In this section, we introduce an approach to collect spam messages in an automated way by directly communicating with the spam botnet control servers. This approach can be used to study both (reverse) proxy- and template-based spamming operations in an automated way.

A straightforward approach to collect spam mails is based on high-interaction honeypots: we execute a spambot on a native Windows machine and let it communicate with the controller such that the bot can either establish a SOCKS tunnel or receive the template and meta-information from the controller. However, we prevent outgoing spam messages by intercepting SMTP communication at the local gateway and emulating the behavior of the target mail server. For example, if the bot wants to connect to `gsmtp183.google.com`, we first intercept this communication and redirect it to the local mail server running at the gateway. Furthermore, we grab the banner from the intended server and then replay the banner to the bot. As a result, the bot is tricked into thinking that it actually communicates with the intended server, whereas it only communicates with our mail server. We can collect all mail messages at the gateway and obtain an overview of the *current* spam messages sent via this spam botnet.

After a certain amount of time, we reset the machine to a clean system using a software-based restore mechanism and execute the next spambot. Different strategies exist to determine when we have collected "enough" unique email messages to reset the honeypot. Simple heuristics include using a predefined timeout or a predefined number of email messages that should be collected, e.g., resetting the honeypot once 5,000 spam messages are collected. Advanced techniques analyze the collected spam messages and reset the honeypot once a complete spam run was observed: our preliminary results indicate that one spam run typically consists of 10 − 100 different domains being advertised in different kind of spam emails. These domains are advertised in a round-robin fashion, and thus we can reset the honeypot once we have observed each URI several times. We have implemented several heuristics to decide if we have already collected enough useful emails and still evaluate which technique works best in practice.

Furthermore, we have implemented a priority queue that enables us to periodically monitor a given spam botnet: Once we have collected enough spam messages from a given binary and thus do not obtain any new information, we revert the honeypot back to a clean state and start the next bot. However, we enqueue the binary for another analysis run since the spam campaign could change and we could observe new spam mails when we execute the bot again later on.

4.2   Towards Proactive Spam Filtering

The spam mails collected with the help of the system proposed in the previous section can be used to generate spam filtering rules in a *proactive* way: since we observe a live spambot, we can be sure that we observe *only* spam messages. Based on the collected information, we can generate detection rules. The easiest rule is an URI blacklist based on the advertised URIs we observe in the collected messages. We can also analyze the spam message in more detail: quite often, the spam engine of a bot contains unique artifacts that can be used to identify the spambot and classify a given message as spam. These artifacts could be specific header fields or the arrangement of certain header fields or body text. Finally, we can generate a model describing the overall structure of the spam message. This model would include the complete template we extracted by analyzing several spam samples. An incoming mail message could then be checked against this model and if it matches, the mail would be classified as spam.

We analyze all collected spam mails and extract common parts to generate a model that matches the spam emails collected from a single spambot. For extraction we use a variation of the longest common substring (LCS) algorithm. We generate all common substrings of all emails contained in a single observed spam run and fill the gaps with placeholders to form a raw template. More specifically, we use the following algorithm to compute a single raw template:

1. First, we read all emails belonging to a single observed spam run and sort them according to their text length. Thus, longer emails are processed first.
2. In the second step, we take the first email from the sorted list and consider it as our first raw template named α.
3. Then, we take the next email from the list and merge it with α to form a second raw template named β, which is then one step more specific than the previous template α.
4. Now, we compare the two raw templates α and β and determine the amount of text that was replaced by placeholders. If the percentage of removed text is below a predefined threshold θ, β becomes our new α, the email used to form β is removed from the list and we continue with step three. That way only emails that do not modify α too much are added to the final template of this run. If the percentage of changed text is above θ, the current β is too generic and is therefore discarded. The email that was used to generate β is moved back to the list of emails and we take the next email from the list to create a new β, as described in step three.
5. As long as emails are in the list we continue with step three. At some point no more emails are left for processing or only those emails are left that did not fulfill the threshold criteria θ. That means that α becomes static. At this point, the raw template is finished and a new raw template generation process begins, with all emails that are left from the previous run.

After the template generation process we end up with a certain number of raw templates, and the number of email that were used to form each. The generated raw templates do not contain any regular expressions yet, but only placeholders. Thus, we generate from each email that was used to form the template a regular expression to replace the placeholders. To achieve this we analyze the variable parts of the emails, i.e., the parts of the email that are replaced by placeholders in the raw template, and store the length of the longest and shortest variable part. Furthermore, we analyze the characters of the variable part to decide if the resulting regular expression should contain digits, characters, or special characters, or all together.

Once all placeholders are replaced with a regular expression, we have a precise template in form of a single regular expression matching all emails of the particular spam run captured in our monitoring environment. Note, that in case a spambot sends messages with permuted words, sentences, or various synonym words, templates can either become too generic or several templates are generated for each message with a permuted sentence for example.

```
Subject: ([\:\'\,\?\w]){3,11} ([\,\'\?\s\w]){14,35}
X-Mailer: Microsoft Outlook Express 6.00.2900.2180

Body:
Lose Weight -Burn Fat -Look great and feel=20
great -
 
http://([A-Za-z]){9,14}.chat.ru
 
And do all this with a miracle weight loss fruit &#8211; ACAI BERRY &#8211;=
Best=20
of all &#8211; it&#8217;s completely FREE for a limited time! Click here to=
 receive your=20
completely free bottle of ACAI BERRY supplemnt!
```

Fig. 2. Final spam template extracted from analyzing over one thousand emails received by a single spambot

Figure 2 shows the results of such a template generation process. The template was generated from 431 spam emails sent by a single spambot. During this spam run only a single campaign was advertised. The figure shows that the template used by the spambot contains very little variable parts. Most of the text is completely fixed, leaving only the subject, and the advertised URL as variable parts within the generated template. Note that the URL is only partially variable, the domain name of the URL is fixed.

In the current template generation process, we only consider the subject, x-mailer, and the complete body of spam messages. Any other information including attachments are stripped from the emails, as most of the header fields like "From:" and "To:" contain only variable parts which do not add more information to the conciseness of the template.

5   Preliminary Results

We obtain malware samples with the help of different honeypot solutions. For example, we use different honeypots to collect samples of autonomously spreading bots and worms, and honeyclients to collect samples of malware that is installed via malicious websites. Furthermore, suspicious samples can be manually submitted to our analysis environment. In total, we receive between 400 and 1,500 unique samples per day using this setup. All samples are analyzed with the help of an automated tool called CWSandbox [19], and a sample that shows signs of spam behavior can then be analyzed in the honeypot environment described above. We keep the samples in a queue and periodically execute them again, such that we can observe changes in the spam runs of a given spam botnet and obtain the latest set of spam messages.

Executing a spambot allows us to efficiently collect spam messages. In the current setup, we use a time-out of 30 minutes after which we reset the honeypot and execute the next malware sample. During this period, the bot typically sends a few hundred up to a few thousand spam messages, we even observed several bots sending more than 50,000 spam messages in this short amount of time.

So far we have executed 40 different spambots in the analysis environment. This resulted in a total of 100.977 spam emails to use for template generation. First checks against a local spam folder with 20.290 spam emails revealed that 30% of the spam email belong to spam campaigns we were able to collect in our observation environment. Some of these spam emails are even more than one year old and still use the same template. As this first test was rather quick and did not consider the full templates we generate, we guess that the detection rate is even higher. The reason why we were not able to use full templates yet is that for the spam campaigns found in the local spam folder we do not have enough emails that were also sent by the bots that ran in our analysis environment. As the detection rate of the spam emails with the help of templates highly depends on the diversity of the emails used to generate the template, a slight variation in the spam campaign can render a template useless.

The following example describes the problem. We used 493 emails from a Casino advertising spam campaign collected during June and November 2008 to evaluate the template generation process. We collected 71 emails in the analysis environment advertising the same campaign on November 10th, 2008. From these 71 emails we generated a single template and tested it against the 493 emails from the spam folder. Only 26 emails matched the template (5% detection rate). The reason for this low detection rate is the low diversity of spam emails collected in the analysis environment during the 30 minutes of execution time: they are all the same. If we take a single slightly different email from the 493 emails and add it to the template generation process, the detection rate rises to 26%. If we add another email to the template generation process, we even achieve 99% detection and all that changes within the template is the advertised URL, the text message is untouched. As a result, the number of emails needed to form a good template depends on the diversity of the spam campaign and the time span the template should be used without update. For the example above it suffices to use three emails for template generation to obtain a 99% detection rate.

6 Conclusion

In this paper, we introduced a technique to learn more about current spambots. We execute a spambot in a controlled environment and collect all mails sent from this bot by emulating mail servers. The technique is proactive in the sense that we do not wait for a message to arrive at an end-users mailbox before using it for classification, but we directly interact with the spambots and botnet controllers. This allows us to obtain information about new spam runs earlier than with current approaches. Furthermore, since we only collect spam messages, we can use them to generate filtering rules. We presented a simple approach to enhance current URIBLs, but the collected information can also be used to extract the message template used by the bot. This information can then be used to examine an incoming message, and if it matches the template, it is highly likely spam.

References

1. Andreolini, M., Bulgarelli, A., Colajanni, M., Mazzoni, F.: HoneySpam: Honeypots Fighting Spam at the Source. In: Proceedings of the SRUTI 2005 (2005)
2. Androutsopoulos, I., Koutsias, J., Chandrinos, K.V., Paliouras, G., Spyropoulos, C.D.: An Evaluation of Naive Bayesian Anti-Spam Filtering. In: Workshop on Machine Learning in the New Information Age (2000)
3. Drucker, H., Wu, D., Vapnik, V.: Support vector machines for spam categorization. IEEE Transactions on Neural Networks 10(5), 1048–1054 (1999)
4. Honeynet Project. Know Your Enemy Lite: Proxy Threats – Port v666 (2008), http://honeynet.org/papers/proxy/index.html
5. John, J.P., Moshchuk, A., Gribble, S.D., Krishnamurthy, A.: Studying Spamming Botnets Using Botlab. In: Proceedings of NSDI 2009 (2009)
6. Jung, J., Sit, E.: An Empirical Study of Spam Traffic and the Use of DNS Black Lists. In: Proceedings of the 4th ACM Conference on Internet Measurement (2004)
7. Kim, J., Chung, K., Choi, K.: Spam Filtering With Dynamically Updated URL Statistics. IEEE Security and Privacy 5(4) (2007)
8. Kreibich, C., Kanich, C., Levchenko, K., Enright, B., Voelker, G.M., Paxson, V., Savage, S.: On the spam campaign trail. In: Proceedings of LEET 2008 (2008)
9. Lemos, R.: McColo Takedown Nets Massive Drop in Spam (2008), http://www.securityfocus.com/brief/855
10. Pathak, A., Hu, Y.C., Mao, Z.M.: Peeking into Spammer Behavior from a Unique Vantage Point. In: Proceedings of LEET 2008 (2008)
11. Provos, N., McNamee, D., Mavrommatis, P., Wang, K., Modadugu, N.: The Ghost in the Browser Analysis of Web-based Malware. In: Proceedings of HotBots 2007 (2007)
12. Ramachandran, A., Feamster, N.: Understanding the network-level behavior of spammers. SIGCOMM Comput. Commun. Rev. 36(4), 291–302 (2006)
13. Ramachandran, A., Feamster, N., Dagon, D.: Revealing Botnet Membership Using DNSBL Counter-Intelligence. In: Proceedings of the SRUTI 2006 (2006)
14. Sahami, M., Dumais, S., Heckerman, D., Horvitz, E.: A Bayesian Approach to Filtering Junk E-Mail. In: Learning for Text Categorization. AAAI Technical Report WS-98-05 (1998)
15. Stewart, J.: Top Spam Botnets Exposed (April 2008), http://secureworks.com/research/threats/topbotnets/
16. Stewart, J.: Spam Botnets to Watch in 2009 (January 2009), http://secureworks.com/research/threats/botnets2009/
17. Venkataraman, S., Sen, S., Spatscheck, O., Haffner, P., Song, D.: Exploiting Network Structure for Proactive Spam Mitigation. In: Proceedings of 16th USENIX Security Symposium (2007)
18. Wang, Y.-M., Beck, D., Jiang, X., Roussev, R., Verbowski, C., Chen, S., King, S.T.: Automated Web Patrol with Strider HoneyMonkeys: Finding Web Sites That Exploit Browser Vulnerabilities. In: Proceedings of NDSS 2006 (2006)
19. Willems, C., Holz, T., Freiling, F.: CWSandbox: Towards Automated Dynamic Binary Analysis. IEEE Security and Privacy 5(2) (2007)
20. Xie, Y., Yu, F., Achan, K., Panigrahy, R., Hulten, G., Osipkov, I.: Spamming Botnets: Signatures and Characteristics. In: Proceedings of SIGCOMM 2008 (2008)

Shepherding Loadable Kernel Modules through On-demand Emulation

Chaoting Xuan[1], John Copeland[1], and Raheem Beyah[1,2]

[1] School of Electrical and Computer Engineering, Georgia Institute of Technology
[2] Department of Computer Science, Georgia State University

Abstract. Despite many advances in system security, rootkits remain a threat to major operating systems. First, this paper discusses why kernel integrity verification is not sufficient to counter all types of kernel rootkits and a confidentiality-violation rootkit is demonstrated to evade all integrity verifiers. Then, the paper presents, DARK, a rootkit prevention system that tracks a suspicious loadable kernel module at a granite level by using on-demand emulation, a technique that dynamically switches a running system between virtualized and emulated execution. Combining the strengths of emulation and virtualization, DARK is able to thoroughly capture the activities of the target module in a guest OS, while maintaining reasonable run-time performance. To address integrity-violation and confidentiality-violation rootkits, we create a group of security policies that can detect all avialiable Linux rootkits. Finally, it is shown that normal guest OS performance is unaffected. The performance is only decreased when rootkits attempt to run, while most rootkits are detected at installation.

Keywords: Rootkit Prevention, Virtual Machine Monitor, Emulator, On-demand Emulation.

1 Introduction and Background

The security issue of the operating system extensions has been studied for years. Unfortunately, the fact is that many commodity operating systems (e.g., Windows XP and numerous Linux distributions) don not provide the defense against those malicious kernel extensions. In recent years, academics propose a "Out-of-the-Box" approach [2][3][4][5][6][32][35][36][37] to protect detection software by placing it outside the target (guest) OS, e.g. hypervisors (virtual machine monitor), external co-processor. This approach creates strong isolation between detection software and malware such that the former is "invisible" to the latter, (most likely) surviving its attacks accordingly.

Rutkowska [7] proposed a taxonomy that classifies rootkits according to how they interact with operating systems. Type I rootkits refers to those that tamper with the static part of an operating system, e.g. kernel text, system call table and IDT; Type II rootkits refers to those that modify the dynamic part of an operating system, e.g., the data section. Since contemporary OSs are not designed

U. Flegel and D. Bruschi (Eds.): DIMVA 2009, LNCS 5587, pp. 48–67, 2009.

to be verifiable, a large amount of dynamic kernel objects that can potentially be exploited by type II rootkits present challenges to security communities [8]. Recent progresses made in rootkit researches [9][10][11][13][14] reveal that hackers may take advantage of some hardware features to construct stealthy rootkits to beat the existing rootkit detectors.

Kernel run-time protection mechanisms can be categorized as detection and prevention. Inherent limitations of rootkit detection mechanisms are discussed in Section 2. Previous run-time rootkit prevention approaches [31][32] focus on protecting the benign kernel code and thwarting malicious kernel code. One key issue here is how to determine the goodness and trustworthiness of any piece of kernel code. Unfortunately, previous approaches did not give in-depth analysis of this problem and just simply assume it is a priori knowledge to end users or protection systems, which is not true in practice. To date, there is no such commodity operating system that strictly control the kernel code loading based on both goodness and trustworthiness of kernel code. Even Microsoft's driver code signing [34] is just employed for the identification of driver code authors, but not for assuring the goodness of signed drivers [33]. The effectiveness and robustness of this mechanism are still being questioned [1][33]. In the end, people have to make decision on whether to install a useful but potentially unsecure driver, which is a challenge that is not addressed by previous approaches.

In this paper, we propose a rootkit prevention approach that tackles the challenge above, while enhancing the existing prevention approaches. The basic idea is to sandbox a suspicious loadable kernel module in an emulator and to assure its goodness by enforcing a group of well-selected security policies. Based on open source software Qemu and Kqemu [12], we designed and implemented a software system, namely DARK that uses on-demand emulation to provide powerful defense against kernel malware. In DARK, when a rootkit tampers with a kernel object or hardware object, its illegal behavior is captured and blocked. In the meanwhile, VM emulation takes place only at the time that a suspicious module is executed. Further, most operations of the VM are performed in virtualization mode. Thus, the substantial execution overhead caused by emulation is avoided. Our contribution in this work includes:

1. Identification of non-integrity-violation rootkits that can escape kernel integrity verifiers.
2. Implementation of a novel rootkit prevention system based on on-demand emulation to sandbox a suspicious kernel module.
3. Creation of a group of security policies to detect and block all rootkits we collected.

The rest of paper is structured as follows. First, we explain the limitation of current rootkit detection mechanisms in Section 2. Section 3 presents the design and implementation of on-demand emulation. Section 4 and 5 describe the details of creating and enforcing security policy. We present the security and performance evaluation results in Section 6 and introduce related work in Section 7, while Section 8 concludes the paper.

2   Limitations of Rootkit Detection Techniques

Run-time rootkit detection methods proposed by researchers can be divided into two categories: specific rootkit detection and generic rootkit detection. Methods in the first category focus on capturing specific type of rootkits. For example, Cross-view diff-based method [6][25] just targets rootkits that conceal disk objects (files and registries); Lycosid [35] is intended to discover hidden process only. On the contrary, methods in the second category are designed to counter broad types of rootkits. To the best of our knowledge, the most generic rootkit detectors known to the public are kernel integrity verifiers [2][3][4][5][21][24][37]. Kernel integrity verifiers concentrate on examining the states of some kernel objects to ensure that illegal tampering of these objects don not occur. They are effective at defeating integrity-violation rootkits. Unfortunately, theses kernel integrity verifiers suffer two fundamental weaknesses: incompleteness of assuring the integrity of dynamic kernel objects; inability of detecting non-integrity-violation rootkits, like confidentiality-violation rootkits and hardware-exploiting rootkits. These two weaknesses are discussed in detail below.

2.1   Dynamic Kernel Objects

Most kernel rootkits are implemented in the form of kernel modules (drivers). Hence, they share the same virtual memory environments as operating system. No matter whether a kernel object (structure, list, text and so on) is exported or not by the OS, a rootkit can always directly access and tamper with it after being loaded to the kernel. In fact, direct kernel object manipulation (DKOM) is one common technique employed by rootkit writers [28]. A kernel object could reside on either permanent memory area (text, dss) or transient memory area (stack and heap); its content could be constant or changeable. A kernel object is static if its memory address is permanent. Otherwise, this object is dynamic. Defending a static kernel object is straightforward, as its location and content are relatively easy to identify. On the other hand, protecting a dynamic object could become challenging due to the following four reasons. First, in comparison with static objects, the population of dynamic objects is much larger, and enumerating all dynamic kernel objects at any time could be impractical. Second, since integrity verifiers have to wake up to work periodically, they miss catching lots of short-lived dynamic objects, e.g., local variables in stacks. Third, a detector's recognition of dynamic objects can be attacked by rootkits so that those objects are invisible to the detector. For examples, rootkits can alter the page table to hide kernel objects from detectors, or remove an element from a link list to make it untraceable. Last, the content of a kernel object can be unpredictable and detectors are unable to differentiated good and bad values. One such example is the entropy pool of Linux kernel, which can be manipulated by rootkits to compromise Linux Pseudo-Random Number Generator (PRNG) [8]. In summary, kernel integrity verifiers cannot assure the integrities of all dynamic objects in a kernel.

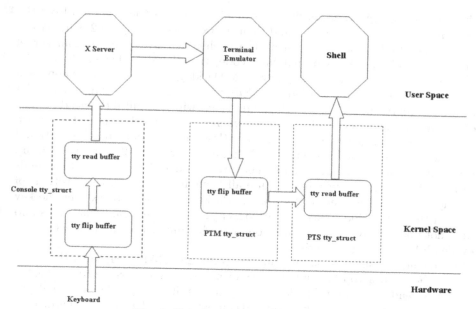

Fig. 1. Key data flow in Linux desktop

2.2 Non-integrity-violation Rootkits

Non-integrity-violation rootkits are rootkits that launch attacks while not manipulating any kernel objects, so kernel integrity verifiers can not catch them. One type of non-integrity-violation rootkits is hardware-exploiting the rootkit, which misuses hardware feature or configuration to achieve their goals. Another type of non-integrity-violation rootkits: confidentiality-violation rootkits. They break the kernel data confidentiality while preserving the data integrity. One class of candidates for the confidentiality-violation rootkits is data theft rootkits, e.g., keyloggers and network sniffers. Next, we demonstrate one confidentiality-violation rootkit: a Linux keylogger (called darklogger) that can sniff keystrokes without illegally changing any kernel object.

Today, common Linux desktop environments like Gnome and KDE use X window systems to manage terminal service: interacting with the keyboard and mouse, drawing and moving windows on the screen. The key data flow in a typical X window system is shown in figure 1. On the X server, the key reading path from keyboard to user space consists of at least two threads working in tandem: a top thread originating from a user process that issues read requests, and a bottom thread originating from the interrupt service routine that reads the key data from the keyboard. Two kernel buffers, *tty flip buffer* (`tty_struct.flip.char_buf`) and *tty read buffer* (`tty_struct.read_buf`), store the key data (interpreted by keyboard driver) and provide the synchronization between the top thread and the bottom thread. When the top thread asks for data and the tty flip buffer is empty, the thread goes to sleep; when the bottom thread fills new key data to the *tty flip buffer*, it awakens the top thread who copies the new data from the *tty flip buffer* to *tty read buffer* and then to user space. In figure 2, when a key is generated by keyboard and travels to the shell, it may be kept in four kernel buffers. By adding hooks or patching code, traditional keyloggers hijack the control flow of kernel's processing key data. Darklogger takes a passive approach based on the observation that *tty read buffer* is a large-size circular buffer and a char data, representing a key, in the buffer is not wiped off until the head pointer of the buffer moves back to its location, where a new char data is written. Since human's keystroke speed is relatively slow (less than 30 characters/second) and the size of tty read buffer is large (4k), it takes more than 2 minutes to fill up the entire buffer. Darklogger is a kernel thread that wakes up every 10 seconds to read the *tty read buffer* and acquire all key data. Based on the positions of the head and tail pointers in the buffer, Darklogger is able to extract the key data of the last period. Because Darklogger just uses the legal kernel APIs and does not maliciously hook any function or modify any kernel data object, it can evade all kernel integrity verifiers.

Following the spirit of sandboxing program [29], DARK captures the interactions between a rootkit and the rest of a kernel. The kernel objects visited (memory read, write and function call) by a rootkit are recorded and analyzed regardless of their locations, lifespan and contents. To DARK, the rootkit defense is an access control problem and its success depends on the effectiveness of the security policies. Last, it should be pointed out that DARK is not designed to withstandrookits that access the kernel in abnormal ways, e.g., directly writing kernel memory or injecting malicious code to kernel by exploiting the vulnerabilities of benign kernel code. These attacks have been well addressed by previous rootkit prevention systems [31][32].

3   On-demand Emulation

Virtual Machine Monitors (VMM) and emulators are two types of hypervisors that support and manage multiple virtual machines (VM). A VMM seeks to achieve high performance by directly executing most instructions of a VM on the host (physical) CPU. In contrast, an emulator translates each VM's instruction to host instructions so to provide different types of virtual CPUs to its VMs, paying the cost of poor performance. Due to their deep inspection capabilities, some researchers use emulators to perform various security related tasks, e.g. malware detection and analysis.

DARK is a hybrid system that combines the strengths of VMMs and emulators to offer better system security and performance. It contains three components: a VMM, an emulator and a virtual machine (VM) where a guest OS is installed. In virtualization mode, the virtual machine runs on top of the VMM to gain nearly native speed. When a suspicious module is to be executed in the VM, the VMM is informed to take control of the VM. Then, the VMM collects the virtual CPU state and MMU status data, and sends them to the emulator. Thus, DARK is switched to emulation mode. Once receiving the VMM's virtual CPU state, the emulator restores the VM's operation and start monitoring the module's activities and enforcing the security policies accordingly. When the execution of the module's code is completed, the emulator suspends the VM and passes its control back to VMM with the current virtual CPU state and MMU status data. The VMM restores the VM and DARK is switched to virtualization mode. The emulation is required only when the target module is executed, and most of VM codes still run on VMM.

3.1   Design

The primary task of the on-demand emulation is to trap the module execution in a VM. However, a module may have many non-privilege instructions and their executions in a VM cannot trigger exception or interrupt, which is the only way of transferring the control from VM to VMM in a virtual machine system. DARK addresses this problem by exploring the paging mechanism of operating systems. A *present bit* in the page table entry indicates whether a virtual page has been assigned a physical page frame. When the CPU accesses a virtual page whose *present bit* is 0, memory management unit (MMU) generates a page fault. Then, an interrupt routine is invoked to allocate a physical page frame and copy the page data from the swap area or disk file (demand paging) to this physical page frame. As Linux never swaps kernel codes to disk, the *present bits* of kernel code pages are always set to 1. DARK can trap a module by clearing the *present bits* of its code pages in the virtualization mode. Later, when the module is to be executed, VM issues a page fault. Thus, the VMM of DARK intercepts the exception and passes the control to emulator, who sets those *present bits* back to 1 and starts executing and monitoring the module in the emulation mode. To maintain the integrity of the existing page fault mechanisms, the page fault handler of guest OS should be modified to properly deal with these manipulated page faults.

Before loading a module to guest OS, the DARK user decides whether to monitor the module or not. If yes, the emulator is notified of the module name. To change the *present bits* of the module before its execution, the guest OS issues a software interrupt through instruction "int 0x90". The VMM catches the interrupt, and hand it over to the emulator. Then, the emulator fetches the module name from the VM image and compares it with the one defined by DARK user to decide if the current module is right target. If two names are different, DARK gives up monitoring and switches back to virtualization. Otherwise, DARK kicks off the monitoring with the following steps. First, the emulator queries the text (code) range of the target module from the module list of the guest OS, and sends it to the VMM. Then, it clears the module *present bits* and transfers the control to VMM, forcing the system into the virtualization mode. Later, when the module is to be executed, the VM generates a page fault, which is trapped to the VMM. The VMM uses the text range of the module to identify that the faulty instruction comes from the target module, and transfers the VM control to emulator. After setting the module *present bits* to 1, emulator restores the VM sessions and starts the monitoring process

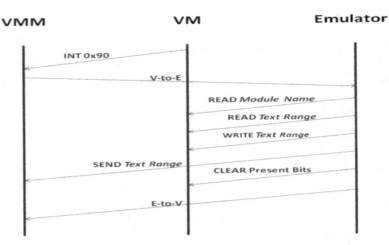

Fig. 2. Partial on-demand emulation process

again. In this way, DARK moves the VM control between VMM and emulator back and forth depending on if the VM executes module code. Figure 2 depicts this on-demand emulation process. When the module is unloaded, DARK turns off on-demand emulation by cleaning up their monitoring records and set the corresponding *present bits* in the VM to 1.

3.2 Implemenation

DARK is built on Qemu and Kqemu [12], who run on any X86 CPU regardless of the hardware virtualization support. Both the guest OS and the host OS are Redhat Linux. Qemu is a hardware emulator that uses binary translation to simulate processor and peripherals, while maintaining a reasonable speed. Kqemu is a kernel module that works with Qemu to provide virtual machine monitor function. In the full virtualization mode of a Qemu/Kqemu system, all user-mode instructions and some kernel-mode instructions of a VM can be directly executed on the host CPU. For security reason, the kernel-mode instructions for memory accesses in the VM have to be intercepted and interpreted by Kqemu. This is done by clearing the global descriptor table (GDT) and local descriptor table (LDT) when VM runs in kernel mode. Thus, any kernel-mode memory access in the VM will cause a general protection fault. Kqemu captures these faults and interprets the instructions in the kernel. Because Kqemu needs Qemu to handle some corner cases such as interpreting HLT instruction, some components of the on-demand emulation framework are already available in orginal Qemu and Kqemu software. To enable the module tracking, DARK modifies the switch control code of the existing on-demand emulation framework. In particular, DARK adds the following business logics to the interrupt handler and V-to-E (virtualization to emulation) control code (in common/module.c and common/kernel.c) of Kqemu:

1. *If an interrupt vector number is 0x90 or 0x91, perfom emulation switching*
2. *For a page fault, if the faulty instruction address is within the text range of target module, perfom emulation switching.*

Moreover, we add one boolean variable to Qemu's E-to-V (emulation to virtualization) control code to ensure that virtualization switch is disabled when the current instruction is from the target module and vice versa.

In addition, we instrument the guest OS kernel (`Linux version 2.4.18`): adding two assembly instructions to `sys_init_module` and `sys_delete_module` functions in `kernel/module.c`. The first instruction issues a software interrupt 0x90 before loading a module; the second one issues the interrupt 0x91 after unloading a module. DARK obtains a module name by reading the module descriptor from the kernel module list. Further, we modify the Linux module loader (insmod.c) to put the module text range in the runsize and `kernel_data` fields of the module descriptor, which allows DARK to read the text range later. In Linux, all processes share one kernel page table that can be accessed from the kernel master page global directory `swapper_pg_dir`. We use this global variable to locate the page table entries of the target module and rewrites the module *present bits* as described in Section 3.1. Last, we alter the page fault handler of the guest OS such that it ignores the page faults caused by the target module execution.

4   Security Policy

DARK does not aim to build perfect security policies to catch all rootkits. In fact, modern operating systems are not designed to be traceable and verifiable, so the creation of such "perfect" policies may be impossible. Rather, similar to SELinux [30], DARK provides a policy framework that gives security administrators the flexibility to write their own security policies. To demonstrate the effectiveness of DARK, we compose a group of security policies that are good enough to detect most existing Linux rootkits and raise the bar for future kernel exploits.

4.1   Policy Framework

DARK treats the rootkit detection as an access control problem: a malicious module needs to illegally access the other part of kernel to perform the attack. DARK's security policy is composed of a group of access control rules whose format is given in table 1.

In table1, *subject* is a kernel module that is to be monitored. A module's home space contains: object (code and global data) section, stack and heap. Any instruction issued from a module space is regarded as a representative of this module, and should be monitored. Note DARK can apply various policies to different modules, which is discussed later. *Operation* indicates the way that a module interacts with the rest of kernel. DARK tracks three types of operations performed by a module: read, write and call. First two are memory access

Table 1. Rule format of Dark

Subject	Operation	Object	Action
{module a, b, c ...}	{read, write, call}	{hardware objects, kernel objects}	{reject, alarm}

operations; call is an action where a module invokes functions exported by OS and other modules. Although a module may influence the kernel objects in other means, e.g., return of an external call, creating a system exception, these three operations are sufficient for DARK to detect the rootkits we know.

Object refers to those system resources and services accessed by a module. Two types of system objects are included in DARK: hardware objects and kernel objects. The former contains dedicated registers, IO ports and IO mapped memory. Many of these hardware objects are crucial to system security. For example, the register IDTR holds the linear address of interrupt descriptor table which is used by CPU to transfer an interrupt to the corresponding Interrupt handler. Hijacking this register allows hacker to amount various attacks, e.g., installing a `virtual-machine-monitor` based rootkits [13][14]. Kernel object is a software concept, and one kernel object is a group of kernel data or code that is semantically meaningful to software developer such as a pointer and a function.

In DARK, a policy rule that contains a hardware object is called system rule; a rule whose object field is a kernel object is called kernel rule. A hardware object that has only one representation in DARK, and it may be a register name, or IO port number or memory address. One kernel object has two representations: one is software-level representation such as variable names and function names, which is used by DARK users to make policies; the other is hardware-level representation and it is a memory address of the corresponding software object. Since DARK enforce policy at hardware level, fore a kernel rule, it's necessary to translate its software-level representation to the hardwarelevel representation, which is called policy translation.

DARK's kernel rules may contain both static kernel objects and dynamic kernel objects. A static kernel object's memory address is determined when the kernel is build, so this object's location is fixed all the time, e.g., system call table. Conversely, a dynamic kernel object's location can only be decided at run time, e.g., a process' page table. A kernel rule containing a static object is called static kernel rule; a kernel rule containing a dynamic object is called dynamic kernel rule. Unlike static kernel rules whose policy translation can be performed before a VM is powered on, policy translation of the dynamic kernel rules has to be postponed to run time.

DARK takes two actions on a policy violation: reject and alarm. Reject denotes that DARK immediately stops executing the target module and prevents any further damages. In Linux, removing a module is more complex and risky than deleting a process from the system, and the former can corrupt the OS's operation integrity and reliability. Current implementation of reject action terminates the VM, and writes a warning message to a log file on the host OS.

Granular failure remediation is of the future work. DARK's alarm action only requires generating the logging messages instead of turning off the whole system. Determination of a reject or alarm action for a rule is based on the consideration of multiple factors: severities to system security, reliability and stability. For those attacks that not only compromise the security but also greatly degrade the system reliability and satiability, reject should be the choice, e.g., runtime patching of the kernel text; For other attacks, terminating the current system operation is not necessary, and alarming is probably sufficient such as sniffing network traffics.

4.2   Established Rules

DARK's policies are constructed based on common knowledge of the OS security and observation of attack patterns of the existing rootkits. Total 19 kernel rules were created and shown in table 2. Among them, four read rules and one call rule are used to address the data theft rootkits as discussed in 2.2. The remaining 14 write rules deal with kernel integrity. Eleven dynamic rules employ seven global variables as the starting points of policy translation. Among them, six global variables are single/double linked lists and the other one (`proc_root`) is associated with binary tree data structure. Note these global variables should be write-protection as well. Otherwise, rootkits may modify the variables to hinder the policy translation. We found that early-stage rootkits tend to manipulate the static kernel objects such as system call table and kernel text. These objects are critical to the system reliability and stability, any illegal modification of them should be rejected at once. Kernel objects contained in Rule 5 and 17 are such examples. On the other hand, some kernel rules are devised to counter the threats in the future, while not being hit by any existing Linux rootkit. For example, it has been reported that some Windows rootkits tamper with the kernel memory management system to hide some kernel objects. It can be foreseen that hackers may apply the same technique to Linux rootkits down to the road. Rule 6 and 10 are designed to achieve such purpose. Rule 9 and 16 in table 3 are optional, because many normal networking drivers may violate them and enforcing these rules possibly generates false alarms. The usages of optional rules depend on user's knowledge to the target modules. In addition to kernel rules, we created 11 system rules, and most of them are applied to special system instructions that handle critical system-level functions, e.g., SGDT and WRMSR.

5   Enforcement

DARK stores the security rules to a local file called policy.dat. This file contains the system rules, static kernel rules and software-level dynamic rules. When a VM is started, DARK forks a thread that performs three tasks: 1. loading the policy.dat to the RAM; 2. periodically translating dynamic kernel rules to the hardware-level representation; 3. transforming all memory-access rules to the hash-table based rules as discussed in Section 5.1. This thread stores all the rules in several global variables, which are used to enforce the policy at run time.

Table 2. Kenrel Rules of Dark

ID	Name	Operation	Kernel Object	Data Type	Action	Dynamic	Optional
1	Console TTY Buffer	Read	`console_table`	`tty_struct`	Alam	No	No
2	Exception Table	Write	`__start_ext__table`	`Exception_table_entry`	Alarm	No	No
3	GDT Table	Write	`gdt_table`	Array	Reject	No	No
4	IDT Table	Write	`idt_table`	Array	Reject	No	No
5	Kernel Text	Write	`_text`	N/A	Reject	No	No
6	MM List	Write	`init_task`	`mm_struct`	Alarm	Yes	No
7	Module List	Write	`module_list`	Module	Alarm	Yes	No
8	Module Text	Write	`module_list`	N/A	Reject	Yes	No
9	Netfilter Hooks	Call	`nf_rejister_hook`	N/A	Alarm	No	Yes
10	Page Table	Write	`init_task`	N/A	Reject	Yes	No
11	Proc Dir Entry List	Write	`proc_root`	`proc_dir_entry`	Alarm	Yes	No
12	Proc Inod Ops List	Write	`proc_root`	`proc_inode_operation`	Alarm	Yes	No
13	Proc file Ops List	Write	`proc_root`	`Proc_file_operation`	Alarm	Yes	No
14	PTM TTY Buffer	Read	`ptm_table`	`tty_struct`	Alarm	Yes	No
15	PTS TTY Buffer	Read	`ptm_table`	`tty_struct`	Alarm	Yes	No
16	Socket Buffer List	Read	`skbuff_head_cache`	`sk_buff`	Alarm	yes	Yes
17	Syscall Table	Write	`syscall_table`	Array	Reject	No	No
18	Task List	Write	`init_task`	`task_struct`	Alarm	Yes	No
19	Task State Segment	Write	`init_tss`	Array	Reject	No	No

When a suspicious module is to be executed, the emulator takes control of the VM and begins policy enforcement. Concretely, DARK intercepts all memory access instructions and some system instructions at the binary translation of Qemu. Note an alternative method is to change the Qemu's simulated MMU to capture the memory accesses. However this method cannot enjoy the benefit of code caching and suffers more performance penalty. For each of the monitored instructions, DARK checks the corresponding rules. If an instruction hit a rule, DARK takes the action defined in the rule. For alarm, DARK writes one warning messages to the system log on the host machine. The message includes the module name, the instruction's address and the rule id. For reject, DARK generates an alarm and then power off the VM by terminating the current Qemu process.

5.1   Hash Table

The data structures that hold memory access rules should be selected prudentially, as inappropriate data structure might hurt system performance. DARK's memory access rules are initially defined as a series of memory intervals. One memory interval, like (0xC03254fa, 0xC03256a0), is called one memory bucket. Some dynamic rules, like socket buffer descriptors, comprise a large amount of memory buckets. If they are stored in linked lists, DARK needs traverse thousands of memory buckets (with various sizes) to inspect one instruction in linear time of n. We present a data transformation method that converts a link list of memory buckets to two hash tables. Since hash table lookups have the complexity of $O(1)$, it can significantly reduce the enforcement overhead.

Similar to the OS concept of a 32-bit page frame, DARK uses 10-bit and 5-bit page frames in the transformation. The memory interval of a bucket is broken into multiple 10-bit or 5-bit page frames and each page frame has one entry in a hash table. Two hash tables stores 10-bit and 5-bit page frame rules respectively. Figure 3 lists the C implementation of the converting routine. The selection of 10 and 5 bit page frames is based on the observation that most memory buckets created by DARK are either large (at the page level) or small (less than 200 bytes). This division ensures that each hash table is not overwhelmed due to the hash conflicts. Given a target memory address, DARK first computes its 5-bit page frame address by removing last 5 bit of the memory address, and searches the frame address from the 5-bit hash table; if not found, it then does the same check for 10-bit hash. Thus, only two bit operations and two hash table lookups are needed at most.

5.2   Code Cache

To reduce the emulation overhead, DARK takes advantage of the performance optimization in Qemu. The key technique is to cache the translated code sequences so that they can be directly executed in the future. Each sequence of instructions ending with a single control transfer instruction is called a block. Qemu translates a block in each main control loop and places the translated block to a code cache. All the translated blocks are organized as a hash table and a cached block can be found fast. A block can be linked to another one if

```
VOID convert_bucket (ULONG start_address, ULONG end_address, int bit) {
        ULONG   mask, page_frame, key, current_address;
        struct value_struct *val;

        mask = (1 << bit) – 1;
        page_frame = 1 << bit;
        current_address = start_address;
        while (1) {
                key = current_address & (~mask);
                val = (value_struct*)malloc(sizeof(value_struct));
                val.start_offset = current_address & mask;
                if (current_addess + page_frame < end_address) {
                        val.end_offset = 0;
                        insert_hash_entry(bit, key, val);
                        current_address += page_frame;
                }
                else { //current_address moves to the last page frame
                        val.end_offset = page_frame – (end_address & mask);
                        insert_hash_entry(bit, key, val);
                        break;
                }
        }
}
```

Fig. 3. Source code of the memory bucket transformation routine

it does not contain the indirect branches, avoiding the extra loop cost. DARK only performs the security check at binary translation, so once a block of code is put into the cache, DARK does not examine it any more. Finally, when the code cache is full, Qemu simply purges all blocks in the cache and refills the cache with new blocks. Since DARK's emulator only caches small-size module code, the chance of overflowing the cache is small.

5.3   Security Log

DARK provides the logging capability that keeps record of the interactions between a module and the rest of the kernel. The log includes: memory write and read, function call and IO operations. For memory read and write, DARK prints out the instruction address, and target memory address and content. For function invocation, DARK records the function address, calling instruction address, the first two parameters and return value of the function. However, parameter semantics of a function are unknown, so DARK logs the first 16 bytes in the stack parameter area of the function. Note that DARK only logs the external memory accesses and function invocation. In addition, we create a tool that interprets log records, identifies all heaps that are assigned to the module, and removes them from the log. Combining this logging capability with Qemu's snapshot can provide the abundant data sources for forensic analysis.

6   Evaluation

This section presents the empirical results of the DARK system. The evaluation is composed of two subsections. In the first subsection, the functional effectiveness of DARK is investigated: whether the security policies are made properly in terms of false positive and false negative detection rates. Then, we conduct the performance evaluation and study the performance impact of on-demand emulation on the VM. DARK is built based on the QEUM 0.8.2 and KQEMU 1.3.0prell. All the experiments are performed on a Dell machine with Intel P4 CPU (2.8 GHz) and 1 GB RAM. The host OS is Fedora Core 5.0 and the guest VM was assigned 256M RAM and 6G hard drive; Guest OS is Red Hat Linux 8.0 with 2.4.18-14 kernel.

6.1   Security

Beside the classification of rootkits given by [7], Petroni [5] classified the rootkits according to their intentions: user-space object hiding (HID), privilege escalation (PE), reentry/backdoor (REE), reconnaissance (REC), and defense neutralization (NEU). In this experiment, we collect 18 rootkits that cover a wide range of attacks. Among them, there are 10 type I rootkits, 8 type II rootkits, 8 HID rootkits, 7 PE rootkits, 3 REE rootkits, 5 REC rootkits and 3 NEU rootkits. In addition, one rootkit from [15] is devised to attack the hardware resources (system BIOS). Unfortunately, the Qemu's BIOS is not updatable, so the rootkit cannot be successfully installed to the test VM. The other 17 rootkits are listed in table 6. A rootkit may have several operation modes and different modes may use different attack tactics. For example, with the technique described in [16],

Table 3. Detection Result of Dark

ROOTKIT	FUNCTION					TYPE	HIT KERNEL RULES		ACTION
	HID	PE	REE	REC	NEU		Load	Operation	
Adore	X	X				I	17	18	Reject
Adore-ng	X	X			X	II	7,12,13	18	Alarm
Adore-ng(hidden)	X	X			X	II	7,12,13	18	Alarm
Darklogger				X		II		15	Alarm
Exception		X			X	I	2	18	Reject
fileh-lkm	X					I	17		Reject
Hookstub		X				I	4	18	Reject
Hp	X	X				II	18	7,12,13	Alarm
KIS	X		X			I	17		Reject
Knark	X	X	X			I	17	18	Reject
Linspy2				X		I	16		Reject
Nfsniffer				X		II	9	16	Alarm
Nushu					X	II		16	Alarm
Pizzaicmp			X			II	9	16	Alarm
Prrf	X	X				II	11,12,13	18	Alarm
Sebek				X		I	7,17		Reject
Srookit	X					I	5		Reject
Vologger				X		I	17	14	Reject
Vologger(local)				X		II		1	Alarm

Adore-ng can optionally hide itself into a benign module, forming a "combo" module. We test the regular Adore-ng and hidden Adore-ng separately. To comprehensively understand the rootkits' behavior, we run several Linux utilities like *ls*, *ps*, *netstat* and *ssh* to verify whether a rootkit works as expected after its installation. Moreover, when a rootkit violates a reject rule, we intentionally instruct DARK not to shutdown the guest VM and make the rootkit continue to run until all testing utilities are finished. Thus, we can catch all security rules that the rootkit hits.

The test result in table 3 suggests that DARK is able to detect all the rootkits with the security rules in table 3. Some rootkits violate multiple rules at the loading stage and operation stage. System call table (rule 17) and task list (rule 18) are primary kernel objects that rootkits target on. Several type I rootkits hijack system call table to hide user-space objects or steal private data. IDT table and kernel exception table are another two static kernel objects that the rootkits tamper with in the test. To type II HID rootkits, proc file system provides exploitable kernel objects that are alternatives to system call table: two such rootkits (adore-ng and prrf) alter the relevant data objects of the proc system to hide processes and network connections. All the PE rootkits modify the user id and group id in the `task_struct` objects to raise a process' privilege level. Another observation is that all rootkits are captured at the loading stage except the Darklogger and Nushu. As we pointed out before, Darklogger is a non-integrity-violation rootkit and does not illegally change any kernel object in the kernel. It just creates a kernel thread and initializes some data structures at the loading stage. Yet, its reading of the PTS buffer is caught by DARK at the operation stage. Nushu manipulates the packets from/to local network adapters by indirectly registering hooks to the kernel through the function `dev_add_pack`. Because this function is not defined in table 3, Nushu escapes the loading-stage inspection. But DARK detects the intrusion when it reads socket buffers at the operation stage. Note that powerful kernel integrity verifiers are still likely to catch the Nushu due to its hooking behavior.

In the experiment, Adore-ng is embedded in the module `iptables_filter` to create a combo module. By comparing the hidden Adore-ng with the regular Adore-ng, we find that they hit the same set of rules. However, the combo module can not be unloaded from the kernel even after we flush the iptable rules and stop the iptable service. After further investigation, we found the reason. Both hidden Adore-ng and the regular Adore-ng modify the kernel module list, which is a list of `module` objects. The regular Adore-ng changes the next fields of the previous and next `module` objects with the purpose of hiding itself, while the combo module alters the `uc.usecount` field of the current `module` object to persist its existence in the kernel. Vlogger is also tested in two operation modes. Although the regular mode offers more powerful features than local mode, the latter turns out to be stealthier: it only alters the dynamic kernel objects and is a type II rootkit.

To estimate the false positive rate of the detection system, we choose 7 categories and total 20 drivers from the Linux source, and execute them in the DARK system. When we test the network drivers, we deactivate the optional rules 9 and 16 to avoid the false alarms. The test result indicates that 19 of 20 drivers pass the test. The failed module is jdb and it is a journaling block device driver used by Ext3 file system for data recovery. This driver alters the `journal_info` filed of two process' `task_struct` objects, leading to the violation of rule 18. This false alarm implies that the rule 18 is too restrictive and should be revised to only include the sensitive fields that task list members. But, on the other side, this violation does not incur the system termination and we believe that overall quality of the security rules is good.

6.2   Performance

Performance evaluation is intended to measure the impact of on-demand emulation on overall system performance. The module `iptable_filter` from Linux source is chosen to be monitored. First, this module operates at the kernel network stack, which is one of major attacking targets of rootkits. Second, running this module in emulation mode is expected to only degrade the performance of the network subsystem in the kernel, and other subsystems should not be affected. `Iptable_filter` registers three hooks to netfilter and applies the iptable rules to network traffics at three guarding points of the netfilter: input, output and forward. We write a number of input and output iptable rules and neither of them actually blocks the network traffics during the test. Three benchmarks: bonnie [17], iperf [18] and lmbench [19], are performed to examine the performance of disk IO, network IO and the entire system respectively.

Comparing with VMM-only system (pure virtualization system), DARK's overhead comes from on-demand emulation, which is composed of two parts: 1. Context switch between virtualization and emulation; 2. Execution overhead in emulator, including binary translation, policy enforcement and execution of translated code sequences. To identify the contribution of each part to the overall cost, we devise another test system: DARK-CS. It does the context switch from virtualization to emulation when an `iptable_filter` function starts to run. Then, emulator returns the control back to VMM immediately and the `iptable_filter` function is actually executed over VMM. Therefore, context switch between virtualization and emulation is the only overhead of DARK-CS. In the experiment, we run each benchmark in DARK, DARK-CS and VMM-only system. Table 4 shows the test result of bonnie. It's observed that the three systems have little

Table 4. Bonnie test result for 100 M files

| | SEQUENTIAL OUTPUT | | | | | SEQUENTIAL INPUT | | | | RANDOM | |
| | Per Char | | block | | Rewrite | | Per Char | | block | | Seeks | |
	K/Sec	%CPU	K/Sec	%CPU	K/Sec	%CPU	K/Sec	%CPU	K/Sec	%CPU	/Sec	%CPU
VMM	8528	64	12755	45	19082	53.0	15805	75	129292	71	3515	84
DARK-CS	8038	61	11715	41	17402	48.2	16860	80	130266	74	4969	85
DARK	8168	67	13949	43	18742	49.8	14480	73	125493	72	5117	83

Table 5. Bonnie test result for 100 M files

	VM as Server (M/Sec)		VM as Client (M/Sec)	
	TCP	UDP	TCP	UDP
VMM	21.81.2	1.050.1	26.82.3	1.130
DARK-CS	19.730.5	1.010	23.991.4	1.080.1
DARK	19.600.6	1.000.1	24.051.0	1.080.1

performance difference when running bonnie. This is because bonnie just accesses the files on disk and `iptable_filter` is not being executed. Bonnie's test result suggests that DARK's overall performance is same as VMM-only system when on-demand emulation doesn't take place.

The iperf test result in table 5 reveals the impact of on-demand emulation on overall system performance. TCP and UDP throughputs of DARK-CS are slightly (about 10%) lower than VMM-only's, which indicates that the overhead of context switching is non-negligible but not significant. CPU state transferring, shadow page table synchronization and page fault handling are three main components of context switching in DARK. However, It is still unknown which component should take the responsibility of performance penalty at the moment. Further, it seems that neither component has much room left for performance improvement. Table 5 also suggests that DARK and DARK-CS have indistinguishable TCP and UDP throughputs. This result can be explained by the code caching technique introduced in section 5.2: to a block of module code, binary translation and policy enforcement are performed only at the first time this block of code is executed, and its translated code sequence in the code cache plays the primary role of deciding the performance in the long run. So code caching is effective to reduce the emulation overhead. We also did the performance test with the Lmbench, and test result confirmed the conclusions we draw above. We can not present the test result under the space constraint.

7   Related Work

Ho [20] proposed the concept of On-demand Emulation that can be used to solve the security problems. His system modified the emulator's hardware support to enable the data tainting at the system level. The system was built on Qemu and Xen VMM, and its main application is prevention of malicious code injection by tracking data received from the network as it propagates through the target VM. DARK does not tamper with any VM's hardware setting, and focuses on kernel rootkit detection.

Kernel Integrity Verification [4][5][21][22][24][37] is one popular rootkit detection approach that follows the spirit of Tripwire [23] in protecting the file systems. It builds a baseline database for the measurable objects (e.g., text, static data) of the target guest and periodically queries current states of those measurable objects to detect intrusions by comparing them with the baseline database. As we mentioned before, these integrity verification methods suffers dealing with dynamic kernel objects and are also incapable of detecting non-integrity-violation rootkits.

Kruegel [27] and Limbo [26] use static and dynamic program analysis techniques to inspect the innocence of a driver off-line. Similar to DARK, both systems create a group of security policies and monitor module behavior. However, they are not run-time rookit detection system, so they suffer fundamental hurdles to static and dynamic program analysis, e.g., code obfuscation, or inaccurate and incomplete analysis result. HookFinder [38] and HookMap [39] are two systems that explore hooking behavior. The former employs the dynmic data tainting to caputer the hooks implanted by rookits, and the later uses the data slicing to identify all potential hooks on the kernel-side execution paths of testing programs such as *ls*, and *netstat*.

SecVisor [31] and NICKLE [32] are two rootkit prevention systems that rely on trusted VMM to enforce life-time kernel integrity. A trusted VMM ensures that only authenticated code can execute in kernel mode, which is a stronger security property than Vista's driver signing. Both systems can protect kernel from code injection attacks including zero-day kernel exploits. DARK is intended to handle the unauthenticated drivers. As long as these drivers follow the behavior specification (security policies) defined in DARK, they are allowed to run in the kernel. So, DARK is an enhancement to the existing prevention solutions.

8   Conclusion

In this paper, we presented a rootkit prevention system to dynamically monitor a suspicious module using on-demand emulation. In addition, we develop a group of security rules to effectively detect rootkits that we gathered, which was demonstrated in the security evaluation. In the end, we show that the performance of a VM is not affected for the majority of system operations. Context switches between emulator and VMM slightly decrease the system performance.

References

1. Rutkowska, J.: Subverting Vista Kernel for Fun and Profit (2006),
   http://www.invisiblethings.org/papers.html
2. Garfinkel, T., Rosenblum, M.: AVirtual Machine Introspection Based Architecture for Intrusion Detection. In: Proceedings of the Symposium on Network and Distributed System Security, NDSS (2003)
3. Zhang, X., van Doorn, L., Jaeger, T., Perez, R., Sailer, R.: Secure Coprocessor-based Intrusion Detection. In: Proceedings of the ACM SIGOPS European Workshop (2002)
4. Petroni, N.L., Fraser, T., Molinz, J., Arbaugh, W.A.: Copilot - a Coprocessor-based Kernel Runtime Integrity Monitor. In: Proceedings of the USENIX Security Symposium (2004)
5. Petroni, N.L., Hicks, M.: Automated Detection of Persistent Kernel Control-Flow Attacks. In: Proceedings of the ACM Conference on Computer and Communications Security, CCS (2007)

6. Jiang, X., Wang, X., Xu, D.: Stealthy Malware Detection through VMM-Based "Out-of-the-Box" Semantic View Recontruction. In: Proceedings of the ACM Conference on Computer and Communications Security, CCS (2007)
7. Rutkowska, J.: Introducing Stealth Malware Taxonomy (2006), http://www.invisiblethings.org/papers.html
8. Baliga, A., Kamat, P., Iftode, L.: Lurking in the Shadows: Identifying Systemic Threats to Kernel Data. In: Proceedings of IEEE Symposium on Security and Privacy (2007)
9. BroFrancis, M.D., Ellick, M.C., Jeffery, C.C., Roy, C.: Cloaker: Hardware Supported Rootkit Concealment. In: Proceedings of IEEE Symposium on Security and Privacy (2008)
10. Heasman, J.: Implementing and Detecting a PCI Rootkit. Technical report, next Generation Security Software Ltd. (November 2006)
11. Heasman, J.: Implementing and Detecing an ACPI BIOS Rootkit. In: Black Hat Europe, Amsterdam (March 2006)
12. Bellard, F.: Qemu and Kqemu (2008), http://fabrice.bellard.free.fr/qemu/
13. King, S.T., Chen, P.M., Wang, Y.M., Verbowski, C., Wang, H.J., Lorch, J.R.: SubVirt: Implementing malware with virtual machines. In: Proceedings of the IEEE Symposium on Security and Privacy, Washington, DC, USA, pp. 314–327. IEEE Computer Society, Los Alamitos (2006)
14. Blue Pill, http://bluepillproject.org/
15. Scythale. Hacking deeper in the system, http://www.phrack.com/
16. Truff. Infecting Loadable Kernel Module, http://www.phrack.com/
17. Bonnie, http://www.textuality.com/bonnie/
18. Iperf, http://dast.nlanr.net/Projects/Iperf/
19. McVoy, L.W., Staelin, C.: Lmbench: Portable Tools for Performance Analysis. In: Proceedings of the USENIX Annual Technical Conference, pp. 279–294 (1996)
20. Ho, A., Fetterman, M., Clark, C., Warfield, A., Hand, S.: Practical Taint-Based Protection using Demand Emulation. In: Proceedings of the ACM SIGOPS/EuroSys European Conference on Computer Systems (2006)
21. Seshadri, A., Luk, M., Shi, E., Perrig, A., van Doorn, L., Khosla, P.: Pioneer: Verifying Code Integrity and Enforcing Untampered Code Execution on Legacy Systems. In: Proceedings of the ACM Symposium on Operating systems Princeiples, SOSP (2005)
22. Microsoft. Windows Kernel Patch Protection (2008), http://www.microsoft.com/whdc/driver/kernel/64bitpatching.mspx
23. Kim, G., Spafford, E.: The Design and Implementation of Tripwire: A File system Integrity Checker. Technical report, Purdue University (1993)
24. Petroni, N.L., Fraser, T., Walters, A., Arbaugh, W.A.: An Architecture for Specification-Based Detection of Semantic Integrity Violations in Kernel Dynamic Data. In: Proceedings of the USENIX Security Symposium (2006)
25. Wang, Y.M., Beck, D., Vo, B., Roussev, R., Verbowski, C.: Detecting Stealth Software with Strider GhostBuster. In: Proceeding of International Conference on Denpendable Network Systems, DSN (2005)
26. Wilhelm, J., Chiueh, T.: A Forced Sampled Execution Approach to Kernel Rootkit Identification. In: Kruegel, C., Lippmann, R., Clark, A. (eds.) RAID 2007. LNCS, vol. 4637, pp. 219–235. Springer, Heidelberg (2007)
27. Kruegel, B.C., Robertson, W., Vigna, G.: Detecting Kernel-Level Rootkits Through Binary Analysis. In: Proceedings of the 20th Annual Computer Security Applications Conference, ACSAC (2004)

28. Hoglund, G., Butler, J.: Rootkits: Subverting the Windows Kernel. Addison-Wesley Professional, Reading (2005)
29. Kiriansky, V., Bruening, D., Amarasinghe, S.P.: Secure execurtion via program shepherding. In: Proceedings of the USENIX Security Symposium (2002)
30. Security-Ehanced Linux, http://www.nsa.gov/selinux/
31. Seshadri, A., Luk, M., Qu, N., Perrig, A.: SecVisor: A Tiny Hypervisor to Guarantee Lifetime Kernel Code Integrity for Commodity OSes. In: Proceedings of the ACM Symposium on Operating Systems Principles, SOSP (2007)
32. Riley, R., Jiang, X., Xu, D.: Guest-Transparent Prevention of Kernel Rootkits with VMM-based Memory Shadowing. In: Lippmann, R., Kirda, E., Trachtenberg, A. (eds.) RAID 2008. LNCS, vol. 5230, pp. 1–20. Springer, Heidelberg (2008)
33. Windows Vista Security Blog,
    http://blogs.msdn.com/windowsvistasecurity/archive/2007/08/16/
    driver-signing-kernel-patch-protection-and-kpp-driver-signing.aspx
34. Windows Driver Signing, http://www.microsoft.com/
35. Jones, S.T., Arpaci-Dusseau, A.C., Arpaci-Dusseau, R.H.: VMM-based hidden process detection and identification using Lycosid. In: Proceedings of the 4th International Conference on Virtual Execution Environments (VEE) (March 2008)
36. Litty, L., Lagar-Cavilla, H.A., Lie, D.: Hypervisor Suppot for Idnetifying Covertly Executing Binaries. In: Proceedings of the USENIX Security Symposium (2008)
37. Baliga, A., Ganapathy, V., Iftode, L.: Automatic Inference and Enforcement of Kernel Data Structure Invariants. In: Proceedings of the 24th Annual Computer Security Applications Conference, ACSAC (2008)
38. Yin, H., Liang, Z., Song, D.: Hookfinder: Identifying and understanding malware hooking behaviors. In: Proceeding of the Annual Network and distributed System Security Symposium, NDSS (2008)
39. Wang, Z., Jiang, X., Cui, W., Wang, X.: Countering Persistent Kernel Rootkits Through Systematic Hook Discovery. In: Lippmann, R., Kirda, E., Trachtenberg, A. (eds.) RAID 2008. LNCS, vol. 5230, pp. 21–38. Springer, Heidelberg (2008)

Yataglass: Network-Level Code Emulation for Analyzing Memory-Scanning Attacks

Makoto Shimamura[1] and Kenji Kono[1,2]

[1] Department of Information and Computer Science, Keio University
[2] CREST, Japan Science and Technology Agency
tima@sslab.ics.keio.ac.jp, kono@ics.keio.ac.jp

Abstract. Remote code-injection attacks are one of the most frequently used attacking vectors in computer security. To detect and analyze injected code (often called *shellcode*), some researchers have proposed network-level code emulators. A network-level code emulator can detect shellcode accurately and help analysts to understand the behavior of shellcode. We demonstrated that *memory-scanning attacks* can evade current emulators, and propose Yataglass, an elaborated network-level code emulator, that enables us to analyze shellcode that incorporates memory-scanning attacks. According to our experimental results, Yataglass successfully emulated and analyzed real shellcode into which we had manually incorporated memory-scanning attacks.

Keywords: Network-level code emulation, Code-injection attack, Memory-scanning attack, Intrusion detection, Intrusion analysis.

1 Introduction

Remote code-injection attacks are one of the most serious threats in computer security today. In the attack scheme, an attacker injects his own malicious code (often called *shellcode*) into a victim server by exploiting various vulnerabilities, such as stack overflow [1], heap overwrite [2,3] and format string attack [4]. Then, he compromises the control flow of the victim to execute it (e.g., by overwriting a return address on the stack). To evade detectors for such attacks [5,6,7], attackers are developing more sophisticated shellcode [8,9,10,11]. For example, *encryption* changes the appearance of malicious code to evade detectors that rely on the byte patterns of the code [5,6]. *Obfuscation* complicates the code so as to confuse static control-flow-based analyzers [7,12]. These techniques diminish the effectiveness of existing detectors and hinder code analysts from extracting malicious behavior from the shellcode.

To detect and extract the behaviors of sophisticated shellcodes, some researchers are proposing network-level code emulators [13,14,15,16,17]. A network-level code emulator inspects a network message, regards it as shellcode, and runs the instructions of the shellcode in an emulated environment. This allows us to decode encrypted shellcode or extract the malicious behavior of obfuscated shellcode. In fact, Polychronakis *et al.* [13,16] and Zhang *et al.* [15]

U. Flegel and D. Bruschi (Eds.): DIMVA 2009, LNCS 5587, pp. 68–87, 2009.

proposed emulators to detect encrypted shellcode. Ma *et al.* [14] used emulation to analyze the relationship between multiple shellcodes. Spector [17] emulates instructions symbolically and analyzes Win32 API calls issued by the shellcode.

In response to the development of network-level code emulation, attackers are trying to evade such emulators by making more sophisticated shellcode. For example, the TAPiON encoder [9] converts shellcode to confuse emulators by inserting meaningless FPU instructions and `rdtsc` instructions. This allows attackers to evade partially-implemented emulators that cannot decode FPU instructions or execute `rdtsc` instructions. Although Polychronakis *et al.*'s emulator [13] could decode shellcode obfuscated by TAPiON, attackers continue to develop new evasion techniques. To maintain the advantage in the never-ending battle against attackers, we must foresee potential problems and possible evasions by network-level code emulators.

Our goal is to improve the effectiveness of network-level code emulation. To achieve this, we describe potential problems with current emulators and how attackers can evade them. *Memory-scanning attacks* [18], originally developed within the context of host-based IDS, effectively prevent network-level code emulators. Memory-scanning attacks disrupt code emulation by accessing memory outside the control of code emulators. Since a network-level code emulator examines network packets, it cannot inherently access the memory regions of a victim process. If shellcode accesses the victim memory, the emulator can not continue its emulation. For example, an attacker scans the victim code region for 0xC3 (`ret` instruction in Intel x86), and then jumps to the location. If this shellcode is executed in the victim process, the control returns immediately to the original location. Unfortunately, the emulator cannot emulate this behavior of shellcode because the code region of the victim is not available to the server. Polychronakis *et al.* [13] mentioned the possibility of using the victim code to evade network-level emulators, but did not discuss this further.

The contribution of this paper is twofold. It:

- **Explains how memory-scanning attacks evade network-level code emulators.** Memory-scanning attacks scan memory regions of the victim process for a useful fragment of code. Polychronakis *et al.* [13] claimed that using the victim code makes shellcode fragile because the shellcode heavily depends on memory layout that tends to change across different software and OS versions. Memory-scanning attacks can be more general and easily applied to existing shellcodes. We explain how memory-scanning attacks successfully evade current emulators and compromise various real-server applications.

- **Proposes Yataglass[1], a network-level code emulator that analyzes memory-scanning attacks.** We propose Yataglass, a network-level code emulator that defends against memory-scanning attacks. Yataglass extracts Win32 APIs or Linux system calls issued by a given shellcode. To detect memory-scanning attacks, Yataglass analyzes evasion code used in

---

[1] Yataglass is named after Yatagarasu, a mythological Japanese tripedal bird that guided the first Japanese Emperor, Jimmu.

memory-scanning attack. The evasion code typically contains a *scanning loop* that searches for a code fragment useful for evasion. Yataglass uses symbolic execution to extract the conditions under which a scanning loop exits. Then, Yataglass prepares a code region that satisfies the extracted conditions to cheat the shellcode to believe it has found the searched-for code fragment. By doing this, Yataglass successfully emulates the behavior of memory-scanning attacks and thus, prevents the shellcodes from evading network-level code emulators.

Note that Yataglass does *not* require a memory image of victim processes. Since Yataglass is supposed to be used in offline analysis, it would be impractical for Yataglass to acquire the memory image of victim processes. To obtain the memory image of a victim process, the shellcode must actually be injected into the victim. Since the memory image of post injection depends on the vulnerability exploited by the shellcode, we cannot reproduce it without actually injecting the code.

We implemented a prototype of Yataglass for the Intel x86 architecture. It extracted Win32 APIs as well as Linux system calls. To demonstrate how effective Yataglass was, we compared it with Spector [17], a state-of-art network-level code emulator. Since the original Spector is not available, we implemented our own version. Unlike Yataglass, Spector lacks the capability of handling memory-scanning attacks. We prepared seven real shellcodes that incorporated memory-scanning attacks for the evaluation. According to our experimental results, Yataglass successfully emulated the behavior of all these shellcodes and produced a list of system calls. However, Spector was disrupted by memory-scanning attacks and failed to emulate the behavior of the shellcodes.

This paper is organized as follows. The next section introduces the concept of network-level code emulators. Memory-scanning attacks are described in Section 3 and Section 4 gives an overview of Yataglass. Section 5 describes Yataglass's symbolic-execution architecture. The experimental results are reported in Section 6. Section 7 discusses possible evasions and more sophisticated memory-scanning attacks. Section 8 compares related work with ours. Finally, we conclude the paper in Section 9.

2   Network-Level Code Emulation

2.1   Emulators for Code-Injection Attacks

The network-level code emulator inspects the payload of network messages, which may include malicious code for remote code-injection attacks. A network-level code emulator has its own virtual registers and virtual stack to emulate instruction execution. Figure 1 shows frequently used registers in the x86 architecture. Using the virtual registers and stack, the emulator executes a shellcode contained in the payload. Since the actual location of the shellcode is not known in advance, the emulator starts execution from every position or uses the help in another NIDS to determine possible shellcode locations. Polychronakis *et al.* [13] chose the former approach, and Spector [17] used the latter one.

Table 1. Frequently used registers in Intel x86 architecture. Registers in upper half are directly accessible in instruction operands and those in lower half are not.

Register names	Description
eax, ebx, ecx, edx	General-purpose registers
esi, edi	Registers for string operations
esp	Stack pointer
ebp	Base pointer (function frame)
eip	Instruction pointer
eflags	Flags for special instructions (e.g., conditions for jcc)

The main advantage of network-level code emulation is twofold. First, it is robust to code conversion such as encryption and obfuscation. Because it executes shellcode, an encrypted shellcode is naturally decoded during execution. Obfuscation is useless because the result of emulation is not affected by obfuscation. Second, the rate of false positives is low. Many researchers have shown that very few innocuous messages can be executed as instructions of significant length [12,13,19]. Thus, network-level code emulators generate fewer false positives than conventional signature-based NIDSs [5,6].

The result of emulation can be used for two main purposes of:

- **Analyzing shellcode.** The network-level code emulator helps us analyze shellcode, because the result of emulation includes all the executed instructions and API calls issued by the shellcode. This result helps analysts understand shellcodes without manual reverse-engineering. For example, Spector [17] uses Win32 API calls issued by shellcode to reveal malicious behavior by the shellcode. Ma *et al.* [14] used execution traces to understand how much variation there was in shellcodes for exploits.
- **Detecting polymorphic shellcode.** A network-level code emulator can detect a message that contains polymorphic shellcode. Existing emulators use various heuristics to detect shellcode. Polychronakis *et al.* [13] and Zhang *et al.* [15] proposed detectors that used two heuristics: 1) the shellcode obtains the instruction pointer (held in the eip register) by executing *GetPC instructions* (call, fstenv, and fnstenv), and 2) it reads its payload to decrypt encrypted instructions. Polychronakis *et al.* later revised their heuristics to detect shellcode that did not use GetPC code and generated code without reading their payloads [16]. Their emulator detected polymorphic shellcode if it executed a memory region that was written to by the shellcode itself.

2.2   Possible Evasions

There are two main evasion vectors possible in network-level code emulators. First, shellcode may inspect the result of system functions. If the emulator cannot emulate the result of system functions, shellcode can detect the fact that it is not running on a real machine. Consequently, it may cease to run to avoid revealing its behavior. For example, shellcode opens a file in a specific format (e.g., a configuration file), and then checks whether the format is correct, and terminates itself if the check has failed. By doing this, an attacker can prevent the emulator from analyzing any further behavior by the shellcode. The defense against this type of evasion is well-known in other areas [20,21,22]. If the emulator traces both branches of a conditional jump, it can continue to execute as if it had successfully passed the check. Thus, we will not discuss this type of evasion further in this paper.

Second, shellcode may refer to instructions embedded inside victim processes. Because existing network-level emulators do not have a memory image of the victim, they cannot correctly emulate the execution of shellcode that refers to the victim memory. *Memory-scanning attacks* belong to this type of evasion. It disrupts existing emulators by jumping to a code fragment inside the victim process. Polychronakis *et al.* [13] mentioned this type of evasion but did not discuss it further. This paper focuses on this type of evasion because, to our knowledge, no solutions have yet been proposed.

3   Memory-Scanning Attack

3.1   Attack scheme

Attackers can disrupt network-level code emulators by using code external to the emulator but embedded in a victim process. This section describes how attackers can use code fragments in a victim process.

An attacker can use code fragments in a victim process in two ways.

- **Jumps to fixed address.** The shellcode jumps to a fixed address and executes a code fragment in the victim process. The attacker can determine the address by preliminary experiments on his own machine. However, as Polychronakis *et al.* pointed out [13], this kind of attack is fragile because the address for useful instructions often differs between the victim machine and the machine used in the experiment. A slight difference in execution environments often leads to a large difference in memory layout. For example, the memory image of the Apache Web server differs on RedHat Linux and Gentoo Linux. An advanced attacker may conduct a two-step attack; the memory layout of the victim process is inspected in the first step, and later the main attack is conducted. We will discuss this in Section 7.
- **Jumps to scanned address (memory-scanning attacks).** The shellcode scans the code region of a victim process for useful instructions and identifies their address. It then jumps there to execute the found instructions. Linn *et al.* [18] pointed out this attack within the context of host-based IDSs. However, to our knowledge, no one has reported this attack can evade network-level code emulators. This kind of attack is less fragile because the attacker does not depend on a specific address for useful instructions.

This paper explains how memory-scanning attacks allow attackers to evade existing network-level code emulators, and we propose a technique of invalidating memory-scanning attacks.

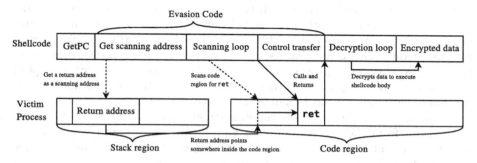

Fig. 1. An example memory-scanning attack. It first gets its own address by using GetPC code and obtains the address for the code region from the return address. After that, it scans a `ret` instruction from the program code, jumps to the found address, then returns and continues to a decryption loop.

In memory-scanning attacks, shellcode contains three code fragments; 1) it obtains the address of a code region from which to start scanning, 2) it executes a *scanning loop* that searches for the address of useful instructions embedded in the victim, and 3) it transfers control to the found instructions.

The scanning address can be determined from the return addresses in the stack. Although the overall memory image is difficult to deduce, the stack layout is much easier to estimate because it is mostly fixed according to the calling convention. To improve matters, we have only to know the offset of the return address from the stack top. This offset is usually constant if the same vulnerability of the same program is exploited. Even if the stack layout is not known, an attacker can scan the stack for a return address. According to the ELF specifications [23], the code regions are located above the addresses 0x8048000. Thus, if shellcode finds a value between 0x8048000 and 0x8060000, the value is a return address with a high degree of confidence.

The simplest form of memory-scanning attack is to scan `ret` instruction (0xC3) and jump there. Figure 1 shows the structure of the shellcode that incorporates a memory-scanning attack. The shellcode consists of five parts: GetPC, obtain scanning address, scanning loop, control transfer, and decryption loop. The shellcode first identifies its own address by using the GetPC code. Because the x86 architecture does not have `eip`-relative memory access, many shellcodes use the GetPC code to access encrypted data in the payload. For example, the GetPC code uses `call` instruction to push the `eip` register into the stack. After that, shellcode obtains a scanning address from a return address as has already been mentioned. Then, it searches the code region for 0xC3, starting from the scanning address. If found, shellcode pushes the address of a decryption loop to the stack and jump there (e.g., by `call` instruction). Then, the control of the shellcode goes to the `ret` instruction and immediately returns.

This simplest form of memory-scanning attack can evade current network-level code emulators. The current emulators stop execution and raise an error when shellcode refers to the code region of a victim process because this region is beyond the control of the emulator. If this error is ignored to force execution, the emulator cannot track the `call` to the code outside the emulator's control. Some might think the emulator can continue execution if this `call` is replaced with `nop` instruction. This is not the case because an attacker can use various sets of instructions in a victim process. If the shellcode uses `pop ebp; ret` (a typical function epilogue), `esp` and `ebp` registers are changed; to continue undisrupted execution, the emulator must change their virtual registers.

We assume that the memory-scanning attack code directly scans for useful instructions from the code region of a victim process. However, an advanced attacker may indirectly scan for useful code fragment (e.g., scans for a prelude to `ret`). We will discuss attacks of this style in Section 7.

3.2 Evasion of Existing Emulation Systems

Memory-scanning attacks can be incorporated into existing shellcodes in various ways. To successfully evade emulation-based detectors and analyzers, the location to which the evasion code is inserted is important. We present some examples where existing detectors and analyzers are evaded.

First, the evasion code can be inserted between the GetPC part and a decryption loop as shown in Fig. 1. This allows attackers to evade detectors that rely on GetPC code [13,15]. If an emulator starts execution from the GetPC part, the execution stops at the evasion. If the execution is started after the evasion, the emulator cannot correctly execute a decryption loop because the GetPC part is mandatory for the decryption loop.

Second, if shellcode dynamically generates code on the stack, the evasion code is inserted just before control is transferred to the generated code. This allows attackers to evade Polychronakis et al. [16]'s advanced detector that counts memory writes and the executed instructions in the written memory.

Last, the evasion code can be inserted just before the call of system functions to hide the arguments and invocations of system functions. This enables attackers to evade emulation-based analyzers [17]. The analyzers might ignore the control transfer to scanned instructions, but the stack pointer is changed at this point. Thus, the analyzer cannot extract the arguments of system functions from the stack. In addition, shellcode can invoke arbitrary functions from the victim program. For example, if the scanning loop scans for `int 0x80` and jumps there, a shellcode can invoke Linux system calls. Arbitrary Win32 APIs can be invoked if shellcode scans for `ret` instruction and pushes the address of the required API on the stack; the `ret` instruction naturally jumps to the specified API.

4   Yataglass Overview

Yataglass is a shellcode analyzer whose analysis output is not disrupted by memory-scanning attacks. Yataglass shares the same goal as Spector [17], a state-of-art shellcode analyzer. The goal of Spector and Yataglass is to help analysts understand the behavior of the shellcode. Both systems generate 1) a low-level output of a fully commented disassembly of the shellcode, and 2) a high-level trace of the system-function calls and their parameters. The primary advantage of Yataglass over Spector is that Yataglass correctly analyzes shellcode that exploits memory-scanning attack. Memory-scanning attacks can evade Spector since it lacks the capability of analyzing scanning loops in detail. In other words, Yataglass is an extension of Spector that enables detailed analysis of scanning loops.

To fight against memory-scanning attacks, Yataglass uses symbolic execution. The symbolic-execution engine of Yataglass infers a code fragment that a scanning loop searches for, forges a code region that contains the code fragment, and deceives the shellcode into finding the code fragment. The symbolic-execution engine carefully traces a scanning loop, and analyzes the exit conditions of the loop to infer the searched-for fragment of code. By doing this, Yataglass disables memory-scanning attacks. Once a memory-scanning attack is disabled, Yataglass can continue to analyze shellcode almost in the same way as Spector. While Spector is tailored to shellcode for Windows, Yataglass has been slightly extended to deal with shellcode for Linux as well as Windows.

Yataglass is designed to take the executable portion of an attack payload as its input. To feed Yataglass executable payloads, we must 1) identify network messages that contain shellcodes, and (2) determine the starting points of code execution within each payload. There are already a number of intrusion-detection systems, such as Snort [5] and Bro [6], which can monitor traffic at the network layer and detect shellcode attacks. Given the output of the IDS, Yataglass starts execution from every position of the payload.

Yataglass uses a custom x86 processor emulator to monitor and record the behavior of shellcode. When Yataglass starts up, it initializes its own virtual stack and registers, and loads the shellcode into its own memory segment. Then, Yataglass executes the shellcode starting with the first instruction, runs until the shellcode executes an invalid instruction, calls system functions to terminate execution (e.g., `exit()`), or switches execution to another program (e.g., `execve()`). At each instruction, Yataglass records the decoded instruction and operand(s). It also records the function name and arguments if it finds a call to a system function during execution.

5   Symbolic Execution in Yataglass

To infer the code fragment that a scanning loop is searching for, Yataglass uses symbolic execution tailored for memory-scanning attacks. Due to the space limitations, we have focused on an extension of Spector.

5.1   Values in Yataglass

To enable symbolic execution, Yataglass treats objects in every register and memory word as *values*. A value is classified into four classes: *number, symbol, expression*, and *unknown*. A number represents concrete data during execution (e.g., a 32-bit integer read from the payload). An expression is a 3-tuple that takes an opcode and two operands. An example of expression is (ADD X Y), where X and Y are values. The concreteness of an expression depends on its operands; an expression is only concrete if both operands are concrete.

Yataglass associates a constraint with each symbolic value. This constraint represents a range of a concrete number that the associated symbol can have. For example, if symbol X can hold a number from 10 to 20, X is associated with the constraint [10, 20]. If symbol Y (8-bit value) is not equal to 120, it is associated with the constraints [0,119], and [121,255]. Using these constraints, Yataglass deals with non-deterministic conditional jumps, and analyzes scanning loops in memory-scanning attack. The detailed use of constraints is explained in Section 5.2.

Yataglass makes a distinction between *unknown* and *symbol* values. A symbol is not concrete but related to the execution of shellcode. For example, Yataglass initially assigns symbol STACK_PTR to esp (stack pointer). However, unknown values are derived from uninitialized memory and usually do not affect the execution of shellcode.

To defend against memory-scanning attacks, Yataglass carefully deals with the code region of a victim process accessed from a scanning loop. Since this region is unknown to the symbolic-execution engine, a naive engine would assign *unknown* values to the entire region. Unfortunately, this is not correct because the values from the code region do affect the execution of shellcode in memory-scanning attacks. In Yataglass, if an unknown code region is accessed from shellcode, a special symbol, $CODE_n$, is assigned to each memory byte in the accessed region. To discern the access to a code region, Yataglass keeps track of code pointers used in shellcode. At the time of initialization, Yataglass assigns another special symbol, $CODE\_PTR_n$, to every memory byte that may be used as a code pointer. For example, Yataglass initializes its own virtual stack with $CODE\_PTR_n$ symbols because shellcode often obtains a code pointer (return address) from the stack. If some memory regions (such as a table to dynamically linked libraries) contain code pointers, they are also initialized with $CODE\_PTR_n$ symbols.

Yataglass optimizes its symbolic execution in similar ways to other symbolic-execution engines [17,20]. It simplifies the result of every operation if possible. We used the following rules to simplify the operation result with symbolic operands X and Y.

- If both X and Y are concrete, then compute and set the result to the destination symbol.
- Check for special cases, such as (SUB X X), (XOR X X), (AND X X), and (OR X X), where the result is equal to zero or X.
- If the operand is addition or subtraction, check all the nested expressions of symbolic operands and cancel out operands if possible. For example, (ADD (SUB X Y) Y) is simplified to X.

This optimization reduces the complexity of symbolic execution in most common cases. In addition, it makes Yataglass robust to encoders like TAPiON [9] that insert garbage operations. For example, TAPiON inserts (XOR (OR X X) X)) and (ADD (SUB X Y) Y) recursively into shellcode. If the simplification is not implemented, 2^n symbols are generated where n is the depth of garbage instructions.

5.2   Conditional Jumps and Inferring Code Fragments

Yataglass's symbolic-execution engine carefully executes conditional loops to infer a code fragment that a scanning loop is searching for. Conditional loops are usually constructed from conditional jumps and some instructions that set the flag register (eflags in x86). When Yataglass encounters a conditional jump, it examines eflags to determine whether the jump is taken or not. If the flags that affect the jump condition are all concrete, Yataglass can continue the execution deterministically. If some flags affecting the condition are not concrete, the execution is non-deterministic and special care must thus be taken.

As pointed out by Borders et al. [17], shellcode tends to execute in a deterministic manner due to its small size and limited functionality. Unfortunately, memory-scanning attacks introduce non-deterministic execution into shellcode. Figure 2 shows a code snippet of a scanning loop. This scanning loop searches for 0xC3 (ret instruction) from the starting address ADDR. The conditional jump in line 5 is non-deterministic because whether the jump is taken depends on the result of cmp in line 4. Since the cmp in line 4 refers to a memory location outside the control of Yataglass, Yataglass cannot know the result of cmp (recall that a scanning loop scans the code region of a victim program).

To overcome this non-determinism, Yataglass forks itself to execute in parallel both the case where the jump is taken and the case where it is not. However, forking at every conditional jump leads to combinatorial explosion because 2^n instances of Yataglass may be generated, where n is the maximum number of iterations of the loop. An instance of Yataglass terminates execution when it detects a conditional jump to an already-executed basic block that leads to the same non-deterministic jump instruction. In Fig. 2, Yataglass forks at line 5, and two instances of Yataglass are executed; 1) one jumps to line 7 and 2) the other continues to line 6 and then jump to line 2. The latter instance encounters an already-executed conditional jump at line 5, and thus terminates itself. However, the other instance exits the loop and continues execution.

To infer the instructions that a scanning loop is searching for, Yataglass determines non-concrete values that set the conditions for the non-deterministic conditional jump of interest. Yataglass associates each flag of eflags with the instruction that set the flag most recently. When Yataglass encounters a conditional jump, it examines eflags and extracts a set of instructions that affect non-concrete flags of eflags. In the example of Fig. 2, the cmp instruction at line 4 sets ZF (zero flag), SF (sign flag), OF (overflow flag), and PF (parity flag), and thus Yataglass associates (CMP $CODE_1$ 0xC3) with these flags. $CODE_1$ is a new symbol that points to a value loaded from CODE_PTR+1 inside the victim's memory.

After extracting the instruction that sets the conditional flag, Yataglass calculates the value of the non-concrete operand for the one case where the jump is taken and for the other where it is not taken. In the example in Fig. 2, Yataglass concludes that $CODE_1$ (or [edi]) equals 0xC3 where the jump at line 5 is

```
# ADDR is an address of code region
1:   mov edi, ADDR          # edi = ADDR (CODE_PTR)
2: loop:
3:   inc edi                # [edi] = CODE₁
4:   cmp byte [edi], 0xC3   # cmp with 'ret'
5:   je loopout             # if(*edi=='ret') goto 7;
6:   jmp loop               # else goto 2
7: loopout:
8:   call edi               # push CONT and jump to 'ret'
9: CONT:
```

Fig. 2. Example of scanning loop

```
# ADDR is an address of code region
1:     mov edi, ADDR          # edi = ADDR (CODE_PTR)
2:  loop:
3:     inc edi                # [edi] = CODE₁
4:     cmp byte [edi], 0xC3   # cmp with 'ret'
5:     jg loop                # if(*edi>'ret') goto 2;
6:     cmp byte [edi], 0xC3   # cmp with 'ret'
7:     jl loop                # if(*edi<'ret') goto 2;
8:  loopout:
9:     call edi               # push CONT and jump to 'ret'
10: CONT:
```

Fig. 3. Example of scanning loop that uses two constraints

taken. Otherwise, $CODE_1$ is not equal to 0xC3. Here, Yataglass imposes constraints ([0, 0xC2] and [0xC4, 0xFF]) on $CODE_1$, which denotes $CODE_1$ is not equal to 0xC3. By doing this, Yataglass can deceive the shellcode to have found the scanned-for instruction. When the control reaches line 8, the value of [edi] (or $CODE_1$) is set to 0xC3.

This mechanism of Yataglass allows us to deal with a more complicated scanning loop as shown in Fig. 3. When Yataglass reaches line 6, the symbol, $CODE_1$, has the constraint [0, 0xC3] (not greater than 0xC3). When Yataglass proceeds to line 7, this constraint is merged with [0xC3, 0xFF]. As a result, Yataglass concludes that $CODE_1$ equals 0xC3.

The x86 architecture supports scas and cmps string instructions that can be used in scanning loops. Figure 4 uses repne scas instruction to find the target instruction, ret. The repne scasb starts scanning a memory region from the address in edi until it either finds the value stored in the al register or the value of ecx becomes zero. To execute both cases, Yataglass forks at the repne scas instruction; one instance of Yataglass assigns al to [edi] and increments edi. The other instance assigns zero to ecx. Figure 5 shows the use of cmps instruction. repe cmpsb compares a byte at esi with a byte at edi until it either finds the difference between the two values or the value of ecx becomes zero. In other words, it compares memory regions. Yataglass forks at the repe

```
# ADDR is an address of code region
1:    mov edi, ADDR        # edi = ADDR
2:    mov al, 0xC3         # al = 0xC3 ('ret')
3:    mov ecx, 0xffffffff  # infinite
4:    repne scasb          # while(ecx != 0){ ecx--; if(al==*edi++)break;}
5:    dec edi              # line 4 sets edi to the found address + 1
6:    call edi             # jump to 'ret'
```

Fig. 4. Example of scanning by scas

```
# ADDR is an address of code region
1:     mov edi, ADDR       # edi = ADDR
2:     mov [esi], 0xC35D   # *esi = 'pop ebp; ret'
3:     mov eax, esi        # save esi
4:  loop:
5:     mov ecx, 0x2        # length + 1
6:     repe cmpsb          # while(ecx != 0){ecx--;if(*edi++!=*esi++)break;}
7:     jecxz loopout       # if (ecx == 0) goto 10
8:     mov esi, eax        # load esi
9:     jmp loop            # goto 4
10: loopout:
11:    sub edi, 0x2        # line 6 sets edi to the found address + 2
12:    call edi            # jump to 'pop ebp; ret'
13: CONT:
```

Fig. 5. Example of scanning by cmps

cmps instruction. One instance of Yataglass infers the content of the scanned-for region from either esi or edi, which points to a concrete instruction sequence. Then it assigns the sequence to the code region and assigns zero to ecx. The other instance decrements ecx and skips the repe cmpsb instruction.

5.3 Implementation

We implemented a prototype of Yataglass. We used libdasm [24] to decode x86 instructions. Yataglass decodes all the x86 instructions including FPU and SSE instructions. However, the FPU, SSE, and privileged instructions are not emulated. It did not cause any problems in our experiment, but attackers can exploit such instructions to evade our emulator.

To analyze shellcodes for Windows, we implemented a stub layer for Yataglass. Yataglass creates a dummy process environment block (PEB) in the bootstrap phase and loads kernel32.dll, user32.dll, and ws2_32.dll. In addition, we implemented some stub functions for Win32 APIs. For example, the stub functions of LoadLibrary() and GetProcAddress() are prepared to emulate shellcodes that use them to obtain addresses of Win32 APIs from DLLs.

We applied two optimizations to Yataglass. First, we implemented basic-block-based instruction decoder [25]. Yataglass decoded the instructions of a basic block before it started to execute the block. It retains decoded instructions in a cache entry. If it detects that a basic block that was decoded before is about to be re-decoded, it obtains the decoded intermediate code from the cache entry. A cache entry is invalidated if Yataglass detects an instruction that rewrites an instruction inside the cached basic block. Second, we implemented signature-based function detection, which was also used in Spector [17]. Most Windows shellcodes share an instruction sequence for searching the addresses of Win32 APIs. We listed up some possible instruction patterns. If Yataglass detects that a shellcode is searching for an API address, it obtains the address of the API by directly analyzing the DLL and immediately returns. Note that even if a shellcode implements the same function whose instruction pattern is not on the list, Yataglass correctly executes it although the speed is slow.

6   Experiments

This section explains how Yataglass can successfully analyze real shellcode into which memory-scanning attacks have been incorporated. For comparison, we also implemented another network-level code emulator which capability corresponds to Spector [17] since the authors of Spector do not release their implementation. In this section, we call our Spector implementation Spector-X. Before showing the effectiveness, we show that memory-scanning attack can be incorporated into realworld shellcode, and actually compromises the real Internet servers such as named [26], wu-ftpd [27], rsync [28], wu-imap [29], Apache Web Server [2], samba [30], and cyrus-pop3d [31].

6.1   Incorporating Memory-Scanning Attacks

To demonstrate memory-scanning attacks can be incorporated into realworld shellcode, we collected seven pieces of real shellcode from SecurityFocus [32] and Milw0rm [33]. Table 2 summarizes the shellcode used in the experiments. The table shows a C source file name of the shellcode, target applications and versions of the shellcode, the site where we obtained the shellcode, the CVE number of exploited vulnerability by the shellcode, the main objective of the shellcode, and what encoder is used for the shellcode, respectively.

Our memory-scanning code is written to incorporate memory-scanning attacks into these pieces of realworld shellcode. Most pieces of shellcode corrupts

Table 2. Realworld shellcode used in experiments

Source	Target application	Obtained from	CVE No.	Objective	Encoding
tsig.c	bind <= 8.2.2	SecurityFocus	2001-0010	Spawns shell	None
7350wurm.c	wu-ftpd <= 2.6.1	milw0rm	2001-0550	Spawns shell	None
rsync-expl.c	rsync <= 2.5.1	SecurityFocus	2002-0048	Embeds backdoor	None
7350owex.c	wu-imap 2000.287	milw0rm	2002-0379	Spawns shell	ToUpper-Evasion
OpenFuck.c	Apache with OpenSSL <=0.9.6d	SecurityFocus	2002-0656	Spawns shell	None
sambal.c	Samba 2.2.8	SecurityFocus	2003-0201	Embeds backdoor	None
cyruspop3d.c	cyrus-pop3d 2.3.2	milw0rm	2006-2502	Embeds backdoor	None

the contents of `esp` register when hijacking the control of a victim process. Thus, we use `ebp` register by default to get a scanning address. However, some pieces of shellcode corrupt `ebp` register but preserves the contents of `esp` register. To deal with this kind of shellcode, we also prepare another version of memory-scanning code, which uses `esp` register to get a scanning address. Since the author of shellcode knows which register (`esp` or `ebp`) is corrupted during the process of hijacking, he can select the correct version of our memory-scanning code. In our experiment, `cyruspop3d.c` corrupts `ebp` register instead of `esp` register.

Our memory-scanning code is carefully written not to include NULL bytes because some pieces of shellcode stop their execution if our code contains NULL bytes. This is because the injected code is often manipulated as if it were a C string. We also applied the well-known technique to evade the effect of `ToUpper()` function. When we exploit some vulnerabilities, the injected code (including our memory-scanning code) is passed to `ToUpper()`. Since the contents of the code is converted through `ToUpper()`, our scanning code is violated if not written carefully to nullify the effect of `ToUpper()`. To nullify the effect of `ToUpper()`, all lower case characters inside the shellcode must be carefully avoided or dynamically generated.

We conducted those attacks to targets into which memory-scanning attack is incorporated. Shellcode generated by `tsig.c`, `7350wurm.c`, and `7350owex.c` successfully spawned a shell using the attacking connection. Shellcode generated by `rsync-expl.c`, `sambal.c` and `cyruspop3d.c` make the victim serve a root shell in a specified port as a backdoor. Shellcode generated by `OpenFuck.c` did not succeed at the first time. After detailed analysis on the shellcode and the target vulnerability, we found that the reason to fail is that the server overwrites a certain location of the shellcode, and thus the shellcode was not correctly executed. We finally succeeded to compromise the server by making the shellcode fragmented to avoid the location. The shellcode spawned a shell.

6.2   Effectiveness of Yataglass

To demonstrate the effectiveness of Yataglass, we demonstrate that Yataglass successfully analyze the seven pieces of shellcode introduced in Section 6.1. Table 3 shows the emulation results. Yataglass successfully analyzed all pieces of shellcode, regardless of incorporation with memory-scanning attack. On the other hand, Spector-X failed to analyze shellcode incorporated with memory-scanning attack. Spector-X stopped its execution when it accessed to the victim's memory. Note that both successfully analyzed the original shellcode.

Figure 6 shows an emulation result of shellcode generated by `rsync-expl.c` with Yataglass. A line of result includes an instruction number (in hexadesimal), an executed instruction address (in hexadecimal), and a mnemonic of executed instruction. For comprehension, we added short notes to the result. According to the result, Yataglass correctly handled a memory-scanning attack (shown from instruction number 004d to 0067). The shellcode first scanned a return address to `eax` from the stack. Yataglass related the obtained value with a symbol *CODE_PTR*. The obtained value was compared with 0x8049001 and 0x8101010 to

Table 3. Summary of emulation results of real shellcodes and their modified versions

Source	Yataglass	Spector-X	Source	Yataglass	Spector-X
tsig.c (original)	√	√	OpenFuck.c (original)	√	√
tsig.c (modified)	√	–	OpenFuck.c (modified)	√	–
7350wurm.c (original)	√	√	sambal.c (original)	√	√
7350wurm.c (modified)	√	–	sambal.c (modified)	√	–
rsync-expl.c (original)	√	√	cyruspop3d.c (original)	√	√
rsync-expl.c (modified)	√	–	cyruspop3d.c (modified)	√	–
7350owex.c (original)	√	√			
7350owex.c (modified)	√	–			

```
Emulation start from 00000000              0054 00ad  d9ee       fldz
No.  Addr. Inst.      Mnemonic      Note    0055 00af  d97424d0   fstenv [esp-0x30]
-------------------------------------------- 0056 00b3  8b7424dc   mov esi,[esp-0x24]
0040 0076  31db       xor ebx,ebx           0057 00b7  89c7       mov edi,eax
0041 0078  53         push ebx              0058 00b9  b05d       mov al,0x5d
0042 0079  686e2f7368 push dword 0x68732f6e 0059 00bb  b9ffffffff mov ecx,0xffffffff
0043 007e  682f2f6269 push dword 0x69622f2f 005a 00c0  fd         std
0044 0083  89e3       mov ebx,esp           005b 00c1  47         inc edi
0045 0085  8d542408   lea edx,[esp+0x8]     005c 00c2  803f5d     cmp byte [edi],0x5d
0046 0089  31c9       xor ecx,ecx                compared CODE_1 and 5d
0047 008b  51         push ecx              005d 00c5  75fa       jnz 0xc1
0048 008c  53         push ebx     # (SUB STACK 0x50)   conditional jump symbol: (CMP CODE_1 0x5d)
0049 008d  8d0c24     lea ecx,[esp]              assign_value: CODE_1 = 0x5d
004a 0090  31c0       xor eax,eax           005f 00c8  47         inc edi
004b 0092  b00b       mov al,0xb   # Syscall No. of execve  005f 00c8  803fc3     cmp byte [edi],0xc3
004c 0094  60         pusha        # Save registers         compared CODE_2 and c3
004d 0095  89ee       mov esi,ebp  # ebp = STACK  0060 00cb  75f4       jnz 0xc1
004e 0097  81c6fcffffff add esi,0xfffffffc # esi = STACK - 4  conditional jump symbol: (CMP CODE_2 0xc3)
004f 009d  8b06       mov eax,[esi] # eax = CODE_PTR        assign_value: CODE_2 = 0xc3
0050 009f  3d01900408 cmp eax,0x8049001 # Avoids null byte 0061 00cd  83c628     add esi,0x28
     # compared CODE_PTR and 0x8049001   0062 00d0  4f         dec edi
     # symbol: (CODE_PTR AT 0xbffe10fc)  0063 00d1  56         push esi
0051 00a4  7cf1       jl 0x97               0064 00d2  55         push ebp
     # conditional jump: (CMP (CODE_PTR AT 0xbffe10fc) 0x8049001)  0065 00d3  ffe7  jmp edi  # jmp to victim's code
     #### forked and child process terminates ####  0066 ----  5d         pop ebp    # CODE_1
     # symbol: (CODE_PTR AT 0xbffe10f8)   0067 ----  c3         ret        # CODE_2
0052 00a6  3d01101008 cmp eax,0x8101010 # Avoids null byte 0068 00d5  61         popa
     compared CODE_PTR and 8101010        0069 00d6  cd80       int 0x80
     symbol: (CODE_PTR AT 0xbffe10fc)     Linux system call 11 (execve) detected!!
0053 00ab  7fea       jg 0x97                   path=//bin/sh |CONCRETE|
     conditional jump: (CMP (CODE_PTR AT 0xbffe10fc) 0x8101010)  argv[0]=//bin/sh |CONCRETE|
     #### forked and child process terminates ####
```

Fig. 6. The emulation result of shellcode generated by rsync-expl.c, incorporated with memory-scanning attack, with Yataglass. Logs of first 64 (0x40) instructions and outputs from forked instances are omitted due to the limited page space.

confirm the value was an address of code region. Yataglass passed the check by setting constraints. Then, the shellcode got the address of itself and calculated an address which would be used as a return address from the victim's memory (address 00d5 of the shellcode). The shellcode scanned the victim's memory for pop ebp and ret. Yataglass assigned 0x5D and 0xC3 to *CODE_1* and *CODE_2*, respectively. After the scanning loops were completed, the shellcode jumped to the victim's memory (*CODE_1*) (at instruction number 0065). Then, the shellcode executed pop ebp, ret and the control returned to the shellcode address 00d5. The control was returned to 0068. Finally, the shellcode executed execve() system call with arguments to spawn /bin/sh.

Figure 7 shows the emulation result of the same shellcode with Spector-X. According to the result, it failed the execution when it tried to touch the victim's memory at instruction number 004f. It could not analyze the shellcode, which finally calls execve() and spawns /bin/sh.

```
Emulation start from 00000000                    0047 008b 51           push ecx
No.  Addr. Inst.       Mnemonic          Note     0048 008c 53           push ebx
------------------------------------------------  0049 008d 8d0c24       lea ecx,[esp]
0040 0076 31db         xor ebx,ebx                004a 0090 31c0         xor eax,eax
0041 0078 53           push ebx                   004b 0092 b00b         mov al,0xb
0042 0079 686e2f7368   push dword 0x68732f6e      004c 0094 60           pusha
0043 007e 682f2f6269   push dword 0x69622f2f      004d 0095 89ee         mov esi,ebp        # ebp = unknown
0044 0083 89e3         mov ebx,esp                004e 0097 81c6fcffffff add esi,0xfffffffc # esi = unknown
0045 0085 8d542408     lea edx,[esp+0x8]          004f 009d 8b06         mov eax,[esi]      # unknown address
0046 0089 31c9         xor ecx,ecx                MEMORY FAIL -- unknown address is used
```

Fig. 7. Emulation result of shellcode generated by rsync-expl.c, incorporated with memory-scanning attack, with Spector-X. First 64 (0x40) instructions are omitted.

7 Discussion

Yataglass successfully analyze shellcode that exploits memory-scanning attack to evade network-level code emulators. In this section, we discuss some possible evasions of Yataglass.

Since the current prototype of Yataglass assumes that memory-scanning code gets an address of a code region from return addresses on stack, an attacker can use this fact to evade the current prototype of Yataglass. First, the scanning code can get a code-region address from a special file /proc/XXX/maps (where XXX is the process ID), which maintains the entire memory map of the process XXX. Yataglass can be easily extended to provide a dummy /proc/XXX/maps since it can detect the function calls to open a file. Second, the scanning code can get a code-region address from function tables such as GOT (Global Offset Table) or PLT (Procedure Linkage Table). These tables are used for resolving the addresses of dynamically linked libraries. To prevent this kind of evasion, it is sufficient for Yataglass to prepare a dummy GOT or PLT. Finally, an attacker can write the target code in data or stack regions and then use mprotect() to make the regions executable. Yataglass can easily prevent this evasion because Yataglass can know the address of and the values stored in the mprotect'ed regions.

The current prototype of Yataglass must be slightly extended to deal with some kinds of scanning loops. First, an attacker can use a scanning loop that identifies *multiple* instructions. In other words, the scanning loop finds out an address that store one of the identified instructions. For example, a scanning loop searches for one of the eight pop instructions in x86, whose opcode ranges from from 0x58 to 0x5F, depending on the target registers (0x58 for pop eax, 0x59 for pop ecx, and so on). In this case, the memory-scanning code 1) saves all the registers, 2) pushes a garbage value to the stack, 3) scans the victim's memory to find one of the eight pop instructions, 4) executes the found pop instruction (by doing this, the garbage value is popped out), and 5) restores all the pushed registers. After this code is executed, the shellcode can continue its execution normally because no registers are changed and the stack is not changed. To deal with this style of scanning loops, Yataglass must be extended to fork itself when a symbol whose value is in some range is used as an instruction. This extension would not lead to an explosion of forked Yataglass because attackers can not write a code that accepts more than 10 different instructions.

Third, Yataglass cannot analyze a shellcode which indirectly scans for code fragment. An attacker may scan for a known fragment of instructions from the target's code for that system function or a function that invokes that system function. In this case, Yataglass can not analyze the shellcode because it can not extract the final system functions from the scanning code. Linn *et al.* [18] already introduced an attack which scans for a 17-byte sequence that comprises the first basic block of the execve system call. To handle this kind of memory-scanning attack, we must extend Yataglass to enable to find the scanned-for sequence from possible scanning patterns.

Fourth, Yataglass may be evaded by two-step attacks. In the first step, the attack code returns an address of useful instructions in the victim process. This address is then used in the second step without any need for scanning. Current Yataglass can not analyze the second shellcode. To solve this problem, Yataglass must be extended to retain the state after the analysis of the first shellcode.

Finally, the current prototype of Yataglass can not deal with shellcode that changes the value of specific variables used in the victim's program. This limitation comes from that Yataglass assumes that we can not know the exact memory layout of victim processes. As already discussed in Section 3.1, shellcode that relies on memory layout is fragile. In particular, since the address space randomization [34] is very popular (for example, current Linux and Windows have this capability), this kind of shellcode is more fragile than before and becoming less attractive to attackers. Even if a network-level code emulator misses this kind of shellcode, the attacked process can defend against the shellcode by itself.

8   Related Work

Since we already described the related network-level code emulators in Section 2.1, this section summarizes other work related to ours.

8.1   Static Analysis-Based Systems

SigFree [19] disassembles payload and counts the number of executable instructions. If this count exceeds the threshold, SigFree regards the payload as shellcode. Andersson *et al.* [35] scan payload for instructions that puts a value into eax register and executes int 80. These detectors are vulnerable to encryption because the code is not interpreted during the detection process.

Kruegel *et al.*'s worm detection method [12] effectively detects a worm outbreak. It extracts possible control flows inside payloads and finds a match between extracted control flows in multiple streams. In contrast, Yataglass extracts detailed behavior of shellcode used by worms. Yataglass is useful to analyze a worm instance. Both help administrators to defend against damages from worms.

8.2   Host-Based Systems

Host-based intrusion detection systems (HIDSs) can extract malicious behaviors by shellcode. For example, Linn *et al.* [18] proposed an HIDS that detects malicious system calls issued by shellcode. This HIDS forces all system calls to be invoked at the addresses known in advance. As a result, this HIDS can collect all malicious system calls invoked by shellcode because those system calls are issued from unknown addresses. ReVirt [36] is a host-based intrusion analysis system that uses virtual machine. It saves all VM states as a checkpoint and logs all non-deterministic events on a virtual machine (e.g., hardware interruption). The collected information allows us to replay intrusions after the server is compromised. Both the HIDSs analyze the compromised server. On the other hand, Yataglass analyzes shellcode. Thus Yataglass allows us to analyze shellcode even if it does not actually compromise victim servers. This feature of Yataglass is useful in many situations. For example, Yataglass can analyze shellcode that is sent to honeypots but does not actually break-in decoy servers.

Andersson et al.'s detector [37] executes shellcode in a sandboxed process and the sandbox then outputs a list of system functions issued by the shellcode. Since the process is protected by a sandbox, an attacker can evade the detector by inspecting the result of system functions. Yataglass is an emulator that can detect conditional jumps that use results of system functions, and thus it can apply the defense against this evasion [20,21,22]. In contrast, their detector runs shellcode on the CPU and thus it is not easy to detect such conditional jumps.

9 Conclusion

Remote code-injection attacks are still one of the most serious problems in network system security. To detect and analyze shellcode used in remote code-injection attacks, network-level code emulation is a promising approach. It is not disrupted by encryption and obfuscation because it runs instructions of shellcode in its emulated environment. Our goal is to improve the efficiency of network-level code emulators by addressing possible evasion techniques.

In this paper, we have shown that *memory-scanning attack* can evade current network-level code emulators and proposed Yataglass, a symbolic execution based emulator to address memory-scanning attack. Memory-scanning attack disrupts code emulation by accessing memory outside the control of code emulators (i.e., victim's memory). Since a network-level code emulator examines network packets, it cannot inherently access memory regions of a victim process. If shellcode accesses the victim's memory, the emulator cannot continue its emulation. Yataglass addressed memory-scanning attack by analyzing evasion code used in memory-scanning attack. The evasion code typically contains a *scanning loop* that searches for a code fragment useful for evasion. Yataglass uses symbolic execution to extract the conditions on which a scanning loop exits. Then, Yataglass prepares a code region that satisfies the extracted conditions. By doing this, Yataglass deceives the shellcode into finding the code fragment and then, the shellcode execute the prepared code. Thus it successfully prevents the shellcodes from evading network-level code emulators.

To show the effectiveness of Yataglass, we prepared seven realworld shellcodes that incorporate memory-scanning attacks and compared Yataglass with Spector [17] of our implementation. Because Spector lacks the capability of handling memory-scanning attack, it was disrupted with all these shellcodes, while Yataglass successfully analyzed their behavior.

Our future work is to address more sophisticated memory-scanning attack. For example, an attacker may scan for code fragments indirectly by using heuristics (e.g, scanning victim's memory for the first basic block of execve() to find the code of execve()). Yataglass is currently limited to scanning loops that directly scans code fragments. We plan to address this kind of attack to improve efficiency of network-level code emulators.

References

1. AlephOne: Smashing stack for fun and profit. Phrack (November 1996)
2. MITRE: OpenSSL SSLv2 Malformed Client Key Remote Buffer Overflow Vulnerability (2002), http://www.securityfocus.com/bid/5363
3. Sotirov, A.: Apache openssl heap overflow exploit (September 2002), http://www.phreedom.org/research/exploits/apache-openssl/
4. Li, W., cher Chiueh, T.: Automated format string attack prevention for win32/x86 binaries. In: Proc. of the 23rd Annual Computer Security Applications Conference ACSAC 2007, pp. 398–409 (2007)
5. Roesch, M.: Snort: Lightweight intrusion detection for networks. In: Proc. of the 13th USENIX Conference on Systems Administration LISA 1999, pp. 229–238 (1999)
6. Paxson, V.: Bro: a system for detecting network intruders in real-time. Computer Networks 31(23–24), 2435–2463 (1999)
7. Chinchani, R., Berg, E.V.D.: A fast static analysis approach to detect exploit code in network flows. In: Valdes, A., Zamboni, D. (eds.) RAID 2005. LNCS, vol. 3858, pp. 284–308. Springer, Heidelberg (2006)
8. The Metasploit Project: Metasploit, http://www.metasploit.com/
9. Bania, P.: Tapion (2005), http://pb.specialised.info/all/tapion/
10. K2: Admmutate (2007), http://www.ktwo.ca/ADMmutate-0.8.4.tar.gz
11. Sedalo, M.: Jempiscode (2006), http://goodfellas.shellcode.com.ar/proyectos.html
12. Kruegel, C., Kirda, E., Mutz, D., Robertson, W., Vigna, G.: Polymorphic worm detection using structural information of executables. In: Valdes, A., Zamboni, D. (eds.) RAID 2005. LNCS, vol. 3858, pp. 207–226. Springer, Heidelberg (2006)
13. Polychronakis, M., Anagnostakis, K.G., Markatos, E.P.: Network-level polymorphic shellcode detection using emulation. In: Büschkes, R., Laskov, P. (eds.) DIMVA 2006. LNCS, vol. 4064, pp. 54–73. Springer, Heidelberg (2006)
14. Ma, J., Dunagan, J., Wang, H.J., Savage, S., Voelker, G.M.: Finding diversity in remote code injection exploits. In: Proc. of the 6th ACM SIGCOMM on Internet Measurement IMC 2006, October 2006, pp. 53–64 (2006)
15. Zhang, Q., Reeves, D.S., Ning, P.: Analyzing network traffic to detect self-decrypting exploit code. In: Proc. of the 2nd ASIAN ACM Symposium on Information, Computer and Communications Security ASIACCS 2007, March 2007, pp. 4–12 (2007)
16. Polychronakis, M., Anagnostakis, K.G., Markatos, E.P.: Emulation-based detection of non-self-contained polymorphic shellcode. In: Kruegel, C., Lippmann, R., Clark, A. (eds.) RAID 2007. LNCS, vol. 4637, pp. 87–106. Springer, Heidelberg (2007)
17. Borders, K., Prakash, A., Zielinski, M.: Spector: Automatically analyzing shell code. In: Proc. of the 23rd Annual Computer Security Applications Conference ACSAC 2007, pp. 501–514 (2007)

18. Linn, C.M., Rajagopalan, M., Baker, S., Collberg, C., Debray, S.K., Hartman, J.: Protecting against unexpected system calls. In: Proc. of the 13th Usenix Security Symposium, August 2005, pp. 239–254 (2005)
19. Wang, X., Pan, C.C., Liu, P., Zhu, S.: SigFree: A Signature-free Buffer Overflow Attack Blocker. In: Proc. of the 15th Usenix Security Symposium, pp. 225–240 (2006)
20. Cadar, C., Ganesh, V., Pawlowski, P.M., Dill, D.L., Engler, D.R.: EXE: automatically generating inputs of death. In: Proc. of the 13th ACM Conference on Computer and Communications Security CCS 2006, October 2006, pp. 322–335 (2006)
21. Moser, A., Kruegel, C., Kirda, E.: Exploring multiple execution paths for malware analysis. In: Proc. of the 2007 IEEE Symposium on Security and Privacy S&P 2007, May 2007, pp. 231–245 (2007)
22. Brumley, D., Hartwig, C., Kang, M.G., Liang, Z., Newsome, J., Poosankam, P., Song, D., Yin, H.: Bitscope: Automatically dissecting malicious binaries. Technical Report CMU-CS-07-133, Carnegie Mellon University (2007)
23. SystemV Application Binary Interface Intel 386 Architecture Processor Supplement, http://www.caldera.com/developers/devspecs/abi386-4.pdf
24. jt: Libdasm (2006), http://www.klake.org/~jt/misc/libdasm-1.5.tar.gz
25. Smith, J.E., Nair, R.: Virtual Machines - Versatile Platforms for Systems and Processes. Elsevier, Amsterdam (2005)
26. MITRE: ISC Bind 8 Transaction Signatures Buffer Overflow Vulnerability (2001), http://www.securityfocus.com/bid/2302
27. MITRE: Wu-ftpd file globbing heap corruption vulnerability (2001), http://securityfocus.com/bid/3581
28. MITRE: rsync Signed Array Index Remote Code Execution Vulnerability (2002), http://www.securityfocus.com/bid/3958
29. MITRE: Wu-imapd Partial Mailbox Attribute Remote Buffer Overflow Vulnerability (2002), http://securityfocus.com/bid/4713
30. MITRE: Samba 'call_trans2open' remote buffer overflow vulnerability (2003), http://securityfocus.com/bid/7294
31. MITRE: Cyrus IMAPD POP3D Remote Buffer Overflow Vulnerability (2006), http://www.securityfocus.com/bid/18506
32. SecurityFocus: http://securityfocus.com/
33. Milw0rm: http://www.milw0rm.com/
34. PaX Team: PaX address space layout randomization (ASLR), http://pax.grsecurity.net/docs/aslr.txt
35. Andersson, S., Clark, A., Mohay, G.M.: Network-based buffer overflow detection by exploit code analysis. In: Proc. of the AusCERT Asia Pacific Information Technology Security Conference, pp. 39–53 (2004)
36. Dunlap, G.W., King, S.T., Cinar, S., Basrai, M., Chen, P.M.: Revirt: Enabling intrusion analysis through virtual-machine logging and replay. In: Proc. of the 5th Symposium on Operating Systems Design and Implementation OSDI 2002, December 2002, pp. 211–224 (2002)
37. Andersson, S., Clark, A., Mohay, G.M., Schatz, B., Zimmermann, J.: A Framework for Detecting Network-based Code Injection Attacks Targeting Windows and UNIX. In: Proc. of the 21st Annual Computer Security Applications Conference ACSAC 2005, pp. 49–58 (2005)

Defending Browsers against Drive-by Downloads: Mitigating Heap-Spraying Code Injection Attacks

Manuel Egele[1], Peter Wurzinger[1], Christopher Kruegel[2], and Engin Kirda[3]

[1] Secure Systems Lab, Technical University Vienna, Austria
{pizzaman,pw}@seclab.tuwien.ac.at
[2] University of California, Santa Barbara
chris@cs.ucsb.edu
[3] Institute Eurecom, France
kirda@eurecom.fr

Abstract. Drive-by download attacks are among the most common methods for spreading malware today. These attacks typically exploit memory corruption vulnerabilities in web browsers and browser plug-ins to execute shellcode, and in consequence, gain control of a victim's computer. Compromised machines are then used to carry out various malicious activities, such as joining botnets, sending spam emails, or participating in distributed denial of service attacks.

To counter drive-by downloads, we propose a technique that relies on x86 instruction emulation to identify JavaScript string buffers that contain shellcode. Our detection is integrated into the browser, and performed *before* control is transfered to the shellcode, thus, effectively thwarting the attack. The solution maintains fair performance by avoiding unnecessary invocations of the emulator, while ensuring that every buffer with potential shellcode is checked. We have implemented a prototype of our system, and evaluated it over thousands of malicious and legitimate web sites. Our results demonstrate that the system performs accurate detection with no false positives.

Keywords: Drive-by download, malicious script, emulation, shellcode.

1 Introduction

A drive-by download is any download of software that happens without the knowledge and consent of a user. Unfortunately, drive-by downloads present a major threat to the Internet and its users [28]. In a typical attack, the mere visit of a web site that contains the malicious content can lead to the infection of a user's computer with malware. The malicious code that is installed as part of the attack then has typically full control over the victim's machine. Often, keystrokes are recorded, passwords are stolen, and sensitive information is leaked out. Also, infected computers may join a botnet [5], a large collection of compromised hosts controlled by the attacker. The computational power of compromised hosts are valuable for attackers as these hosts can be misused for spam campaigns [17] or denial of service attacks [20].

The typical steps of a drive-by download attack are shown in Figure 1. It can be seen how the attacker first prepares a web site with malicious content. When this site is

U. Flegel and D. Bruschi (Eds.): DIMVA 2009, LNCS 5587, pp. 88–106, 2009.

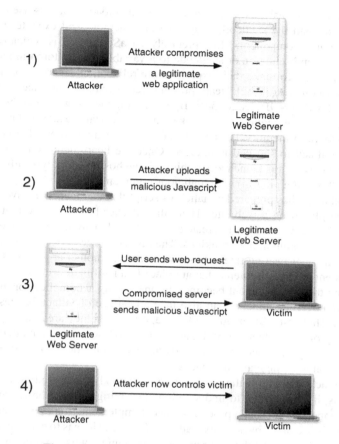

Fig. 1. The typical steps of a drive-by download attack

later visited by a victim, hostile script code is downloaded and executed by the victim's browser. This script exploits a vulnerability in the browser or an installed browser-plugin. Once successful, the payload (shellcode) of the exploit downloads malware that provides full control to the attacker.

Most current drive-by downloads target browser plug-ins that are developed and distributed by third parties [28,29]. The reason is that these plug-ins are less tested than the core browser, and thus, more likely to contain security vulnerabilities. Also, plug-ins are typically distributed as binary executables (at least in the case of Microsoft's Internet Explorer). As many plug-ins are written in non-safe languages such as C, they are susceptible to a wide range of vulnerabilities that are common for applications written in such languages. These vulnerabilities include buffer overflows, memory corruption issues, and pointer overwrites. Finally, plug-ins are often executed in the context of the browser, and as a result, can get full access to the browser and the underlying operating system.

As mentioned previously, as part of a drive-by download, attackers use client-side scripting code to load the shellcode (payload) into memory and execute the exploit against a vulnerable component. More precisely, JavaScript [11] is typically used to assign the binary representation of shellcode to a variable that is stored in the address space of the browser. To make their exploits more reliable, attackers resort to a technique called *heap spraying* [7,32]. Heap spraying creates multiple instances of the shellcode, combined with a NOP sledge [34][1]. By leveraging the knowledge of how a script engine manages its heap memory, an attacker can, to a certain extent, influence where variables are stored in memory. As a result, the area of heap memory that needs to be sprayed for an attack to succeed is reduced. Once the heap memory has been "prepared," the actual exploit is launched. To this end, the hostile script typically invokes a vulnerable method (of a plug-in) with malicious arguments.

When the attacker has prepared a malicious script that can launch a drive-by download, it can be placed on a web site. Then, the attacker has to ensure that potential victims visit this site. One way is to create a new site and manipulate search engines so that they list this site high in their rankings. The higher a page is ranked, the higher the chance is that an unsuspecting Internet user will visit it. Another approach is to embed malicious content in advertisements that are placed on legitimate web pages. Here, the site embedding the advertisement becomes an unknowing accomplice for distributing the attack. Moreover, an attacker can also take advantage of vulnerabilities found in popular web applications. By exploiting these applications, they are able to place their content directly on the vulnerable web site. Automated SQL injection attacks [6,16], for example, modify the database back-ends of web applications in order to include iframe tags that load the malicious pages.

Drive-by attacks belong to the most common methods for spreading malware today [29]. Thus, it is important to find solutions that mitigate the problem and protect users. In this paper, we present a proof-of-concept implementation of a system that detects shellcode-based drive-by download attacks. Our basic idea is to check the variables (strings) that are allocated by the browser (the script engine) when executing client-side scripts. When such a variable contains shellcode, we assume that the script is hostile, attempting to setup the environment for an exploit. Thus, the script is terminated, before any vulnerable function is invoked. We implemented our system in the Mozilla Firefox browser. However, our conceptual solution is general and works for arbitrary browsers. The main contributions of this paper are as follows:

- We propose a technique that uses emulation to automatically identify shell-code-based drive-by download attacks in a browser.
- We describe a proof-of-concept implementation of our approach that is integrated into the Mozilla Firefox browser.
- We present experimental results that show the feasibility of our approach. We have evaluated our prototype on more than one thousand malicious and several thousand benign sites. Our experimental results demonstrate that the system is able to accurately detect drive-by downloads with no false positives.

---

[1] A NOP sledge consists of a sequence of NOP instructions that increase the chance of successfully hitting the shellcode when hijacking the control flow of the vulnerable application.

2   Anatomy of a Drive-by Attack

In this section, we first provide a short overview of JavaScript to enable the reader to understand script-based drive-by downloads. Then, we present and discuss a real-world attack to illustrate the problem that we aim to defend against.

2.1   JavaScript Basics

JavaScript is an implementation of the ECMA-262 standard that defines an object-oriented scripting language [11]. The JavaScript specification defines a set of core components, such as data types (e.g., `String`, `Integer`, `Object`), special objects (e.g., `Date`, `Math`), and operators. The most prominent use of JavaScript is for supporting dynamic content on the client-side (in web browsers). However, JavaScript is also often embedded in other software, such as Adobe's Acrobat PDF reader. Systems that use JavaScript typically provide *environments* that allow a script to interact and communicate with other components. The document object model (DOM), for example, is part of the environment provided by the web browser. It allows scripts to manipulate the web pages that are displayed and to react to user actions and inputs.

The JavaScript interpreter of the Mozilla foundation is called SpiderMonkey [11]. Microsoft's implementation of ECMA-262 is called JScript [22]. This implementation adds facilities to the environment that allow a script to instantiate and communicate with ActiveX components [21]. These components are the preferred way of providing plug-ins for the Internet Explorer. On request, the libraries implementing the components are loaded into the address space of the Internet Explorer process, and the necessary objects are instantiated. ActiveX plug-ins, thus, have the same privileges that the browser has, often including full access to the file system and the network.

Among the data types, `strings` deserves special attention. ECMA-262 defines strings as sequences of 16-bit integers, commonly interpreted as UTF-16 characters. Popular JavaScript engines, such as SpiderMonkey, implement strings as immutable. That is, once a string variable is initialized, the value does not change for the rest of its lifetime. String operations, such as substituting characters (i.e., `replace` method of the string object), do not modify the original value. Instead, a new additional string variable is instantiated with the modified content. We will see that this fact has important ramifications for the implementation of our defense technique.

2.2   An Example of a Real-World Drive-by Download

In this section, we describe a typical drive-by download attack. We actually encountered this specific attack during our experiments. On September 2, 2008, our high-interaction client honeypot visited the URL `http://www.thewebleaders.com`. This page contained an `iframe` that loaded the script presented in Listing 1.1.

The most noticeable property of the script is that it uses obfuscated variable and function names to make it difficult for a human analyst to understand the script's purpose. Manual analysis reveals that the function defined in Line 1 serves as a decryption routine. The two values that make up the key for decryption are the location currently visited by the browser (`location.href`, Line 2), and the source code of the decryption function itself (`arguments.callee`, Lines 3,4). Using the current location as

```
1    function XfNLVA421(IaP1EoKdg) {
2        var I833Nad64 = location.href;
3        var hOtmWAGmO = arguments.callee;
4        hOtmWAGmO = hOtmWAGmO.toString()
5        ...
6        try {
7            eval(jiiIUpFi3);
8        } catch(e)
9        ...
10   }
11   XfNLVA421('a7A7a7A7ac9bB5b261...');
```

Listing 1.1. Excerpt of an obfuscated, real-world malicious script

part of the key to the decryption function allows the attacker to prevent the analysis of the script when it is loaded from a different location. That is, when the script is captured, and during a later analysis served locally, the decryption will fail. The last step of the function uses the decrypted content in an eval[2] statement (Line 7). Nesting the eval in a try-catch block suppresses the errors that would be seen by the analyst if the eval would fail. This failure would happen, for example, in case the key is wrong.

```
1    function IxQUTJ9S() {
2        if (!Iw6mS7sE) {
3            var YlsElYlW = 0x0c0c0c0c;
4            var hpgfpT9z = unescape("%u00e8%u0000%u5d00%uc583% ...");
             ...
5            for (var CCEzrp0s=0;CCEzrp0s<Wh_74Nkm;CCEzrp0s++) {
6                je9rIXgu[CCEzrp0s] = QdV7IGyr + hpgfpT9z;
7            }
             ...
9        }
     ...
11   var Kp1uYOjP = new ActiveXObject('Sb.SuperBuddy');
12   if (Kp1uYOjP) {
13       IxQUTJ9S();
14       oH9mUjOd(9);
15       Kp1uYOjP.LinkSBIcons(0x0c0c0c0c);
```

Listing 1.2. Excerpt of a real-world, decrypted malicious script

After decryption, the string passed to eval contains the code excerpt presented in Listing 1.2. Line 4 loads x86 shellcode into variable hpgfpT9z. Subsequently, the heap is sprayed by filling the memory with a large number of strings that contain a NOP

---

[2] ECMA-262 specifies that an implementation must provide an eval function. This function takes an argument of type string and interprets its argument as an ECMAScript program. That is, the eval function executes the argument it receives as a script.

sledge and a copy of the shellcode (Lines 5-7). In Line 11, the SuperBuddy ActiveX component is instantiated. If a valid object can be created, then the vulnerable method LinkSBIcons is invoked (Line 15). The LinkSBIcons vulnerability is known as CVE-2006-5820 [4]; the argument of LinkSBIcons is used as a function pointer, thus diverting control flow to the sprayed heap.

3   Automatically Detecting Drive-by Attacks

As described in the previous section, drive-by downloads that target memory corruption vulnerabilities have to prepare the environment before they can successfully launch their exploits. To this end, they use client-side script code to allocate (often large numbers of) strings that are filled with x86 (shell)code. The key idea of our detection approach targets precisely this behavior. More specifically, to detect drive-by downloads that exploit memory corruption vulnerabilities, we monitor all strings that are allocated by the JavaScript interpreter. These strings are checked for the presence of shellcode. Of course, all checks occur *before* a vulnerability can be abused to redirect control flow to the shellcode. When our system detects that a script creates a string that contains shellcode, the execution of the script is stopped.

The prototype implementation of our detection technique was implemented and integrated into the Mozilla Firefox browser and SpiderMonkey, its JavaScript engine. We chose Firefox as our prototype platform as this is an open source browser. Obviously, we would have liked to have integrated our solution into the Internet Explorer. Unfortunately, we did not have access to the source code. Nevertheless, we note that our solution is conceptually generic, and is not dependent on a specific browser. We have chosen to target JavaScript because it is by far the most common language for writing scripts on the web. Of course, an attacker could make use of a different language than JavaScript to deliver an exploit (and some indeed use Visual Basic Script). However, it would be straightforward to include our technique also into other script engines.

In the following sections, we describe our technique in more detail. In particular, we discuss how we keep track of the strings that are allocated, and how we detect the shellcode that an attacker may attempt to inject. Then, we discuss two optimizations that are applied to make the proposed approach fast enough to be used in practice.

3.1   Tracking Object (String) Allocations

For a drive-by attack to succeed, it is important that the bytes constituting the shellcode are stored at successive addresses in memory. Otherwise, these bytes would not be interpreted as valid x86 instructions. Of course, one could consider to split a sequence of instructions over multiple segments and connect these segments with jumps, but at least the bytes of each segment need to be consecutive to be valid. In JavaScript, the only way to guarantee that bytes are stored in a consecutive manner is by using a string variable. Here, consecutive characters of the string are allocated in adjacent memory locations.

To detect the shellcode that a malicious script might construct on the heap, we have to keep track of all string variables that the program allocates. To this end, we modified the SpiderMonkey JavaScript interpreter that is embedded in Firefox. More precisely, we added code to all points in the interpreter where string variables are created. These points were found at three locations: one for the allocation of global string variables, one for local string variables, and one for strings that are properties (members) of objects. The code that we added simply keeps track of the start address of a new string variable and its length. Here, it is important to recall that strings in JavaScript are immutable. As a result, whenever a character in a string is modified, or when two strings are concatenated, the resulting string is created in a new memory area. Thus, string manipulation is automatically handled by the code introduced for creating a new string variable.

In addition to the start address and the length of new string variables, we also keep track of the two sub-strings that are used in a string concatenation operation. That is, whenever a new string is created as a result of a concatenation operation, we keep pointers to the sub-strings. This is needed for an optimization that is discussed later.

An attacker might consider to use integer arrays to store the shellcode in successive memory addresses. However, JavaScript supports arrays of integers that follow this (packed) memory layout only for 31-bit values, where the remaining bit is always set to indicate that the value is an integer. The fact that one bit is set in each four-byte integer makes it more difficult for the attacker to craft his shellcode. Also, support for packed integer arrays can be easily disabled. For integer values that are larger than 31-bit, and for all other data types, JavaScript handles arrays differently. More precisely, such arrays only store identifiers (pointers) that reference objects that are allocated elsewhere. Since these objects contain additional management information and are allocated from a pool of memory, it is very difficult for an attacker to reliably predict where these objects will end up. As a result, our system focuses on the content of string variables. Of course, when attackers develop techniques to store shellcode in objects that are allocated in the object pool, we could easily add checks for these objects as well.

3.2 Checking Strings for Shellcode

Given information about the addresses and lengths of the strings in memory, the next question that needs to be answered is how shellcode can be automatically detected within these strings. More precisely, we have to discuss how shellcode can be recognized, and the points in time when this analysis is launched.

For the detection of shellcode, we are leveraging *libemu* [19]. libemu is a small library written in C that offers basic x86 emulation and shellcode detection. It is efficient in detecting shellcode and being used in projects such as Nepenthes and Honeytrap. To recognize shellcode in a string (character buffer), libemu checks, starting from each character, whether there is a sequence of valid instructions of sufficient length. When such an instruction sequence is found, libemu reports shellcode. Since most bytes can be disassembled to valid x86 instructions, libemu also uses a number of heuristics to discriminate random instructions from actual shellcode. We currently use a value of 32 bytes as the threshold for the minimal length of a shellcode sequence. We found that this value works well in our experiments, and it is also significantly shorter than all Windows shellcode encountered in the wild [26].

Note that an attacker might try to evade detection by distributing shellcode fragments over multiple strings. In this case, to be successful, each fragment must end in a jump instruction to the next fragment. Moreover, since the total length of each fragment must not exceed 32 bytes, there is almost no space for a NOP sledge. As a result, the attacker must guess the jump offset quite precisely. While modern heap manipulation techniques allow for a certain control over the heap layout, we believe that such an attack is very difficult to launch in practice. Moreover, randomizing the allocation of individual objects in the heap would be easy to do and render this hypothetical evasion vector infeasible. Note that randomizing object allocations does not help against current drive-by attacks that store the complete shellcode in one string. The reason is that the location of a particular string might not be know precisely, but the attacker can allocate thousands of such self-contained, malicious strings (sometimes worth tens or hundreds of megabyte). Then, hitting a single string is sufficient to successfully run the shellcode.

The goal of our detection approach is to ensure that the attacker *cannot* execute shellcode *before* we analyze all (string) objects that he has created. The straightforward approach to do this is to invoke the emulator whenever a new string object is created. Of course, every string object is only checked once. Nevertheless, this naive approach incurs a significant performance penalty.

3.3   Performance Optimizations

To reduce the performance penalty that is incurred when checking every string that is allocated, two approaches are possible. First, one can reduce the total number of invocations of the emulation engine. Second, one can reduce the amount of data that the emulator needs to inspect. Our prototype supports techniques to leverage speedups from both of these approaches.

Since vulnerabilities exploited by drive-by download attacks are almost always found in the browser or its plug-in components, we consider the JavaScript interpreter as safe. As a result, while executing JavaScript core functionality, a script is allowed to create string objects without checks, even ones that contain shellcode. To transfer control flow to such a string buffer with shellcode, the malicious script must exploit a vulnerability in an "external" component, leaving the JavaScript core part. Thus, to detect any shellcode before it can be executed, it is not required to perform emulation immediately after creating a new string object. Instead, it is possible to only record information on all created string objects, and postpone emulation to the time at which control flow leaves the interpreter, entering an external component or the browser.

The delayed checking allows us to collect information about the involved string objects and leverage this knowledge to decrease the overall amount of data that has to be checked. First, we use information about string concatenation, a frequent operation. Consider that we observe the fact that a given string a consists of the concatenation of strings x and y. This allows us to skip the analysis (emulation) of x and y when a was already scanned and found to be clean. A second venue for optimization is the JavaScript garbage collector. By invoking garbage collection on every transition from the interpreter to the environment, we are able to discard all objects from the emulation that are freed by the garbage collector. We have modified the garbage collector routines to remove the freed contents from the list of objects to emulate (after zeroing their content).

Note that although the detection is delayed, it is still complete in the sense that no machine instructions residing in the memory space of a JavaScript object can potentially be executed before being checked by our shellcode detector.

4   Evaluation

This section discusses how we evaluated our prototype as well as the experimental results. The evaluation was carried out in three parts. First, we evaluated our system for false positives by accessing a large number of popular benign web pages. Second, we used our system on pages that launch drive-by downloads and evaluated the detection effectiveness. Third, we examined the performance overhead of our system.

4.1   False Positive Evaluation

In the context of our system, a false positive is a page that is detected as malicious without actually loading shellcode to memory. To evaluate the likelihood of false positives, we extended our prototype system to visit a list of $k = 4,502$ known, benign pages. These pages were taken from the Alexa ranking of global top-sites, and simply consisted of the top k pages. We consider this to be a realistic test set that reflects a wide range of web applications and categories of content.

For the batch evaluation of URLs, we implemented a Firefox extension that visits all URLs provided in a file. After a timeout, the extension automatically visits the next URL in the list. More precisely, the extension moves to the next URL two seconds after the page finished loading, or ten seconds after page loading started. The hard limit of ten seconds was necessary to handle scripts that continuously issued page reloads.

Our prototype did not produce any false positives for this dataset. This might look suspicious at first glance: The x86 instruction set is known to be densely packed, thus, almost any sequence of bytes makes up valid instructions. However, one has to consider the fact that JavaScript uses 16-bit Unicode characters to store text. That is, even if a given sequence of ASCII characters results in a valid x86 instruction most of the time, the JavaScript representation of the same characters most likely does not, since every other byte would contain the value 0x0. Of course, an attacker can encode the shellcode appropriately. However, benign pages typically do not contain strings that map to valid instruction sequences.

4.2   Detection Effectiveness

In a next step, we evaluated the capabilities of our technique to identify drive-by attacks that rely on shellcode to perform their malicious actions. To this end, we evaluated our system on the traces of 1,187 web browsing sessions that are known to contain drive-by attacks. These traces were collected by visiting URLs that are advertised in spam emails. We retrieved a list of such URLs from the Spamcop [33] web service, as well as from mails collected in the spam trap of a medium-size security company.

To filter those URLs that actually host drive-by attacks, we used the Capture Honeypot Client (HPC) [2]. Capture visits the URLs with a browser on a virtual machine (VM). After a site is loaded, the state of the VM is inspected, and all modifications to the file system and registry as well as new processes are logged. In addition to the logged information, the system records a trace of all network communication that was taking place. Capture simply visits a URL in a browser and performs no additional actions. Thus, by filtering URLs that caused a new process to be launched, we were able to identify those sites that perform drive-by attacks. The system running in the VM was a Windows XP Professional (Service Pack 2) installation. No additional security patches were applied, and automatic updates were turned off. Additionally, the Flash and QuickTime plug-ins were installed.

Once a URL was identified to host a drive-by attack, we used Chaosreader [14] to extract application level data from the network traces. Chaosreader is able to recognize a variety of application data from network traces. Among others, Chaosreader identifies HTML documents, binary images, or gzip compressed data, saving each response to an HTTP request in a distinct file. Files that were found to be compressed were decompressed before continuing.

Extracting a single file for every response to an HTTP request made further postprocessing necessary. For example, if an HTML page references a JavaScript URI via an `src` attribute of a `script` tag, this results in another request in which the browser fetches the JavaScript. The response contains only JavaScript code without surrounding HTML tags. Visiting such a file in a web browser results in its contents being interpreted as text, and thus, no interpretation of the code takes place. We used a simple heuristics to add the necessary HTML and `script` tags to such files. More precisely, whenever a file does not already contain valid HTML, and it does contain any of the most used JavaScript reserved words (e.g., `function`, `var`), it is wrapped in appropriate tags.

Once the HTML and JavaScript files were restored, they were uploaded on a local web server. In total, 11,910 URLs (files) were associated with the 1,187 traces (since a trace can contain multiple resources that are accessed by the browser, for example, due to redirection or embedded content). Our prototype system was instructed to visit each of these URLs. The modifications required to process encrypted attack scripts are detailed in Section 5. One might ask why we did not simply use our system to visit malicious pages that are live on the Internet, but, instead, replicate malicious sites and their scripts locally. The reason is that malicious sites on the Internet are frequently taken down. Additionally, many malicious sites only perform attacks on the first visit of a client. Thus, changing the prototype and revisiting the same location could not detect attacks hosted on such pages. In our setup, we have created a corpus that allows us to replicate our experiments and better debug and understand cases in which the detection fails initially.

When running our prototype detection system on the resources associated with 1,187 traces, we detected 956 instances of shellcode. This yields an initial detection effectiveness of 81%. We then examined the remaining 231 traces to understand why our system did not detect shellcode while the Capture honeypot client indicated an attack.

Manual analysis revealed four main causes that result in our prototype failing to detect a threat. One group (with 62 traces) contains drive-by downloads that do not make use of memory exploits. In particular, a popular attack against the Sina Downloader ActiveX component exploits insecure component behavior. More precisely, this component contains functions that allow a script to download a file and to start a program. This makes it trivial for an attacker to download malware and start it, without ever corrupting memory. However, note that this attack targets an old vulnerability (from 2006) that is very specific to a particular component. Thus, it is not a general class of vulnerabilities that our approach misses, but a specific problem in a component that basically offers all the functionality required by the attacker.

The second group of attacks (with four traces) that were missed by our system are due to exploits that use Visual Basic (VB) script code to prepare the environment and launch the exploit. As mentioned previously, our current prototype only instruments the JavaScript engine. However, similar techniques could easily be added to the VB script engine.

The third group of missed attacks (with 127 traces) are due to the way our experiments are carried out. Recall that we do not visit live pages on the Internet, but invoke individual resources (files) that we extracted from network traces. In some cases, the malicious code is distributed over several scripts that are in different files. In these cases, the browser does not see and analyze the complete, malicious script at once. This typically leads to JavaScript errors, and failure to inject shellcode into the heap. This, however, does not reflect a deficiency in our approach. If these sites were visited with a browser protected by our proposed technique, all scripts would be fetched and executed by the web browser in the same context, thus, allowing to detect the threat.

Finally, a forth group (with 38 traces) was not recognized as malicious because it contains traces that were false positives of the Capture honeypot client. More specifically, they were .cab archive files. Whenever a .cab file is downloaded, Windows automatically starts the Windows Management Instrumentation to handle this resource. While this activity results in a new process being launched, it is not because of a malicious drive-by download but due to legitimate activity. However, Capture considers the start of a new process as an indication of a successful attack.

Given the discussion of the four cases above, we argue that only the traces associated with attacks against the Sina Downloader ActiveX and similar components should be considered false negatives for our system. As a result, we can compute a detection rate of $\frac{956}{956+62} = 93.9\%$. Also, we observe that we detected all drive-by attacks that exploited a memory corruption vulnerability, which is by far the most common type of exploit found in the wild.

After evaluating the detection capabilities of our system, we also performed further analysis of the ActiveX components created by the malicious scripts. Our results show that most malicious sites perform their attacks through only a handful of vulnerable components. Figure 2 depicts a breakdown of the distribution of the involved components. It is interesting to observe that the two most prominent components (SuperBuddy and QuickTime viewer) account for almost 50% of the targets of the attacks. Note that the figure lists the 1,688 ActiveX components that were created during our evaluation. Nonetheless, not every created component lead to a successfull exploit.

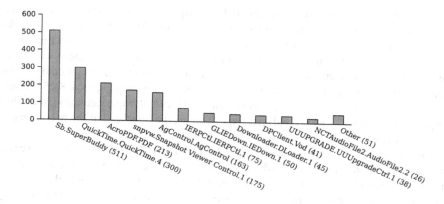

Fig. 2. ActiveX components involved in drive-by downloads

4.3 Performance

Our approach uses x86 instruction emulation to detect shellcode within JavaScript strings. This happens online; that is, the analysis must be performed at the time the browser loads a page. Since emulation is a resource intensive task, careless invocations of the emulator may lead to a significant performance overhead. We have pursued several strategies to minimize the overhead, as explained in Section 3.3. In this section, we describe the results of our performance evaluation.

Our experiment measures the wall-clock time required to load a set of web pages. We have chosen the 150 most popular web sites (according to Alexa). The same set of pages was processed three times. First, we ran an off-the-shelf Mozilla Firefox browser without performing any additional tasks. Second, we used our modified version of the browser that provides protection against drive-by download attacks, without any performance optimizations. Third, we used the browser with protection and performance optimizations.

All measurements have been carried out on a machine with an Intel Core 2 Duo processor running at 2.66 GHz and 4 GB of main memory. Internet connectivity was established using an ADSL line with a bandwidth of 1 MBit/s.

The results of our performance evaluation are presented in Table 1. On average, an unmodified Firefox browser took 3.51 seconds to load one web page from our testing set. This time includes the download of the content over the Internet, parsing and

Table 1. Page load times (sec) with and without drive-by download protection

		Total time[s]	Time/page[s]	Overhead/page	Factor
Off-the-shelf browser		527	3.51		
Protected browser	w/o optimizations	1,237	8.25	4.74	2.35
	w/ optimizations	876	5.84	**2.33**	**1.66**

rendering of the page, and execution of all JavaScript code. In comparison, a modified version of the browser, which provides protection against drive-by download attacks, takes additional time. The overhead can be attributed to the effort spent on tracing the allocated string objects, and more importantly, emulation of their content when executing functionality from the JavaScript environment. A basic implementation of our system, without application of performance optimization measures, took 8.25 seconds per page. This is a significant performance penalty. Our final implementation, including all optimizations took, 5.84 seconds per page. That is, the overhead of the naive version could be reduced in half.

Browsing the Web is an interactive occupation, and it is desirable for the user to experience as little latency as possible when loading a new page. Obviously, the decrease in performance introduced by our approach seems significant. However, note that the time users typically spend on consuming the downloaded content (e.g., reading an article) by far outweighs the time that is spent on waiting for new content to be loaded. Thus, we believe that the benefit of a secure browsing experience, without the risk of falling prey to a drive-by download attack, well compensates the inflicted performance penalty.

5   Implementation Details

As mentioned previously, our system has been implemented by extending Mozilla Firefox and SpiderMonkey. However, all drive-by download attacks in our dataset target the Internet Explorer (IE). The astute reader might wonder how our system can actually detect such attacks, since they are not supposed to work with Firefox. In the following, we provide some (what we believe) interesting details on how we implemented our system to detect IE attacks with a modified Firefox browser. Of course, when our technique would be integrated with Internet Explorer, such extensions would not be necessary. Also, the system as introduced can readily detect drive-by downloads that target Firefox. Moreover, we discuss some additional issues that needed to be addressed because of our experimental setup.

Simulating ActiveX components. Attacks that aim to exploit a vulnerability in a specific plug-in often perform a check for the availability of this plug-in. That is, such attacks only reveal their malicious behavior when the vulnerable component is present. In the case of ActiveX plug-ins, this is done by trying to instantiate the vulnerable component. If the plug-in object is instantiated successfully, it usually means that the component is present.

Unfortunately, Mozilla Firefox does not support ActiveX plug-ins. However, as most drive-by attacks rely on ActiveX to be present, we had to modify the browser appropriately. More precisely, we extended Firefox such that it creates dummy objects for instantiation requests to ActiveX components. Thus, whenever a malicious script attempts to instantiate an ActiveX component, the call succeeds and the corresponding dummy object is created.

These objects accept all method invocations, and also log method calls together with their respective arguments. Note that although it is not the main focus of our work, this information can be used to identify the vulnerability that is used to divert the control flow.

Browser fingerprinting. Browser fingerprinting is a technique applied by attackers to serve only exploits that match the specific browser of the sites' visitors. To this end, instead of bluntly trying a series of attacks, a script is executed to determine the browser, its version, and installed plug-ins. Based on the knowledge gathered by this script, it fetches only those exploit scripts that match this setup (e.g., if no QuickTime plug-in is detected, no QuickTime related exploits are tried). Even when no fingerprinting is performed as described above, the malicious script most likely verifies that it is executed in a browser that it intends to exploit. Therefore, the script queries the properties of the navigator object and only continues if the information matches its authors' intentions. Since our prototype is implemented in Mozilla Firefox, this would have prevented all scripts that perform such techniques from executing. However, the recorded traces hold proof of a successful drive-by attack. Thus, we modified our prototype to pretend to be the same browser and version[3] that was used when the traces were recorded.

To assure that the script is executing in Microsoft's Internet Explorer, attackers rely on inaccuracies of the JScript parser. More precisely, the JScript parser is more tolerant with regards to semicolons than SpiderMonkey.

```
1    try {
2        ...
3    } catch (e) {};
4    finally {
5        ...
6    }
```

Listing 1.3. Illustration of different parsing behavior

Listing 1.3, for example, illustrates this with a try-catch-finally construct. While the JScript parser gladly accepts this syntax (notice the semicolon after the catch block in Line 3), the SpiderMonkey engine terminates the script with an error (i.e., "finally without try") at Line 4. These different parsing behaviors introduce further means for an attacker to make sure the script is interpreted by the Internet Explorer. As we could observe such attacks in the wild, we had to modify the parser of our prototype to reflect the behavior of the JScript parser.

Dynamic encryption keys. Most malicious scripts are encrypted in some way. The attackers' motivation to disguise malicious scripts is obviously the intention to encumber the analysis of such scripts. Encryption is a straightforward approach to do so.

An encrypted script contains a decryption routine and a cipher text. During execution, the cipher text is decrypted by the routine, and the result is executed via JavaScript's eval function. Two possibilities exist where the decryption routine derives the correct key from. (1) the key might be part of the script itself (e.g., stored in a variable), or (2) the key is dependent on the environment of the script. While in the first case, decryption is automatically handled by the interpreter, the second case requires

---

[3] Corresponding to the user-agent string: Mozilla/4.0 (compatible; MSIE 6.0; Windows NT 5.1; SV1).

that the environment presents the right information for the queried value. In our evaluation dataset, many decryption keys were partly derived from the current URL of the browser. Since the scripts were hosted at a local web server, the URLs were different, thus leading to wrong decryption keys. For wrong key values, the decryption routines produce only garbage and, as a result, no malicious behavior can be observed. Since, on the other hand, the values were correct when the network traces were recorded, we modified our prototype to report the URL that was visited during the recording of the trace as the current location. This allowed the scripts to decrypt the cipher text correctly, and we were able to analyze and detect their malicious behavior.

Batch processing time-outs. Some malicious scripts use the setTimeout function of JavaScript to delay their actions. During our batch processing of URLs, we use a time-out of ten seconds before moving to the next page. As a result, the usage of such timers could prevent detection. To mitigate this problem, we had to assure that these timeouts expire before the batch processing extension moves to the next URL. To this end, we modified Firefox to replace all delays of setTimeout calls with a delay of 50ms.

Interestingly, during our evaluation, we encountered a malicious script that implemented a custom version of a setTimeout-equivalent function. More precisely, the script looped and measured the expired time between the initial run of the loop and the current time. Once the desired delay was reached, execution continued. This sample did not use the setTimeout function and thus, the extension switched to the next URL before the malicious content was executed. Notice, however, that not detecting the malicious script in this sample is an artifact of the batch processing and does not indicate a weakness in our proposed approach. In fact, after removing the sleep function, the system did detect the malicious script, the shellcode it used, and the involved ActiveX components.

6   Related Work

Many researchers have proposed methods to analyze, detect, and mitigate the threat posed by malicious software. For malware analysis, two different approaches exist. While dynamic analysis actually executes the malware, static analysis is performed without running the software in question. Dynamic approaches execute the malware in a controlled environment, and observe the interaction of the malicious component with the environment. Hooking API function calls results in detailed information of the behavior of a program.

CWSandbox [36] uses hooking to log the invocations of Windows API function. Similarly, Anubis [1] performs its analysis via virtual machine introspection [13] on an application that is executed in an emulated machine. A mixture of static and dynamic techniques is applied by Kirda et al. [18] to detect malicious browser plug-ins. Egele et al. performed information flow analysis on browser plug-ins [9] to identify spyware components that leak sensitive information. Information flow analysis is also the key idea of Panorama [37], where Yin et al. implemented a system to discover rootkits. While powerful, existing analysis techniques are typically too heavyweight to be used for detection on a client machine. In contrast to that, our proposed technique detects drive-by download attacks by monitoring potentially malicious scripts directly in the browser.

Previous studies have shown that drive-by download attacks pose a real threat to the Internet and its users. The mechanisms used by attackers to mount their attacks are investigated by Provos et al. in [29]. The life cycle of an infected machine is analyzed by Polychronakis in [27]. In [28], Provos et al. present a measurement study that reports that the results for 1.3% of all Google search queries contain at least one link pointing to a page that performs a drive-by attack. Also, Frei et al. [12] analyzed the vulnerability landscape of web browsers in the Internet. Apparently, only 60% of the users that navigate the Internet everyday use the latest, most secure version of their web browser. Based on a Secunia report [31], the authors argue that many browser plug-ins commonly in use have known vulnerabilities. The fact that many users only reluctantly update their web browsers and plug-ins makes it feasible for attackers to distribute attacks that target old vulnerabilities. As many of the vulnerabilities leading to control flow hijacking are present in ActiveX components, Dormann and Plakosh [8] propose fuzzy testing as a means of detecting such flaws before distributing a component.

Detecting shellcode in network traffic has a long standing history. Network intrusion detection systems, such as Snort [30] or Bro [23], rely on signatures to identify malicious network streams. While signature detection works well for known static threats, advanced polymorphic shellcode and engines that can automatically produce such shellcode can sometimes evade these detection techniques. Based on abstract payload execution, Toth and Kruegel have proposed a mechanism to detect buffer overflow attacks [34]. More precisely, their prototype implementation identifies long valid sequences of instructions in HTTP requests, thus detecting the NOP sledge that commonly accompanies shellcode. Continuing this work, Polychronakis et al. [24,26] proposed to apply lightweight emulation on network data to identify polymorphic shellcode. This approach relies on the so-called GetPC heuristic. That is, a shellcode is only identified if a sequence of instructions is emulated that reads the current program counter value. The class of non-self-contained shellcode, however, contains code that reaches its goal without showing such behavior. In [25], the authors extend their detection techniques to also identify this class of attacks. While network-traffic-based techniques are useful, they typically cannot be used to detect drive-by downloads. The reason is that, although JavaScript contents of a web page are transmitted over the network, this code is often obfuscated. Furthermore, the shellcode contained in the JavaScript scripts are not transmitted in binary form. Instead, the ASCII representation of the individual bytes is transmitted. This sequence does not yield a valid instruction sequence in general.

Analyzing malicious JavaScript has recently gained more attention by the scientific community. Hallaraker and Vigna [15] present an approach to audit the execution of JavaScript code. These audit logs can be compared to high-level policies to detect potential attacks. Similarly, Feinstein and Peck introduced Caffeine Monkey [10], a tool that supports the collection and analysis of malicious JavaScript. To this end, they extended the Mozilla SpiderMonkey JavaScript engine by adding run-time logging facilities. Chenette et al. [3] aim at automatically reversing the obfuscation of malicious JavaScripts. Their approach relies on hooking techniques to monitor calls to relevant

JavaScript functions, such as eval or document.write. These systems focus on auditing JavaScript activity, while our approach aims at detecting malicious drive-by downloads.

Vogt et al. propose a system that prevents cross-site scripting attacks performed by malicious JavaScript code [35]. To protect a user from JavaScript that tries to steal sensitive information, the propagation of such information through the JavaScript engine is tracked. Requests to a domain containing information originating from another domain raise an alert, and allow the user to stop further execution of the script.

7 Conclusion

Drive-by downloads belong to the most threatening vectors of attack that are currently used by cyber-criminals to illegitimately gain control of victims' computers. In this paper, we present a novel approach that helps protect a user against drive-by attacks that rely on shellcode.

Our system is integrated into the web browser where it monitors JavaScript code that is downloaded and executed. More precisely, our system traces all string objects that are created during run-time, and it uses x86 instruction emulation to determine whether a string buffer contains executable shellcode. The detection of the shellcode takes place before a vulnerability can be exploited (and control flow redirected). Hence, an attack can be mitigated before the security of the browser is compromised.

Our approach includes optimizations to assure a reasonable performance overhead while delivering excellent detection results for drive-by attacks that exploit binary vulnerabilities in browser plug-in software. We have built a prototype implementation with which we have verified the capability of our approach to successfully detect real-world drive-by download attacks. Our evaluation shows that our approach is feasible in practice.

Acknowledgments

This work has been supported by the Austrian Science Foundation (FWF) under grant P18764, SECoverer FIT-IT Trust in IT-Systems 2. Call, Austria, Secure Business Austria (SBA), and the WOMBAT and FORWARD projects funded by the European Commission in the 7th Framework.

References

1. Bayer, U.: Anubis - analyzing unknown binaries, http://www.anubis.iseclab.org
2. Capture-HPC Client Honeypot / Honeyclient (2009),
   https://projects.honeynet.org/capture-hpc
3. Chenette, S.: ToorConX - the ultimate deobfuscator (2008),
   http://www.toorcon.org/tcx/26_Chenette.pdf
4. Superbuddy activex control vulnerability (2006),
   http://cve.mitre.org/cgi-bin/cvename.cgi?name=CVE-2006-5820
5. Dagon, D., Gu, G., Lee, C., Lee, W.: A Taxonomy of Botnet Structures. In: Annual Computer Security Applications Conference, ACSAC (2007)

6. Dan Goodin (The Register). SQL injection taints BusinessWeek.com,
   `http://www.theregister.co.uk/2008/09/16/businessweek_hacked/`
   (last accessed, December 2008)
7. Daniel, M., Honoroff, J., Miller, C.: Engineering Heap Overflow Exploits with JavaScript.
   In: 2nd USENIX Workshop on Offensive Technologies, WOOT 2008 (2008)
8. Dormann, W., Plakosh, D.: Vulnerability detection in activex controls through automated
   fuzz testing (2008), `http://www.cert.org/archive/pdf/dranzer.pdf`
9. Egele, M., Kruegel, C., Kirda, E., Yin, H., Song, D.X.: Dynamic spyware analysis. In:
   USENIX Annual Technical Conference, pp. 233–246 (2007)
10. Feinstein, B., Peck, D.: Caffeine monkey: Automated collection, detection and anal-
    ysis of malicious javascript (2006), `http://www.dc414.org/download/`
    `confs/defcon15/Speakers/Feinstein_and%20_Peck/Whitepaper/`
    `dc-15-feinstein_and_peck-WP.pdf`
11. M. Foundation. SpiderMonkey (JavaScript-C) Engine,
    `http://www.mozilla.org/js/spidermonkey/`
12. Frei, S., Dübendorfer, T., Ollmann, G., May, M.: Understanding the web browser threat.
    Technical Report 288, ETH Zurich, 06 2008 (2008)
13. Garfinkel, T., Rosenblum, M.: A virtual machine introspection based architecture for intru-
    sion detection. In: 10th Annual Network and Distributed System Security Symposium, NDSS
    2003 (2003)
14. Gregg, B.: fetch application data from snoop or tcpdump logs,
    `http://chaosreader.sourceforge.net/`
15. Hallaraker, O., Vigna, G.: Detecting malicious javascript code in mozilla. In: 10th Inter-
    national Conference on Engineering of Complex Computer Systems (ICECCS 2005), pp.
    85–94 (2005)
16. Leyden, J.: Drive-by download attack compromises 500k websites,
    `http://www.channelregister.co.uk/2008/05/13/zlob_trojan_`
    `forum_compromise_attack/` (last accessed, February 2009)
17. Kanich, C., Kreibich, C., Levchenko, K., Enright, B., Voelker, G.M., Paxson, V., Savage, S.:
    Spamalytics: An empirical analysis of spam marketing conversion. In: ACM Conference on
    Computer and Communications Security (2008)
18. Kirda, E., Kruegel, C., Banks, G., Vigna, G., Kemmerer, R.A.: Behavior-based spyware de-
    tection. In: USENIX Security (2006)
19. x86 shellcode detection and emulation, `http://libemu.mwcollect.org/`
20. Moore, D., Voelker, G., Savage, S.: Inferring Internet Denial of Service Activity. In: Usenix
    Security Symposium (2001)
21. M.D. Network. ActiveX Controls,
    `http://msdn.microsoft.com/en-us/library/aa751968.aspx`
22. M.D. Network. JScript Windows Script Technologies,
    `http://msdn.microsoft.com/en-us/library/hbxc2t98.aspx`
23. Paxson, V.: Bro: A System for Detecting Network Intruders in Real-Time. Computer Net-
    works 31 (1999)
24. Polychronakis, M., Anagnostakis, K.G., Markatos, E.P.: Network-level polymorphic shell-
    code detection using emulation. In: Büschkes, R., Laskov, P. (eds.) DIMVA 2006. LNCS,
    vol. 4064, pp. 54–73. Springer, Heidelberg (2006)
25. Polychronakis, M., Anagnostakis, K.G., Markatos, E.P.: Emulation-based detection of non-
    self-contained polymorphic shellcode. In: Kruegel, C., Lippmann, R., Clark, A. (eds.) RAID
    2007. LNCS, vol. 4637, pp. 87–106. Springer, Heidelberg (2007)
26. Polychronakis, M., Anagnostakis, K.G., Markatos, E.P.: Network-level polymorphic shell-
    code detection using emulation. Journal in Computer Virology 2(4), 257–274 (2007)

27. Polychronakis, M., Provos, N.: Ghost turns zombie: Exploring the life cycle of web-based malware. In: First USENIX Workshop on Large-Scale Exploits and Emergent Threats (2008)
28. Provos, N., Mavrommatis, P., Rajab, M.A., Monrose, F.: All your iframes point to us. In: USENIX Security Symposium (2008)
29. Provos, N., McNamee, D., Mavrommatis, P., Wang, K., Modadugu, N.: The Ghost In The Browser Analysis of Web-based Malware. In: First Workshop on Hot Topics in Understanding Botnets, HotBots 2007 (2007)
30. Roesch, M.: Snort - Lightweight Intrusion Detection for Networks. In: 13th Systems Administration Conference, LISA (1999)
31. Secunia PSI study: 28% of all detected applications are insecure (2007), http://secunia.com/blog/11/
32. Sotirov, A.: Heap Feng Shui in JavaScript, http://www.phreedom.org/research/heap-feng-shui/heap-feng-shui.html (last accessed, November 2008)
33. Spamcop - the premier service for reporting spam, http://www.spamcop.net/
34. Toth, T., Krugel, C.: Accurate buffer overflow detection via abstract payload execution. In: Wespi, A., Vigna, G., Deri, L. (eds.) RAID 2002, vol. 2516, pp. 274–291. Springer, Heidelberg (2002)
35. Vogt, P., Nentwich, F., Jovanovic, N., Kruegel, C., Kirda, E., Vigna, G.: Cross site scripting prevention with dynamic data tainting and static analysis. In: 14th Annual Network and Distributed System Security Symposium, NDSS 2007 (2007)
36. Willems, C., Holz, T., Freiling, F.: Toward automated dynamic malware analysis using cwsandbox. IEEE Security and Privacy 5(2), 32–39 (2007)
37. Yin, H., Song, D.X., Egele, M., Kruegel, C., Kirda, E.: Panorama: capturing system-wide information flow for malware detection and analysis. In: ACM Conference on Computer and Communications Security, pp. 116–127 (2007)

Polymorphing Software by Randomizing Data Structure Layout

Zhiqiang Lin, Ryan D. Riley, and Dongyan Xu

CERIAS and Department of Computer Science, Purdue University, USA
{zlin,rileyrd,dxu}@cs.purdue.edu

Abstract. This paper introduces a new software polymorphism technique that randomizes program data structure layout. This technique will generate different data structure layouts for a program and thus diversify the binary code compiled from the same program source code. This technique can mitigate attacks (e.g., kernel rootkit attacks) that require knowledge about data structure definitions. It is also able to disrupt the generation of data structure-based program signatures. We have implemented our data structure layout randomization technique in the open source compiler collection gcc-4.2.4 and applied it to a number of programs. Our evaluation results show that our technique is able to achieve software binary diversity. We also apply the technique to one operating system data structure in order to foil a number of kernel rootkit attacks. Meanwhile, programs produced by the technique were analyzed by a state-of-the-art data structure inference system and it was demonstrated that reliance on data structure signatures alone may lead to false negatives in malware detection.

1 Introduction

A widely adopted methodology for implementing software is data abstraction, which involves the abstraction of data structures and enables programmers to isolate a data definition from its representation and operations. Software is implemented to access and process data structures. Software implementation, if not obfuscated, will expose certain data structure definitions as well as their layouts. This observation has been exploited recently in network protocol reverse engineering [11, 40, 29, 20, 30, 16].

Knowledge about data structure layout is often used by attackers. For example, a buffer overflow attack relies on the attacker knowing that the program buffer is adjacent to a function pointer or return address [22]. Kernel rootkits, especially those that manipulate kernel objects directly, require that the attacker know the layout of specific kernel objects in order to manipulate them. In network application penetration testing, if the attacker knows the structure of the protocol message, he can reduce the fuzz space and speed up the test [39, 21]. These attacks can be foiled if we can prevent attackers from obtaining an accurate data structure layout of the victim program.

U. Flegel and D. Bruschi (Eds.): DIMVA 2009, LNCS 5587, pp. 107–126, 2009.

Data struct layouts are also used as attack signatures in some defense techniques. For example, in protocol analysis, the data structure associated with a protocol payload can be used to construct the exploit signature for runtime network intrusion detection. In malware analysis, it has been reported recently that data structure layout can be used to generate malware signatures [19].

Forrest et al. [23] has suggested that monoculture is one of the main reasons why computers are vulnerable to large-scale, reproductive attacks. As such, randomization can be introduced to increase the diversity of software. This strategy has been widely instantiated in existing work such as address space randomization (ASR) [38, 41, 8, 10], instruction set randomization (ISR) [6, 28], data randomization [12, 17], and operating system interfaces randomization [13, 27]. Given the success of existing randomization strategies, we propose another instantiation of software randomization: Data structure layout randomization (DSLR).

In this paper, we demonstrate that software can be diversified by DSLR. We propose an approach to instrument a compiler (as the compiler knows about a program's semantics) so that it will generate a different data structure layout each time the same source program is compiled. We instrument the compiler to scan the data structure definitions (e.g., `struct` and `class`) marked by the programmer as randomizable and then reorder their member fields and insert garbage fields. We note that DSLR is different from the software obfuscation techniques [15]. Those techniques are used in software protection and aim at making it harder to reverse engineer the data structure definitions in a *single* binary. On the other hand, DSLR makes it difficult to derive data structure signatures from *multiple* copies of the same software.

The benefit of DSLR to malware defense is two-fold: First, DSLR can mitigate attacks that rely on knowing the data structure layout of victim programs. Second, the feasibility (and simplicity) of DSLR suggests that malware signatures based on data structure layout may not always be effective when used alone for malware detection.

We have implemented our DSLR technique in an open source compiler collection, `gcc-4.2.4`, and applied it to a number of programs. The detailed design and implementation are presented in Section 3 and Section 4, respectively. Our evaluation results in Section 5 show that DSLR can achieve software binary diversity. DSLR can be used generate diverse kernel data structure definitions to mitigate a number of kernel rootkit attacks. Meanwhile, we demonstrate that DSLR introduces noise to a state-of-the-art data structure inference system when generating a program's data structure signature. Finally, DSLR imposes very low performance overhead on `gcc` and on the original, un-randomized program.

2   Technical Challenges

In this section, we examine two technical challenges in realizing DSLR: Which data structures to randomize and how to randomize them.

2.1   Randomizability of Data Structures

Data structure layout, at the binary level, is reflected by the offsets of the encap-sulated object fields. The encapsulated objects include `struct`, `class`, and stack variables declared in functions (as they are related to a particular stack frame and addressed by `EBP`). The first two types have been exploited to derive mal-ware signatures [19]. We believe that a function's local variable layout can also be leveraged to compose signatures and thus we will also discuss randomizing them.

However, randomizing just any data structure will not work in general as manifested in the following examples: (1) If a data structure is used in network communication, the communicating parties may not understand each other if the data structure is randomized. (2) If a data structure definition is public (e.g., defined in shared library `stdio.h`), it cannot be randomized. (3) There is a special case in GNU C that allows zero-length arrays to be the last element of a structure (a zero-length array is actually the header of a variable-length object). If a zero-length array is declared as the last element in a `struct`, that element cannot be randomized, otherwise it cannot pass `gcc` syntax checking. (4) A programmer may directly use the data offset to access some fields. (This is particularly true in programs which mix assembly and C code.) (5) To initialize the value of a structure, the programmer uses the order declared to initialize the structure. These fields cannot be randomized, as the program may crash. In light of these cases, we declare a data structure as randomizable if and only if it is not exposed to any other external programs and does not violate the original `gcc` syntax and programmer intention.

Data structure randomizability is closely related to program semantics. It would be ideal if the compiler could automatically spot all the randomizable data structures. In practice, however, only the programmer can designate randomiz-able data structures with confidence. Even if we could define some heuristics to automatically spot those randomizable data structures, we could not claim both completeness and safety. In this paper, we simply require that programmers use new keywords to specify randomizable data structures.

2.2   Data Structure Randomization Methods

The second challenge is how to randomize a data structure. The simplest ran-domization method would be to reorder its layout. Our primary goal is to create binary diversity for the same software – the more variation, the better. There-fore, we will design a randomization method which reorders the member fields of each data structure to be randomized. Suppose a program has n such data structures and each has m fields, then the number of possible combinations after randomization would be $(m!)^n$.

However, field reordering alone is still not sufficient. For example, suppose a data structure has only two members which are both of `int` type. No matter how we reorder these two fields, the layout of this data structure is still "`int` and `int`". As a result, to randomize a data structure containing multiple members of the same type, we have to use a different randomization method. To this end, we insert garbage fields into these data structures.

3   DSLR Design in GCC

In this section we present the detailed design of DSLR in a specific compiler system. As C/C++ is commonly used in system and user level programming, we have implemented our DSLR technique in the popular, open-source compiler gcc [1].

By instrumenting gcc to reorganize the fields in encapsulated data structures, DSLR will fill the memory image with a random layout each time the program source is compiled. Hence, we need to decide where to instrument gcc.

For a program source, gcc first builds an initial Abstract Syntax Tree (AST). It then converts the language-specific AST into a uniform, generic AST. The generic AST will be transformed into another representation called GIMPLE (a representation form which has at most three operands). After GIMPLE, the source code is converted into the static single assignment (SSA) representation [5] to facilitate more than 20 different optimizations on SSA trees. After the SSA optimization pass, the tree is converted back to GIMPLE which is then used to generate a register-transfer language (RTL) tree. RTL is a hardware-based representation that corresponds to an abstract target architecture with an infinite number of registers. There are also a number of optimization passes such as register allocation, code scheduling, and peepholes performed at the RTL level.

Given these internal steps in gcc, the possible instrumentation points for DSLR are AST, GIMPLE, SSA, and RTL. We instrumented at the AST level for the following reasons: (1) the AST retains a lot of original information from the program source code, such as the type and scope information for data structures and functions; (2) The AST representation is easier to understand and the structure of the tree is concise and relatively convenient for us to modify; (3) When generating the AST, gcc has not yet determined the layout of the data structures, and as such we can reorder the data structure members and reconstruct the AST without needing to compute specific memory addresses.

The data structures to be randomized can be divided into three categories: struct, class and the function stack variables. We reorder the inner AST representations of these data structures, which will eventually lead to the reorganization of the memory layout. Note that these data structures have their own scopes. When the AST for these data structures is generated, all the member variables in each data structure are chained together and represented by a link list. To perform randomization, we can just capture the head node of the list, reorder the nodes of the list based on a random seed, and insert some "garbage" nodes into the list if necessary.

Figure 1 shows a simple example. A data structure test has three fields: int a, char b, and int* c. When compiled with the original gcc, the order of the fields is in the originally declared order (Figure 1(b).) When compiled with our

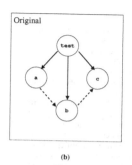
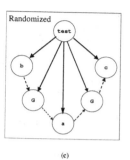

(a)   (b)   (c)

Fig. 1. Example of data structure randomization: (a) the original definition, (b) the original AST, and (c) the randomized AST. The "G" nodes represent the garbage fields added to the data structure. The dotted arrows represent the order of the fields.

DSLR-enabled gcc, the order of the fields is randomized. We also add 2 garbage fields. Figure 1(c) shows the randomized AST representation of struct test.

As discussed in Section 2, to enhance data structure layout diversity we adopt the following strategy: (1) different data structures at the same project building time will be reordered differently (with different randomization seeds); and (2) the same data structure at different project building times will be reordered differently. We use project building time instead of compile time because when building a project, gcc usually compiles each file individually (as specified in the Makefile), and we need to ensure that the same data structure has a uniform layout across one entire build. Suppose a program has two data structures, S1 and S2, which have 4 and 5 fields respectively. When we build the program using our modified gcc, S1 and S2 will be randomized differently. In addition, the same data structure (e.g., S1) will have different layouts in memory at different project building times. Hence, the number of possible layouts for this program would be 4! * 5!. We believe such a strategy will greatly improve the binary diversity of the program, as the chances of generating identical instances would be $1/(\prod_{i=1}^{j} |S_i|!)$, where j is the total number of data structures to be randomized and $|S_i|$ represents the total number of fields (members) in data structure S_i.

4   DSLR Implementation in GCC

Our DSLR prototype is implemented in gcc-4.2.4 with over one thousand lines of C code. We modified gcc's AST representation to perform the randomization. Our prototype consists of four key components: (1) keyword recognizer, which recognizes the new keywords we introduce to specify data structure randomizability and garbage padding; (2) re-orderer, which reorders the field variables in a data structure definition according to a random seed; (3) padder, which inserts the garbage fields into a data structure; and (4) randomization driver, which controls the randomization process. In the remainder of this section, we present the details of these components.

```
...
<function-definition>        ::= {<declaration-specifier>}*<declarator>{<declaration>}*<compound-statement>
<declaration-specifier>      ::= <storage-specifier>
                              | <obfuscate-specifier>
                              | <type-specifier>
                              | <type-qualifier>
<obfuscate-specifier>        ::= __obfuscate__(( <obfuscate-list> ))
<obfuscate-list>             ::= <obfuscate-property>
                              | <obfuscate-list>, <obfuscate-property>
<obfuscate-property>         ::= ε | __reorder__ | __garbage__
<struct-or-union-specifier>  ::= <struct-or-union> <identifier> "{" {<struct-declaration>}+ "}" <obfuscate-specifier>
                              | <struct-or-union> "{" {<struct-declaration> <obfuscate-specifier>}+ "}"
                              | <struct-or-union> <identifier> <obfuscate-specifier>
<class-specifier>            ::= <class> <identifier> "{" {<class-declaration>}+ "}" <obfuscate-specifier>
                              | <class> "{" {<class-declaration> <obfuscate-specifier>}+ "}"
                              | <class> <identifier> <obfuscate-specifier>
...
```

Fig. 2. A partial BNF definition of our extend grammar for C/C++

4.1 Keyword Recognizer

We introduce several new keywords to instruct **gcc** regarding which data structures to randomize and how.

The first keyword is __obfuscate__. It is implemented similar to the way __attribute__ is already implemented in [3]. Similar to __attribute__, we offer options for __obfuscate__ to tell gcc which randomization method(s) it should apply. For that we define two other keywords: __reorder__ and __garbage__. The first one informs gcc that the data structure layout should be reordered and the latter one tells gcc to insert some garbage fields into the data structure.

There are three types of data structures that can be randomized and marked with the __obfuscate__ keyword: (1) **structs** in C, (2) **classes** in C++, and (3) stack variables declared in a function. Figure 3 shows usage examples of these keywords.

```
1 class Test
2 {
3     int a;
4     char b;
5     int *c;
6     ...
7 } __obfuscate__ (( __reorder__ ));
```

(a)

```
1 #include <stdio.h>
2 struct Test
3 {
4     int a;
5     char b;
6     int *c;
7 } __obfuscate__ (( __reorder__ , __garbage__ ));
8 __obfuscate__ (( __reorder__ )) int main(void)
9 {
10     int loc1 = 1;
11     char loc2 = 'n';
12     char loc3[4];
13     printf(" The address in struct:
14                 %x , %x , %x\n", &t.a, &t.b, &t.c);
15     printf(" The address in local:
16                 %x, %x, %x\n",&loc1,&loc2,&loc3);
17     return 0;
18 }
```

(b)

Fig. 3. Sample code (a) showing how to randomize a class in C++ and (b) showing how to randomize a **struct** and stack variables in the **main** function

Since we implemented DSLR at the AST level, there are two modifications when implementing the new keywords. The first is in lexical analysis, which makes the compiler recognize the new token. The second is to build our own *parser* for the keyword.

4.2   Reorderer

When generating the AST for a program, gcc will chain the members of a particular data structure to a list. If it encounters the keyword _-reorder_-, it will invoke the re-orderer when gcc finishes constructing the entire chain, and then it can reorder the members according to the random seed generated by the randomization driver.

We implement the re-orderer at different points for each category of data structures. To randomize the layout for a struct, we insert the re-orderer into function c_parser_struct_or_union_specifier, which handles structs and unions, just after this function has constructed every item in a struct or union. Note that it is not necessary to randomize the members in a union as it only contains one instance of the declared members at runtime. To randomize a class, we insert our re-orderer into function unreverse_member_declarations. For local variables, we insert it into the function c_parser_compound_statement_ nostart.

4.3   Padder

We implement the padder to insert garbage fields between fields of a data structure. The padder will be combined with the re-orderer to perform the randomization, and it will be inserted in the same places as the re-orderer. When gcc recognizes the keyword _-garbage_-, the padder will insert garbage fields of various sizes. Such garbage creates noise in the memory image and makes it more difficult to identify the true data structure. The size of garbage items is determined by the randomization driver.

4.4   Randomization Driver

The randomization driver supports the re-orderer and padder and is directly related to the effectiveness of DSLR. When encountering a randomizable data structure during project building, it will first check whether this data structure already has a 32-bit random value stored in a project build file. If so, it will use that random value; otherwise it will generate a random value via the glibc function random and store it in the project build file for future use. The project build file is a project-wide file that records the random value and the number of fields of each data structure to be randomized. It is critical to ensuring layout consistency across a single project build. In particular, when building projects such as the Linux kernel and its drivers, it should use the same project build file, otherwise the kernel may use different data structure layouts and cause crashes. Similarly, it checks whether the total number of elements of that data structure has been counted. If not, it will count the number of fields in that data structure and store it in the project build file.

After knowing the random value and the total number of fields for a data structure to be randomized, it takes two basic methods to perform the re-ordering and padding.

Reordering Method. Suppose our randomization driver gets a random value R and the total number of fields for a particular data structure m. It will follow the reordering method shown in Algorithm 1.

Algorithm 1. *Reordering Method*

1: **Input**: random value R, total number of fields m, and the original order of field variables: pos[1..m]
2: **Output**: the reordered fields in pos'[1..m]
3: **Initialization**: j ← m;
4: **Reorder**(j, pos[1..j]){
5:     i ← R%j + 1;
6:     pos'[j] ← pos[i]; /*move the i-th element in pos to the rightmost available position in pos'*/

7:     if(j==1) return;   /*no element left in pos, and hence return*/
8:     if(i!=j) pos[i] ← pos[j];
9:     **Reorder**(j-1, pos[1..j-1]);
10: }

In the algorithm, `pos[i]` represents the position of the ith member/field variable in the original data structure. Based on the original ordering of the member variables, the method recalculates the positions of the member variables according to the random value R. We verify that Algorithm 1 is able to generate all $m!$ layouts for a data structure containing m members.

Padding Method. When we insert garbage fields between the member variables of a data structure, the padding method determines the size of the garbage fields. We limit the size to 1, 2, 4, or 8 bytes. To do that we partition the random value R into four parts: x_1, x_2, x_3, and x_4, and each part has 8 bits. We then reduce these 8 bits to 2 bits by calculating x_i mod 4 ($i \in \{1, 2, 3, 4\}$). These four random values fall into the range of 0 to 3, which correspond to 8-byte, 4-byte, 2-byte, and 1-byte sizes, respectively. Suppose there exists a data structure which contains five member variables and the four random values (after the mod operation) are 1, 3, 2, and 0. Then we insert 4 garbage fields between the members using padding size of 4, 1, 2, and 8 bytes, respectively. Note that if the data structure requires both reordering and padding, the two methods will be applied in that order. We note that padding will not interfere with any subsequent optimization steps performed by `gcc`.

5   Evaluation

In this section, we present our evaluation results. We first assess the effectiveness of our DSLR technique in Section 5.1, and then measure the performance impact of DSLR on both `gcc` and the generated binaries in Section 5.2.

5.1   Effectiveness

Estimating Data Structure Randomizability. We applied our DSLR-enabled gcc to a number of goodware and malware programs. We use open-source goodware such as openssh, and malware programs collected from offensive computing [2] and VX Heavens [4]. We first manually estimate the randomizability of data structures in these programs by inspecting their source code. As discussed in Section 2, it is difficult to accurately determine all the randomizable data structures in a program and we delegate that task to programmers. In our experiments, we used the following heuristics for randomizability estimation: For each data structure, we manually check if it is used/involved in one of the following scenarios: (1) network communication, (2) disk I/O, (3) shared library, (4) assembly code, (5) pointer arithmetic, and (6) struct data initialization. If so, the data structure is deemed un-randomizable.

Table 1 summarizes the results. We define k_i ($i \in \{0, 1, 2\}$) as the total number of structs, classes, or functions in a program. We also define j_i ($i \in \{0, 1, 2\}$) as the total number of data structures we consider randomizable. Hence, j_0/k_0, j_1/k_1, and j_2/k_2 represent the randomizability ratios for struct, class, and function (shown in the 3rd, 4th, and 5th columns in Table 1), respectively. We note that some of the function stack layouts could not be randomized. The reason is that they contain goto statements (thus the label order is fixed).

Table 1. Result of randomizability estimate and layout diversity

Benchmark program	LOC(K)	Randomizability of Data Structure			Possible Layout
		struct	class	funcs	ω
42 Virus	0.88	1/1	-	24/24	4E5
Slapper	2.44	26/30	-	69/70	5E47
pingrootkit	4.81	26/27	-	57/57	5E15
Mood-nt	5.31	36/37	-	121/122	8E119
tnet-1.55	11.56	14/17	-	179/179	7E82
Suckit	24.71	110/111	-	143/144	9E159
agobot3-pre4	245.44	23/31	50/50	340/346	2E1106
patch-2.5.4	11.53	5/7	-	123/123	4E3
bc-1.06	14.29	20/21	-	166/166	6E56
tidy4aug00	15.95	9/18	-	341/341	2E52
ctags-5.7	27.22	51/79	-	488/488	3E668
openssh-4.3	76.05	63/80	-	820/838	4E1271

Layout Diversity. bc_struct is a data structure in the bc-1.06 binary. As shown in Figure 4, this data structure compiled by the DSLR-enabled compiler (with random number 669) has its layout changed significantly: not only has the field order been changed, it also contains 6 additional garbage fields.

We then estimate the layout diversity of these programs. It is rather cumbersome to experiment with all possible layouts. Instead, we numerically compute the number of binary variants that our compiler will be able to generate for each program, based on the result of the data structure randomizability estimation (j_i ($i \in \{0, 1, 2\}$) of each program). The numerical results are shown as ω in the

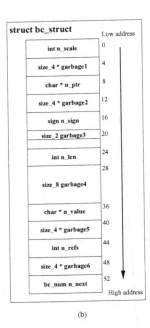

typedef enum{PLUS,MINUS} sign;
typedef struct bc_struct * bc_num;

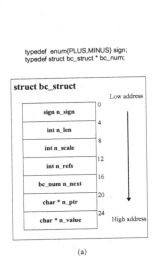

(a)   (b)

Fig. 4. Data structure layout comparison: (a) original layout, and (b) randomized layout

last column of Table 1, which is the total number of binary instances of each program. Note $\omega = \prod_{i=1}^{j_0+j_1} |S_i|!$, where $j_0 + j_1$ is the total number of **structs** and **class**es to be randomized and $|S_i|$ is the total number of fields (members) in data structure S_i.

Binary Code Diversity. A direct consequence of randomizing data structure layout is that the binary code generated will also be diversified. The reason is that the field variables in **structs**, **class**es, and even local variables, are accessed by data offsets which will be changed due to the randomization. Therefore, it would be interesting to evaluate the difference between the DSLR-generated code and the original un-randomized code.

To evaluate code diversity, we first compiled each benchmark program with an unmodified copy of **gcc** to get the original binary, whose size is represented by I_0 shown in the 2nd column of Table 2. We then used the DSLR-enabled **gcc** to compile the same program and generate three instances. Their code sizes are represented by I_1, I_2, and I_3, respectively. Next, we compared the original binary with the newly generated binaries using a tool called **bsdiff** [33]. The difference is represented by δ_i. **bsdiff** is a patch tool which generates the difference between two binaries. Different from other binary diff-ing tools, **bsdiff** adopts an "approximate matching" algorithm, which counts the byte-wise difference in two directions (both forward and backward) rather than in one direction (often

Table 2. Evaluation of binary code diversity

Benchmark program	Code Diversity							
	$I_0(K)$	$I_1(K)$	$\delta_1(\%)$	$I_2(K)$	$\delta_2(\%)$	$I_3(K)$	$\delta_3(\%)$	$\overline{AVG_\delta}$
42 Virus	27.37	27.39	7.0	27.39	6.5	27.40	8.0	7.2%
Slapper	36.03	33.83	12.0	33.85	13.2	33.82	14.3	13.2%
pingrootkit	84.08	84.29	5.0	84.28	3.9	84.28	5.1	4.7%
Mood-nt	74.52	75.25	9.6	75.32	9.5	75.35	9.8	9.6%
tnet-1.55	174.17	175.15	7.6	175.03	7.7	174.96	6.9	7.4%
Suckit	99.61	102.20	6.3	102.17	6.8	102.17	6.4	6.5%
agobot3-pre4	904.42	909.97	8.3	912.72	8.5	909.55	7.2	8.0%
patch-2.5.4	216.56	217.51	6.1	217.48	6.2	217.51	6.2	6.2%
bc-1.06	150.39	151.64	8.8	151.55	8.2	151.57	8.2	8.4%
tidy4aug00	119.54	119.54	6.7	119.54	6.8	119.54	7.5	7.0%
ctags-5.7	527.11	531.69	16.2	531.69	16.4	531.64	16.7	16.4%
openssh-4.3	997.64	1003.39	8.5	1003.53	8.2	1003.52	8.1	8.3%

forward). As such the results generated by `bsdiff` are more accurate. Note that the results of `bsdiff` are highly compact [33], and thus the differences reported by `bsdiff` are relatively small. According to `bsdiff`, DSLR can achieve a difference between 3-17%. The last column of Table 2 $\overline{AVG_\delta}$ shows the average percentage over the three instances.

Defending Against Kernel Rootkits. A kernel rootkit is a piece of malicious software that compromises a running operating system kernel. Usually an attacker will use them to hide his presence on a running system. An important feature of modern kernel rootkits is their ability to hide the existence of running processes from an administrator. It is important, for example, that malicious processes not appear in `ps` listings. To evaluate our DSLR-enabled compiler as a defense solution, we used it to randomize the `task_struct` data structure in the Linux kernel (version 2.6.8) to protect against these process hiding attacks by a number of kernel rootkits. Six rootkits were tested to determine if they were able to hide a process under the randomized kernel. A summary of the results is shown in Table 3. Detailed results for each rootkit are as follows:

adore-ng. The adore-ng rootkit is a loadable kernel module (LKM) rootkit. This means that it is loaded into the kernel like a driver. After being loaded, adore-ng modifies function pointers contained in various kernel data structures. It avoids the system call table, as hooking the system call table would make it easily detectable. Adore-ng also has a user-level component, `ava`. When `ava` authenticates with the rootkit, a flag is added to the `flags` element of the `task_struct` for the `ava` process. Under the newly randomized kernel the `flags` element cannot be accurately located, and so `ava` cannot be properly authenticated. This renders the rootkit useless.

enyelkm. While still being an LKM, enyelkm differs from adore-ng in that it does not have a user-level control component. Instead, options are chosen at compile time. By default, enyelkm hides any running process whose name contains the string OCULTAR. It finds these processes by traversing the process list and scanning the process names. Under the randomized kernel the linked list within task_structs is randomly located, making enyelkm's attempts to traverse the list fail. This causes process hiding to be unsuccessful.

override. Much like enyelkm, override is configured at compile time. Override makes extensive use of current, which is a macro that resolves to be the address of the task_struct for the currently running process. When running on the new kernel, the randomized elements of this data structure cause override to crash the kernel.

fuuld. Fuuld is a data-only rootkit written by one of this paper's authors during previous research. It uses a technique known as direct kernel object manipulation (DKOM) to modify kernel objects directly without the need to execute code in the kernel. It operates by using /dev/kmem to search for and remove processes from the process list. When the task_struct structure is randomized, it is unable to properly traverse the process list.

intoxnia-ng2. The intoxnia rootkit is another LKM rootkit. Unlike adore-ng, however, intoxnia compromises the kernel by only hooking the system call table. Interestingly, this simplistic attack method is not troubled by the randomization of task_struct. This is because intoxnia hides a process by filtering the data returned by the system call getdents to ensure that directory listings from the /proc file system do not reflect hidden processes. Neither the process list, nor any elements in it, are involved. The data structures that intoxnia does modify are arguments to system calls, which cannot be randomized because they are part of the user-level library as well.

mood-nt. The mood-nt rootkit installs itself directly into the running kernel using the /dev/kmem interface. It then proceeds to hook the system call table and hide processes using a technique similar to that of intoxnia. As such, this rootkit was also uninhibited by the randomization of task_struct.

Many kernel rootkits operate by inserting malicious code into the kernel and modifying existing function pointers to cause the kernel to execute it. Five of the above rootkits (adore-ng, enyelkm, override, intoxnia, and mood-nt) employ this attack strategy. Existing work [24,37,35] is able to effectively prevent these attacks. However, a different type of rootkit attacks – data-only attacks – exist. In this case, a rootkit program will directly modify kernel data structures using a memory interface device such as /dev/kmem. The fuuld rootkit above employs this strategy. As evidenced by its effectiveness against the fuuld rootkit, DSLR appears to be a promising approach to defending against data-only attacks.

Table 3. Effectiveness of DSLR against kernel rootkits

Rootkit	Attack Vector	Prevented?
adore-ng 0.56	LKM	✓
enyelkm 1.2	LKM	✓
override	LKM	✓
fuuld	DKOM – /dev/kmem	✓
intoxnia ng2	LKM	×
mood-nt	/dev/mem	×

Given that the rootkit author must know the layout of kernel data structures in order to modify them, randomizing that layout will significantly raise the bar for such attacks.

Evaluation against Laika. We also performed effectiveness evaluation of DSLR against Laika [19], a data structure inference system. The released version of Laika only supports taking snapshots of Windows binaries, whereas we implement DSLR in gcc, which cannot compile Windows programs. To assess the effectiveness of DSLR, we had to manually randomize the data structures in a Windows-based program by following our randomization methods. We then used the Windows compiler to generate the binary code. We used three Windows-based programs: agobot, 7-zip, and notepad. For some reason, Laika could not process the binary image of notepad. Hence we only present the results with 7-zip and agobot.

For each application, we generated three binary instances and used Laika to detect their data structure layout similarity. In particular, Laika uses a mixture ratio [19] to quantify similarity: the closer the value is to 0.5, the higher the similarity. When detecting similarity, Laika has the option of filtering out pointers. Table 4 summarizes the results. The code difference among the instances of each program is around 5%. For 7-zip, when pointers are filtered out, Laika reported mixture ratios around 0.502. With pointers, it reported mixture ratios around 0.511. It looks like the binaries of 7-zip do not appear significantly different to Laika. We believe that the reason is the following: 7-zip only has 25 data structures randomized. But it has more than 80 un-randomizable data structures which are in the library. These data structures dominated. Hence the mixture ratios are close to 0.5. Agobot, on the other hand, contains 49 data structures and 50 classes in its own code, so the mixture ratios went higher: 0.57 without pointers and 0.63 with pointers. The mixture ratios indicate that, by randomizing the data structure layout, we introduced noise to Laika. Also, even though Laika indicated high similarity among 7-zip instances, it is still debatable how to account for the library code when detecting data structure similarity, as two different applications (with a small number of user-level data structures) may use lots of similar library data structures (such as those in the runtime support) in their implementations.

Table 4. Evaluation of DSLR against Laika

Benchmark Program	LOC	Un-randomized Binary	Randomized Binary	Code Difference	Mixture Ratio	
					w/o Pointer	w/ Pointer
7zip-4.64	41.01K	498K	502K	4.26%	0.50184625	0.50942826
			503K	5.08%	0.50244766	0.51070610
			504K	5.88%	0.50325966	0.51487480
agobot3-0.2.1-priv4	497.09K	1.17M	1.18M	6.18%	0.57368920	0.70016150
			1.19M	6.10%	0.57586336	0.60932887
			1.19M	6.34%	0.56068546	0.58418036

5.2 Performance Overhead

Finally, we evaluate the performance overhead incurred by DSLR. Since we modified gcc, we would like to know how much overhead DSLR imposes on gcc. In our experiments, we built each program 3 times. g_1, g_2, and g_3 represent the normalized gcc performance overhead. The 2nd, 3rd, and 4th columns of Table 5 show these results. On average DSLR imposed around 2% performance overhead, which is mainly caused by random value lookup, field count, and field reordering.

Since DSLR will change the program's data structure layout and subsequently change the binary code produced, we would also like to know the program's performance overhead due to DSLR. We measured the corresponding runtime overhead of the compiled binaries. The 6th, 7th and 8th columns of Table 5 show these results. DSLR imposed less than 4% overhead. The normalized overhead is obtained by running each binary 10 times. Note that for those virus and daemon malware programs, we did not measure their performance overhead (i.e. the N/As in Table 5) as they ran in the background and were thus difficult to measure. We notice that some randomized binaries reported a slightly better performance than their un-randomized counterparts. The reason may lie in the data locality improvement caused by DSLR.

Table 5. Normalized performance overhead

Benchmark program	Overhead imposed to gcc				Overhead imposed to application			
	g_1	g_2	g_3	$\overline{AVG_g}$	o_1	o_2	o_3	$\overline{AVG_o}$
42 Virus	3.6%	3.2%	2.7%	3.2%	N/A	N/A	N/A	N/A
Slapper	2.5%	2.8%	2.1%	2.5%	N/A	N/A	N/A	N/A
pingrootkit	3.0%	2.8%	2.7%	2.8%	N/A	N/A	N/A	N/A
Mood-nt	2.2%	2.1%	1.8%	2.0%	N/A	N/A	N/A	N/A
tnet-1.55	0.8%	1.2%	1.1%	1.0%	N/A	N/A	N/A	N/A
Suckit	1.2%	1.5%	2.3%	1.7%	N/A	N/A	N/A	N/A
agobot3-pre4	2.9%	3.3%	3.0%	3.1%	N/A	N/A	N/A	N/A
patch-2.5.4	1.6%	1.0%	1.2%	1.3%	-0.9%	1.2%	-2.0%	-0.6%
bc-1.06	3.0%	0.9%	2.4%	2.1%	1.1%	1.0%	-0.8%	0.4%
tidy4aug00	1.7%	1.5%	1.8%	1.7%	1.6%	-1.3%	1.1%	0.5%
ctags-5.7	2.9%	1.8%	1.1%	1.9%	-1.8%	-0.7%	-0.7%	-1.1%
openssh-4.3	1.7%	2.4%	1.8%	2.0%	2.7%	1.8%	-0.9%	1.2%

6   Limitations and Future Work

The first limitation of DSLR is that right now we do not support other languages such as Java, as we instrument gcc at the language-specific AST level. Our next step will involve either adding support to these languages, or studying the details of other gcc internal representations such as GIMPLE and RTL so that DSLR support can be made more generic.

The second limitation is that the randomizability of a data structure cannot be determined accurately and automatically. Instead, we rely on programmers' knowledge and judgment. As discussed in Section 2, the fundamental challenge in automatically determining the randomizability of a data structure is safety and completeness. To automate the identification, we could approximate the result by performing some sort of data flow analysis to identify certain un-randomizable data structures. For example, if we do not aim at achieving completeness, we could adopt several heuristics to achieve automation, such as using the execution context to determine if a data structure is used in network I/O and excluding it from DSLR if so.

The third limitation is that we do not support other randomization techniques such as struct/class splitting. Right now we only increase the field number by adding garbage fields, and we do not decrease the field numbers, which can be achieved by struct/class splitting techniques used in the obfuscation community [15]. Our future work includes adopting those obfuscation techniques to make it generate more polymorphic data structure layouts.

The fourth limitation is in software distribution. When compiled by the DSLR-enabled gcc, a program can have a large number of binary variants. It will cause some inconvenience in software distribution. One possible solution is: upon the request for a copy of the software, a binary instance would be generated and shipped on-demand. Another way would be to maintain a binary repository for large-scale on-line distribution.

7   Related Work

7.1   Security through Diversity

Address Space Randomization (ASR). ASR is a technique which dynamically and randomly relocates a program's stack, heap, shared libraries, and even program objects. This is either implemented by an OS kernel patch [38], or modifying the dynamic loader [39], or binary code transformations [8], or even source code transformations [10]. The goal is to obscure the location of code and data objects that are resident in memory and foil the attacker's assumptions about the memory layout of the vulnerable program. This makes the determination of critical address values difficult if not impossible. Most ASR approaches cannot achieve data structure layout randomization, as the relative addresses of member variables do not get changed. Also, they need system support such as a loader kernel support, but we cannot assume that the remote system always has ASR. Even though the source code transformation approach [10] can to some extent generate polymorphic layout for static data in different runs, it still involves loader support, and does not randomize the variable member layout for dynamic data.

Instruction Set Randomization (ISR). ISR is an approach to preventing code injection attacks by randomizing the underlying system instructions [6,28]. In this approach, instructions become data, and they are encrypted with a set of random keys and stored in memory. During program execution, a software translation is involved for decrypting the instructions before being fetched. ISR does not randomize any data structure layout.

Data Randomization. Similar to ISR, program data can also be encrypted and decrypted. PointGuard [17] is such a technique which encrypts all pointers while they reside in memory and decrypts them only before they are loaded into CPU registers. It is implemented as an extension to the gcc compiler, which injects the necessary encryption and decryption wrappers at compilation time. Recently, Cadar et al. [12] and Bhatkar et al. [9] independently presented a new data randomization technique which provides probabilistic protection against memory exploits by XORing data with random masks. This is also implemented either as a C compiler extension or a source code transformation.

Operating System Interfaces Randomization. Chew and Song proposed using operating system interface randomization to mitigate buffer overflows [13]. They randomized the system call mapping, global library entry points, and stack placement to increase the heterogeneity. Similarly, by combining ASR and ISR, RandSys [27] randomizes the system service interface when loading a program, and at run-time de-randomizes the instrumented interface for correct execution.

Multi-variant System. N-variant systems [18] are an architectural framework which employs a set of automatically diversified variants to execute the same task. Any divergence among the outputs will raise an alarm and can hence detect the attack. DieHard [7] is a simplified multi-variant framework which uses heap object randomization to make the variants generate different outputs in case of an error or attack. DieFast [32] further leverages this idea to derive a runtime patch and automatically fix program bugs. Reverse stack execution [36], i.e, reverse the stack growth direction, can prevent stack smashing and format string attacks when executed in parallel with normal stack execution in a multi-variant environment.

Compared with the above randomization approaches, DSLR exploits another randomization dimension with different goals, application contexts, and implementation techniques.

7.2 Data Structure Layout Manipulations and Obfuscations in Compilers

Propolice [22] is a gcc extension for protecting applications from stack-smashing attacks. The protection is implemented by a variable reordering feature to avoid the stack corruption of pointers.

There are several other data structure reorder optimizations in the compiler to improve runtime performance by improving data locality and reuse. Pioneering the approach is the one proposed by Hagog et al. [26] which is a cache aware data layout reorganization optimization in gcc. They perform structure splitting and field reordering to transform struct and class definitions. Recently, struct-reorganization optimizations have undergone the conversion from GIMPLE to Tree-SSA [25]. To handle multi-threaded applications (because of the false sharing), Raman et al. [34]

proposed structure layout transformations that optimize both for improved spatial locality and reduced false sharing.

Similar to code optimizations to improve program performance, there exist code obfuscation techniques which aim to reduce the understand-ability of a program by reverse engineering. As data structures are important components and key clues to understand code, one of the most important obfuscations is data structure obfuscation. Common obfuscation techniques [15] include obfuscating arrays (such as splitting, regrouping [42], flattening, folding [14], and reordering arrays), obfuscating classes (such as splitting a class, inserting a new class, reordering class members), and obfuscating variables (such as substituting code for static data, merging and splitting variables [14]). These techniques are particularly useful to thwart the intermediate code analysis of Java and .NET, which tend to be easily analyzable [31].

Compared with these two approaches, DSLR has different goals. The reordering optimization techniques mentioned above aim to improve the performance, and their reordered layout is fixed/deterministic for all the compiled binaries. For data structure obfuscation techniques, the data structure layout they generate is again fixed. When taking snapshots of the memory to infer the signature, these techniques do not increase the diversity of data structure layout. However, we do not aim to obfuscate the data structure for a single binary. Instead, we aim to generate polymorphic layouts among multiple binary copies.

8 Conclusion

We have presented a new software randomization technique – DSLR – that randomizes the data structure layout of a program with the goal of generating diverse binaries that are semantically equivalent. DSLR can be used to mitigate malware attacks that rely on knowledge about the victim programs' data structure definitions. In addition, the simple implementation of DSLR poses a new challenge to data structure-based program signature generation systems. We have implemented a prototype of DSLR in `gcc` and applied it to a number of programs. Our evaluation results demonstrate that DSLR is able to achieve binary code diversity. Furthermore, DSLR is able to foil a number of kernel rootkit attacks by randomizing the layout of a key kernel data structure. Meanwhile, DSLR is able to reduce the similarity between binaries generated from the same source program.

Acknowledgment

We would like to thank Anthony Cozzie for his kind help with his Laika system for the evaluation of DSLR. We would also like to thank the anonymous reviewers for their very helpful comments. This research was supported in part by the US National Science Foundation (NSF) under grants 0546173 and 0716444. Any opinions, findings, and conclusions or recommendations in this paper are those of the authors and do not necessarily reflect the views of the NSF.

References

1. Gnu compiler collection (gcc) internals,
   http://gcc.gnu.org/onlinedocs/gccint/
2. Offensive computing, http://www.offensivecomputing.net/
3. Using the gnu compiler collection (gcc),
   http://gcc.gnu.org/onlinedocs/gcc-4.2.4/gcc/
4. Vx heavens, http://vx.netlux.org/
5. Aho, A.V., Lam, M.S., Sethi, R., Ullman, J.D.: Compilers: Principles, Techniques and Tools, 2nd edn. Addison-Wesley, Reading (2006)
6. Barrantes, E.G., Ackley, D.H., Palmer, T.S., Stefanovic, D., Zovi, D.D.: Randomized instruction set emulation to disrupt binary code injection attacks. In: Proceedings of the 10th ACM conference on Computer and communications security (CCS 2003), pp. 281–289. ACM, New York (2003)
7. Berger, E.D., Zorn, B.G.: Diehard: probabilistic memory safety for unsafe languages. In: Proceedings of the 2006 ACM SIGPLAN conference on Programming language design and implementation(PLDI 2006), pp. 158–168. ACM, New York (2006)
8. Bhatkar, E., Duvarney, D.C., Sekar, R.: Address obfuscation: an efficient approach to combat a broad range of memory error exploits. In: Proceedings of the 12th USENIX Security Symposium, pp. 105–120 (2003)
9. Bhatkar, S., Sekar, R.: Data space randomization. In: Zamboni, D. (ed.) DIMVA 2008. LNCS, vol. 5137, pp. 1–22. Springer, Heidelberg (2008)
10. Bhatkar, S., Sekar, R., DuVarney, D.C.: Efficient techniques for comprehensive protection from memory error exploits. In: Proceedings of the 14th conference on USENIX Security Symposium, Berkeley, CA, USA (2005), USENIX Association
11. Caballero, J., Yin, H., Liang, Z., Song, D.: Polyglot: Automatic extraction of protocol format using dynamic binary analysis. In: Proceedings of the 14th ACM Conference on Computer and and Communications Security (CCS 2007) (2007)
12. Cadar, C., Akritidis, P., Costa, M., Martin, J.-P., Castro, M.: Data randomization. Technical Report MSR-TR-2008-120, Microsoft Research (2008)
13. Chew, M., Song, D.: Mitigating buffer overflows by operating system randomization. Technical Report CMU-CS-02-197, Carnegie Mellon University (2002)
14. Cho, S., Chang, H., Cho, Y.: Implementation of an obfuscation tool for c/c++ source code protection on the xscale architecture. In: Brinkschulte, U., Givargis, T., Russo, S. (eds.) SEUS 2008. LNCS, vol. 5287, pp. 406–416. Springer, Heidelberg (2008)
15. Collberg, C., Thomborson, C., Low, D.: A taxonomy of obfuscating transformations (1997)
16. Comparetti, P.M., Wondracek, G., Kruegel, C., Kirda, E.: Prospex: Protocol specification extraction. In: Proceedings of 2009 IEEE Symposium on Security and Privacy, Oakland, CA (May 2009)
17. Cowan, C., Beattie, S., Johansen, J., Wagle, P.: Pointguard: protecting pointers from buffer overflow vulnerabilities. In: Proceedings of the 12th conference on USENIX Security Symposium, Berkeley, CA, USA (2003), USENIX Association
18. Cox, B., Evans, D., Filipi, A., Rowanhill, J., Hu, W., Davidson, J., Knight, J., Nguyen-Tuong, A., Hiser, J.: N-variant systems: a secretless framework for security through diversity. In: Proceedings of the 15th conference on USENIX Security Symposium, Berkeley, CA, USA (2006), USENIX Association

19. Cozzie, A., Stratton, F., Xue, H., King, S.T.: Digging for data structures. In: Proceeding of 8th Symposium on Operating System Design and Implementation (OSDI 2008) (December 2008)
20. Cui, W., Peinado, M., Chen, K., Wang, H.J., Irun-Briz, L.: Tupni: Automatic reverse engineering of input formats. In: Proceedings of the 15th ACM Conference on Computer and Communications Security (CCS 2008), Alexandria, VA (October 2008)
21. Cui, W., Peinado, M., Wang, H.J., Locasto, M.: Shieldgen: Automatic data patch generation for unknown vulnerabilities with informed probing. In: Proceedings of 2007 IEEE Symposium on Security and Privacy, Oakland, CA (May 2007)
22. Etoh, H.: GCC extension for protecting applications from stack-smashing attacks, ProPolice (2003), http://www.trl.ibm.com/projects/security/ssp/
23. Forrest, S., Somayaji, A., Ackley, D.: Building diverse computer systems. In: Proceedings of the 6th Workshop on Hot Topics in Operating Systems (HotOS-VI), Washington, DC, USA, p. 67. IEEE Computer Society, Los Alamitos (1997)
24. Garfinkel, T., Rosenblum, M.: A Virtual Machine Introspection Based Architecture for Intrusion Detection. In: Proc. Network and Distributed Systems Security Symposium (NDSS 2003) (February 2003)
25. Golovanevsky, O., Zaks, A.: Struct-reorg: current status and future perspectives. In: Proceedings of the GCC Developers' Summit (2007)
26. Hagog, M., Tice, C.: Cache aware data layout reorganization optimization in gcc. In: Proceedings of the GCC Developers' Summit (2005)
27. Jiang, X., Wang, H.J., Xu, D., Wang, Y.-M.: Randsys: Thwarting code injection attacks with system service interface randomization. In: Proceedings of the 26th IEEE International Symposium on Reliable Distributed Systems (SRDS 2007), Washington, DC, USA, pp. 209–218. IEEE Computer Society, Los Alamitos (2007)
28. Kc, G.S., Keromytis, A.D., Prevelakis, V.: Countering code-injection attacks with instruction-set randomization. In: Proceedings of the 10th ACM conference on Computer and communications security (CCS 2003), Washington D.C., USA, pp. 272–280. ACM, New York (2003)
29. Lin, Z., Jiang, X., Xu, D., Zhang, X.: Automatic protocol format reverse engineering through context-aware monitored execution. In: Proceedings of the 15th Annual Network and Distributed System Security Symposium (NDSS 2008), San Diego, CA (February 2008)
30. Lin, Z., Zhang, X.: Deriving input syntactic structure from execution. In: Proceedings of the 16th ACM SIGSOFT International Symposium on Foundations of Software Engineering (FSE 2008), Atlanta, GA, USA (November 2008)
31. Low, D.: Protecting java code via code obfuscation. Crossroads 4(3), 21–23 (1998)
32. Novark, G., Berger, E.D., Zorn, B.G.: Exterminator: automatically correcting memory errors with high probability. In: Proceedings of ACM SIGPLAN Conference on Programming Language Design and Implementation (PLDI 007), San Diego, California, USA. ACM Press, New York (2007)
33. Percival, C.: Naive differences of executable code (2003), http://www.daemonology.net/bsdiff/
34. Raman, E., Hundt, R., Mannarswamy, S.: Structure layout optimization for multithreaded programs. In: Proceedings of the International Symposium on Code Generation and Optimization (CGO 2007), Washington, DC, USA, pp. 271–282. IEEE Computer Society Press, Los Alamitos (2007)
35. Riley, R., Jiang, X., Xu, D.: Guest-Transparent Prevention of Kernel Rootkits with VMM-Based Memory Shadowing. In: Lippmann, R., Kirda, E., Trachtenberg, A. (eds.) RAID 2008. LNCS, vol. 5230, pp. 1–20. Springer, Heidelberg (2008)

36. Salamat, B., Gal, A., Yermolovich, A., Manivannan, K., Franz, M.: Reverse stack execution. Technical Report No. 07-07, University of California, Irvine (2007)
37. Seshadri, A., Luk, M., Qu, N., Perrig, A.: SecVisor: A Tiny Hypervisor to Guarantee Lifetime Kernel Code Integrity for Commodity OSes. In: Proceedings of the ACM Symposium on Operating Systems Principles (SOSP 2007) (October 2007)
38. PaX Team. Pax address space layout randomization (aslr),
    http://pax.grsecurity.net/docs/aslr.txt
39. Wang, X., Li, Z., Xu, J., Reiter, M.K., Kil, C., Choi, J.Y.: Packet vaccine: Black-box exploit detection and signature generation. In: Proceedings of the 13th ACM Conference on Computer and Communication Security (CCS 2006), pp. 37–46. ACM Press, New York (2006)
40. Wondracek, G., Milani, P., Kruegel, C., Kirda, E.: Automatic network protocol analysis. In: Proceedings of the 15th Annual Network and Distributed System Security Symposium (NDSS 2008), San Diego, CA (February 2008)
41. Xu, J., Kalbarczyk, Z., Iyer, R.K.: Transparent runtime randomization for security. In: Proceedings of the 22nd International Symposium on Reliable Distributed Systems (SRDS 2003), pp. 260–269. IEEE Computer Society, Los Alamitos (2003)
42. Zhong, Y., Orlovich, M., Shen, X., Ding, C.: Array regrouping and structure splitting using whole-program reference affinity. In: Proceedings of the ACM SIGPLAN 2004 conference on Programming language design and implementation, PLDI 2004 (2004)

On the Effectiveness of Software Diversity: A Systematic Study on Real-World Vulnerabilities

Jin Han, Debin Gao, and Robert H. Deng

School of Information Systems, Singapore Management University
{jin.han.2007,dbgao,robertdeng}@smu.edu.sg

Abstract. Many systems have been introduced to detect software intrusions by comparing the outputs and behavior of diverse replicas when they are processing the same, potentially malicious, input. When these replicas are constructed using off-the-shelf software products, it is assumed that they are diverse and not compromised simultaneously under the same attack. In this paper, we analyze vulnerabilities published in 2007 to evaluate the extent to which this assumption is valid. We focus on vulnerabilities in application software, and show that the majority of these software products – including those providing the same service (and therefore multiple software substitutes can be used in a replicated system to detect intrusions) and those that run on multiple operating systems (and therefore the same software can be used in a replicated system with different operating systems to detect intrusions) – either do not have the same vulnerability or cannot be compromised with the same exploit. We also find evidence that indicates the use of diversity in increasing attack tolerance for other software. These results show that systems utilizing off-the-shelf software products to introduce diversity are effective in detecting intrusions.

1   Introduction

Software diversity has many advantages over mono-culture in improving system security [12,21]. Linger [16] proposed methods that systematically generate stochastic diversification in program source to increase system resistance and survivability. Obfuscation techniques (e.g., instruction-set randomization [2,15] and address space randomization [3]) were proposed to safeguard systems against code-injection attacks and other memory error exploits. N-variant systems [4] execute a set of automatically diversified variants on the same inputs, and monitor their behavior to detect divergence that signals anticipated types of exploits, against which the variants are diversified.

Instead of artificially introducing diversity, some recent work focused on utilizing existing diverse software for network protection [17] and intrusion detection [8]. Some of these systems (e.g., the HACQIT system [14,18] and its successor [22]) employed output voting to monitor outputs from diverse replicas, while others (e.g., Behavioral Distance [8,9,10]) monitor the low-level behavior of the diverse replicas.

U. Flegel and D. Bruschi (Eds.): DIMVA 2009, LNCS 5587, pp. 127–146, 2009.
© Springer-Verlag Berlin Heidelberg 2009

An interesting and important assumption made by many of these systems utilizing off-the-shelf diverse software is that the diverse software is vulnerable only to different exploits. With this assumption, replicas constructed using diverse off-the-shelf software will not be compromised by the same attack. This is a reasonable assumption because most of the off-the-shelf diverse software is developed independently by different groups of developers, and so the same mistake/vulnerability is unlikely to be introduced. However, to the best of our knowledge, there has not been a systematic analysis to evaluate the extent to which this assumption is correct. Such analysis also guides users in choosing between artificially introducing diversity (e.g., instruction-set randomization, address space randomization, and N-variant systems) and utilizing off-the-shelf software products to introduce diversity.

In this paper, we present a systematic analysis on the effectiveness of utilizing off-the-shelf diverse software for improving system security. In particular, we evaluate the extent to which different off-the-shelf software suffers from the same vulnerability and exploit. This is achieved by carefully analyzing over 6,000 vulnerabilities published in the year of 2007.

To get a better idea of what is to be analyzed and how this analysis benefits systems that utilize off-the-shelf diverse software, consider an example in which a system uses behavioral distance [8,9,10] for intrusion detection (see Fig 1). In this example, a web service is provided by two diverse web servers running on two diverse operating systems. The same input, which may potentially be an attack input, is processed by both servers. Similar architectures, e.g., diverse servers on the same operating system, have also been introduced [14,18,22].

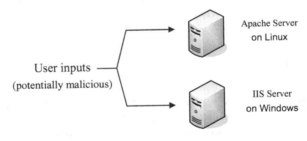

Fig. 1. An example (Behavioral Distance) of utilizing off-the-shelf diverse software

This system detects an intrusion when deviations are found in the two replicas when they are processing the same input. Such deviations may be detected in server outputs [14,18,22] or in the low-level behavior, e.g., system calls [8,9,10]. A very important observation is that such deviations occur only if the two replicas behave differently when processing the same malicious input. The system assumes that either the two replicas do not have the same vulnerability, or they cannot be exploited simultaneously with a single attack.

In order to evaluate the extent to which this assumption is valid, several questions need to be answered:

– Among the large number of vulnerable software products, how many of them have potential substitutes that provide similar functionality? For those that are software substitutes of one another, do they have the same vulnerability? If they do have the same vulnerability, can they be exploited with the same attack?

– Among the large number of vulnerable software products, how many of them can run on multiple operating systems? For those that run on multiple operating systems, do vulnerabilities of the software on one operating system propagate to the same software on a different operating system? If so, can they be exploited by the same attack when running on different operating systems?

To the best of our knowledge, there is no closely related work which could answer these questions. We systematically analyzed more than 6,000 vulnerabilities published in the year of 2007. In summary, our results show that more than 98.5% of the vulnerable application software products have software substitutes (and therefore can be used in a replicated system to detect intrusion), and the majority of them either do not have the same vulnerability, or cannot be compromised with the same exploit code. In addition, among the application software products, nearly half are officially supported to run on multiple operating systems. Although the different operating system distributions of the same product are likely (more than 80%) to suffer from the same vulnerability, the attack code is different in most cases. We also found evidence that indicates the use of diversity in increasing attack tolerance in other categories of vulnerable software.

It is not the objective of this paper to build systems utilizing software diversity or to evaluate how difficult it is to manage such systems. Instead, we measure the extent to which software diversity could be utilized to increase system security in using off-the-shelf software products.

In the rest of this paper, we first present the data source we utilized and some preliminary analysis (see Section 2). We then focus our analysis on the application software vulnerabilities in which we analyzed whether diverse software products providing the same services could suffer from the same vulnerability (see Section 3), and whether the same software product running on different operating systems will suffer from the same vulnerability and exploit (see Section 4). In Section 5, we present analysis on other vulnerable software products. Finally, we conclude in Section 6.

2   Source of Information and Preliminary Analysis

The main source of information we used for our analysis was the NVD/CVE (National Vulnerability Database/Common Vulnerabilities and Exposures) vulnerability database. We analyzed all the vulnerabilities recorded in CVE in the year of 2007, which consist of 6,427 vulnerability entries[1]. To obtain detailed information on the vulnerabilities and the corresponding software products, we

---

[1] The CVE 2007 database published on April 25, 2008 was used (http://nvd.nist.gov/download/nvdcve-2007.xml).

also consulted other sources including SecurityFocus, FrSIRT, CERT, Milw0rm, Secunia, OSVDB, IBM X-Force, as well as vulnerability advisories, security announcements, and bug lists from software vendors. After removing 87 entries that were rejected by CVE, the total number of vulnerabilities that we focused on was 6,340.

Note that the limited information introduced errors in our analysis. First, not all vulnerabilities are published. We only analyzed vulnerabilities found and published in 2007. Second, we may not have found all information on some published vulnerabilities. This is due to the limited resources we have, although we did our best in searching various public resources; it might also be the fact that some information about the vulnerabilities is not publicly available.

Our first step in the analysis was to find whether the vulnerable software has any substitutes (software products that offer similar functionality). We also categorized the vulnerabilities into five different types for further analysis.

2.1   Software without Substitutes

To implement a replicated system with diverse replicas (e.g., the one shown in Fig 1), we need to find (at least) two software products that provide the same service (*software substitutes*) and/or software products that run on multiple operating systems. If the software product does not have any substitutes and runs only on a single operating system, then diversity using off-the-shelf software cannot work and one has to introduce diversity via other artificial means (e.g., address space randomization). Therefore, we first analyze all the vulnerable software products in the CVE database to see if they have any substitutes.

We find that most software products do have substitutes and those that do not have mostly fall into one of the following three categories:

- **Hardware specific software:** This includes hardware drivers and firmware only provided by corresponding hardware vendors.
- **OS specific software:** This includes utilities that are specific to an operating system, e.g., Mac Installer, Windows Login window. They are only provided by the OS vendor.
- **Domain specific and customized software:** This includes that used in medical, biological, nuclear and other specific domains. The customized software refers to that developed for a specific company, e.g., management software that is used in a specific company, ActiveX controls developed and used for online transactions on a specific web site.

Table 1 shows some examples of software products that do not have substitutes. An interesting observation is that we did not find many vulnerable software products from the CVE database that are domain specific or customized. This does not necessarily mean that these software products do not have vulnerabilities. Domain specific and customized software products are used in a more controlled environment and it is less likely that they are reported in public vulnerability resources.

Table 1. Examples of software products without substitutes

Vendor	Product	CVE entry
ATI	Display driver	CVE-2007-4315
NVIDIA	Video driver	CVE-2007-3532
Intel	2200BG Wireless driver	CVE-2007-0686
HP	Help and Support Center	CVE-2007-3180
HP	Quick Launch Button	CVE-2007-6331
Alibaba	Alipay ActiveX control	CVE-2007-0827
Microgaming	Download Helper ActiveX	CVE-2007-2177

2.2 Vulnerable Software Categorization

Some vulnerabilities exist in application software that runs as user-space programs on an operating system. Others may exist in scripts that run on top of another software program. The analysis we performed varies according to the type of vulnerable software products. Therefore, we first put the vulnerable software into different categories.

- **Application software:** Application software is the most interesting because it is relatively easy to find the software substitutes. It is usually compiled into binary format and run as a process of its own in the user space. Word processors, web browsers, web servers and computer games are some examples of application software. It also includes plug-ins, extensions, and add-on's to application software, except those for a web server (see the next category).
- **Web script modules:**[2] These are light-weighted software modules which only run on web servers. We put them into a separate category instead of a sub-category of application software because of the large number of vulnerabilities in them. Examples include Content Management Systems (CMS), forums, bulletin boards, and other script modules.
- **Operating systems:** This category includes the operating system kernel and utilities that are closely related to the operating system, e.g., Apple Installer and the login window of Microsoft Windows.
- **Languages and libraries:** These include programming languages and libraries for general programming use, e.g., PNGlib (for decoding the PNG image) and SMTPlib (for implementing the SMTP protocol).
- **Others:** For example, firmware (including Routers, IP phones, hardware firewalls, etc.), software that runs on mobile phone, video game consoles (e.g., XBox) and so on.

Fig 2 shows the number of vulnerabilities in each software category and the corresponding percentage.

---

[2] They may be called web applications (e.g., in SANS [5]). We call this category web script modules, instead, to avoid the misunderstanding that it also contains web servers and browsers.

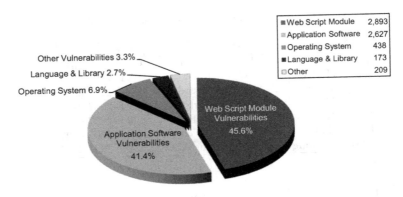

Fig. 2. Vulnerabilities in different software categories

2.3   Vulnerabilities in Application Software

As shown in Fig 2, 41.4% of the vulnerabilities found in 2007 are in application software. We focus our analysis on this category because it contains most of the commonly used and critical software, and it is usually what an intrusion detection system tries to protect. Not only that, it is also easy to find substitutes for an application software product, which makes it a natural candidate for introducing diversity. This is also the category for which information is best available and therefore the results of our analysis are most accurate.

The first analysis we did was to find the number of vulnerable application software products that do not have substitutes. As discussed in Section 2.1, this is important because one of the two ways of utilizing off-the-shelf software products to introduce diversity is to use software substitutes (the other is to run the same software on multiple operating systems). If many vulnerable application software products do not have any substitutes, then we will have to rely on the other way of introducing diversity.

We found 1,825 distinct application software products in all the 2,627 application software vulnerabilities[3], out of which only 25 (1.4%) do not have software substitutes. Some of the examples were shown in Table 1. This result coincides with our expectation in view of the highly competitive software industry market.

We have found that most software products in this category have software substitutes. The next question is whether these software products and their corresponding substitutes have the same vulnerability or not. In order to do this analysis, we further classify the application software vulnerabilities (Box 1 in Fig 3) into two sub-categories: vulnerabilities that exist in multiple software products (Box 2) and vulnerabilities that exist in a single software product (Box 3).

---

[3] A total number of 4,120 different names of software products were found in the descriptions of these vulnerabilities. Many of them were duplicates with different naming conventions or different product versions. After eliminating these duplicates, we found 1,825 distinct software products.

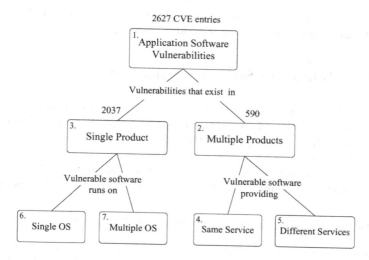

Fig. 3. Analysis on application software vulnerabilities

The results of the classification are obtained by examining the vulnerable product information and the description of each vulnerability in the CVE database. Fig 3 shows that majority of the vulnerabilities (2037 out of 2627) exist in only a single software product, which is an evidence in favor of introducing diversity since the replicas constructed in a replicated system are unlikely to suffer from the same vulnerability. We look into each of the two categories for further analysis.

Among the vulnerabilities that exist in multiple software products (Box 2 in Fig 3), we want to find out whether software products suffering from the same vulnerability are substitutes of one another (i.e. whether they provide the same service). This analysis is important because only software products providing the same service can be used in an intrusion detection system using software diversity (such as the behavioral distance system shown in Fig 1). If software programs and their substitutes suffer from the same vulnerability (Box 4), then such intrusion detection systems will not be effective in detecting intrusions. We present our detailed analysis for this in Section 3. If multiple software products – which suffer from the same vulnerability – are not providing the same service (Box 5), then they are not used simultaneously for constructing the intrusion detection system and therefore will not affect the effectiveness of diversity using off-the-shelf software products.

Among those vulnerabilities that exist in a single product (Box 3 in Fig 3), we want to find out how many of these software products can execute on multiple operating systems. For those that run on multiple operating systems (Box 7), it is also important to find out whether their vulnerabilities can be exploited in the same way when they are running on multiple operating systems. We present our analysis of these problems in Section 4. If a software product can only run on a single operating system (Box 6), then it cannot be used in a replicated system in which replicas are constructed using the different distributions of a single software product on multiple operating systems.

3 Vulnerabilities in Software Substitutes

As shown in Fig 3, there are 590 entries of vulnerabilities in multiple software products. Each of these vulnerabilities exists in more than one software product, which may or may not provide the same service. In this section, we first briefly show our method for finding vulnerabilities in software substitutes and our findings using this method (Section 3.1), and then discuss the attack code for exploiting the same vulnerability in these software substitutes (Section 3.2).

3.1 Finding Vulnerabilities in Software Substitutes

An interesting observation is that the same vulnerability may be represented in multiple entries in the CVE database. For example, entries CVE-2007-2761 and CVE-2007-2888 correspond to the same vulnerability (see Table 2). For this reason, we cannot simply rely on different CVE entries to distinguish different vulnerabilities.

Different CVE entries that refer to the same vulnerability usually have similar descriptions. We use Vector Space Model [19], one of the classical models in information retrieval, to compare the descriptions for all CVE entries. The similarity between two vulnerability descriptions is calculated using

$$\mathsf{sim}(d_1, d_2) = \frac{\vec{d_1} \cdot \vec{d_2}}{|\vec{d_1}| \times |\vec{d_2}|} = \frac{\sum_{i=1}^{t} w_{i,1} \times w_{i,2}}{\sqrt{\sum_{i=1}^{t} w_{i,1}^2} \times \sqrt{\sum_{i=1}^{t} w_{i,2}^2}}$$

where $\vec{d_1}$ and $\vec{d_2}$ are the descriptions of two vulnerability entries, $w_{i,j}$ is the weighting for the ith term in description d_j which is assigned with the frequency of the term. The threshold for the similarity score is set to 0.65 by manual tuning to obtain a good trade-off between the number of false positives and false negatives.

After the automatic comparison process using Vector Space Model and additional manual verification and correction, 410 distinct vulnerabilities are obtained from the 590 vulnerability entries that exist in multiple software products. We then performed a detailed analysis for each vulnerability and found that 29 of them (which involve 69 CVE entries) fall into the category in which the same vulnerability exists in multiple software products providing the same services (software substitutes). Some examples are shown in Table 2.

The result shows that although many vulnerabilities (410) exist in multiple software products, only a small portion of them (29) exist in multiple software products that provide the same service. Note that although the Vector Space Model helped a lot in finding similar descriptions in different vulnerability entries, some manual analysis was needed to obtain the results shown above.

Table 2. Two examples of the same vulnerability in software substitutes

CVE Entry	Description
CVE-2007-2761	Stack-based buffer overflow in MagicISO 5.4 build 239 and earlier allows remote attackers to execute arbitrary code via a long filename in a .cue file.
CVE-2007-2888	Stack-based buffer overflow in UltraISO 8.6.2.2011 and earlier allows user-assisted remote attackers to execute arbitrary code via a long FILE string (filename) in a .cue file.
CVE-2007-0548	KarjaSoft Sami HTTP Server 2.0.1 allows remote attackers to cause a denial of service (daemon hang) via a large number of requests for nonexistent objects.
CVE-2007-3340	BugHunter HTTP SERVER (httpsv.exe) 1.6.2 allows remote attackers to cause a denial of service (application crash) via a large number of requests for nonexistent pages.
CVE-2007-3398	LiteWEB 2.7 allows remote attackers to cause a denial of service (hang) via a large number of requests for nonexistent pages.

3.2 Exploit Code

In this step of the analysis, we further examine the 29 vulnerabilities that exist in software products providing the same services. If it happens that these software products are used to construct replicas in a replicated system (e.g., a behavioral distance system in Fig 1), then both replicas suffer from the same vulnerability. We want to find out whether the exploit codes on them are the same. If they are the same, then both replicas will be compromised by a single attack, and the intrusion detection system will fail to detect the intrusion.

We manage to find all the exploit codes (on multiple products) for 20 out of the 29 vulnerabilities. Exploit codes for the rest do not seem to be readily available to the public. By comparing the exploit codes for each of the 20 vulnerabilities for all the corresponding software substitutes, we found that the exploit code is the same across multiple software products for 14 of the 20 vulnerabilities.

It is not surprising that the same vulnerability will be exploited in the same way, even on different software products. A couple of notes are worth mentioning though. First, some of these vulnerabilities are about denial of service (DoS) attacks, which are usually not the type of intrusions a replicated system utilizing software diversity tries to detect [8,9]. For example, the same exploit code for sending a large number of requests for non-existent pages will cause a denial of service in the three software products in the second group in Table 2. Therefore, this result is not necessarily a strong evidence against the effectiveness of using off-the-shelf software to introduce diversity. Second, we have not studied the effect of using multiple operating systems at this point. In some cases, the exploit codes may be dependent on the operating system, especially in code injection attacks (see the next section).

3.3   Summary

To summarize, our analysis of the application software products shows that 22.5% (590 out of 2627) of the vulnerability entries are vulnerabilities in multiple software products, among which 7.1% (29 out of 410) are vulnerabilities in multiple software products that provide the same service. For those vulnerabilities in multiple software products providing the same service, there are roughly 70% (14 out of 20) chances that the same exploit code can be used to compromise these software products. Although strictly speaking these three numbers cannot be multiplied together directly[4], they are very good indications that diverse off-the-shelf application software products can be utilized effectively in replicated systems to detect intrusion and increase system resilience against software attacks.

4   Software Products Running on Multiple Operating Systems

Having analyzed the branch of vulnerabilities that exist in multiple software products in Fig 3 in Section 3, we now focus on the branch of vulnerabilities that exist in a single software product. As shown in Fig 3, this category consists of the majority of vulnerabilities in application software. Therefore, understanding how software products in this category can be utilized to introduce diversity is important. Here we focus on diversity via running software on multiple operating systems, since the vulnerability exists only on a single product and diversity via running software substitutes will definitely work. Running the same software on multiple operating systems is also a cheaper way of introducing diversity due to its lower cost in managing the replicated system.

In this section, we first briefly show the different operating systems we considered (Section 4.1), and then examine whether the software products in this category run on multiple operating systems (Section 4.2). Finally, similar to our analysis in Section 3.2, we analyzed the corresponding exploit code in Section 4.3.

4.1   Different Operating Systems

Fig 4 shows the different operating systems that we consider in our analysis. We classify operating systems into four families: Microsoft Windows, Unix/Unix-like, Mac and others (see Fig 4). This is mainly due to their different kernels and binary executable formats (Portable Executable for Windows systems, ELF for Unix and Unix-like systems, and Mach-O for Mac). Note that it is an important requirement that these operating systems are diverse so that the same exploit is unlikely to compromise the same program running on different operating systems. Although Mac OS X shares part of the kernel code with BSD operating systems, we show in Section 5.2 that they rarely share common vulnerabilities.

---

[4] Due to the lack of knowledge about the number of vulnerabilities each software has, the commonality of each software product in terms of the number of requests per unit time, the consequence of a compromise, and etc.

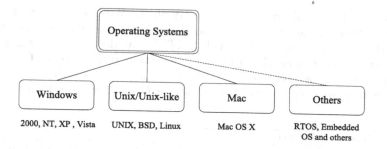

Fig. 4. Different operating systems

4.2 Software Products Running on Multiple Operating Systems

Next, we want to find out whether software products in this category (in which vulnerabilities exist only in one software product) can run on multiple operating systems. Since a lot of manual work is required in this analysis, we randomly picked 300 out of the 2,037 vulnerability entries for analysis. Results are shown in Fig 5.

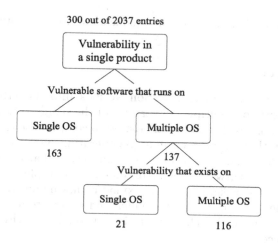

Fig. 5. Vulnerable software on multiple operating systems

Fig 5 shows that more than 54% (163 out of 300) of the software products we analyzed officially supports only one operating system. However, note that it is still possible to construct diverse replicas using software substitutes that provide the same service for them.

Among the rest of the 45.7% software products that are supported to run on multiple operating systems, 15.3% (21 out of 137) do not share the same vulnerability among different operating system versions (e.g., the first entry in

Fig 6, in which the vulnerability exists only on the Windows version of Mozilla Firefox, but not on the Unix and Mac versions). From our analysis, this is mainly due to the fact that many of these vulnerabilities are design errors, which easily propagate across versions that run on multiple operating systems. One typical example is the vulnerability entry CVE-2007-5264, in which the client's information is sent unencrypted to the game server (second entry in Fig 6).

CVE Entry	Description
CVE-2007-3285	Mozilla Firefox before 2.0.0.5, when run on Windows, allows remote attackers to bypass file type checks and possibly execute programs via a (1) `file:///` or (2) `resource:URI` with a dangerous extension, followed by a NULL byte (%00) and a safer extension. (Vulnerability in only one of the OS versions of the software product)
CVE-2007-5264	Battlefront Dropteam 1.3.3 and earlier sends the client's online account name and password unencrypted to the game server. A remote attacker with administrative privileges could exploit this vulnerability to obtain user account, product key and other sensitive information. (Vulnerability in multiple OS versions of the software product)

Fig. 6. Vulnerabilities in software products that run on multiple OSes

4.3   Exploit Code

Similar to Section 3.2, in this subsection we look into the 116 vulnerabilities (each of which exists on multiple OS versions of the single software product), to see whether the same exploit code can be used to compromise the corresponding software program that executes on multiple operating systems.

We first consider a naive attacker, who is not aware that a replicated system where the vulnerable software is being executed on multiple operating systems. We assume that the attacker is trying to exploit a known vulnerability to execute some attack code, e.g., to overflow a buffer and overwrite a return address in order to execute a shellcode. There are at least two reasons why such an exploit is unlikely to succeed.

First, the source of the same software product on different OSes may be different. This could cause many differences in, e.g., memory layout which is critical for a successful buffer overflow. For example, calculating time intervals on Windows usually requires two variables (SYSTEMTIME and FILETIME) and a conversion between the two, whereas it usually takes only one variable (timeval) on Linux.

Second, even when the source is exactly the same for different OS distributions of the same product, the attack code to be executed may be different due to the different APIs and system calls across different operating systems. It is highly unlikely that the same machine code can be used on different operating systems, e.g., to open a shell. The system interface could be different even across OSes in the same family, e.g., different versions of Microsoft Windows. Table 3 shows some of the typical system calls and their corresponding system call numbers on different versions of the Windows operating system.

Table 3. System calls on Windows

System Call	NT	2000	XP	2003 Server	Vista
NtClose()	0x000f	0x0018	0x0019	0x001b	0x002f
NtOpenFile()	0x004f	0x0064	0x0074	0x007a	0x00b8
NtReadVirtualMemory()	0x0089	0x00a4	0x00ba	0x00c2	0x0102
NtTerminateProcess()	0x00bb	0x00e0	0x0101	0x010a	0x014f

Next, we consider a more sophisticated attack in which the attacker is aware that a replicated system running the vulnerable software on multiple operating systems is in use. If the attacker wants to evade the intrusion detection system, he/she will most likely have to design and implement an exploit code that first figures out which operating system is running and subsequently execute the corresponding exploit code (see Algorithm 1).

Algorithm 1. Exploiting the same software running on multiple OSes

```
os_ret ← os_test();
if is_win(os_ret) then
    win_attack_code();
else if is_unix(os_ret) then
    unix_attack_code();
else if is_mac(os_ret) then
    mac_attack_code();
end if
```

Note that Algorithm 1 is very different from one in which the attacker knows the operating system (and its version) to be exploited before sending the attack code. Many attack tools first interact with the vulnerable server to find out which operating system is running by using operating system fingerprinting techniques [7,23]. After that, the attack packets specifically designed for the corresponding operating system are sent to the vulnerable server. This type of attacks will not work here because 1) the replicated system (e.g., Fig 1) usually removes any non-determinism in the system, which makes operating system fingerprinting impossible or inaccurate; 2) the same operating-system-specific attack will be duplicated and sent to all replicas, and the attack only compromises the vulnerable replica (the difference of the behaviors of the compromised and uncompromised replicas makes such operating-system-specific attacks easily detectable).

There are at least two difficulties in implementing Algorithm 1. One is to implement `os_test()` which not only executes on all different operating systems but returns different outputs when executing on different operating systems. The other is that such an exploit code, which is at least several times that of the exploit code for any specific operating system, is usually too long to fit in the limited buffer available in the vulnerable program. We have not found a real attack that employs the technique shown in Algorithm 1.

Another observation is that only three cross-OS viruses have been reported in Kaspersky Lab's viruslist according to the statement issued by Kaspersky Lab[5]. According to Kaspersky Lab, all the three viruses are proof-of-concept malicious programs written purely with the intention of demonstrating that such viruses are possible. None of these viruses actually had any practical applications so far.

4.4 Summary

In this section, we analyze the vulnerabilities that exist in a single application software product. Our analysis shows that:

- 45.7% (137 out of 300) of the vulnerable software products involved in this category are officially supported on multiple operating systems;
- Among those that are officially supported on multiple operating systems, 84.7% have the vulnerability propagated across multiple OS versions;
- At least two factors (different memory layout and different machine instructions) make it difficult to construct an exploit that can compromise software running on multiple operating systems simultaneously. No such practical attacks have been reported.

These findings show that roughly 50% of the software products are candidates for a replicated system running the same software on multiple operating systems. Even if the same vulnerability exists on multiple replicas, compromising them simultaneously remains difficult. However, due to the fact that most of these vulnerabilities are shared among the different OS versions of the same software, utilizing diverse operating systems is not as effective as utilizing software substitutes.

5   Vulnerabilities in Other Software Products

In this section, we present our analysis on the other three categories, namely web script modules, operating systems, language and libraries.

5.1   Web Script Modules

Software in this category consists of light-weighted products that run on web servers to provide web-based applications. Examples include forums, bulletin

---

[5] http://www.kaspersky.com/news?id=184875287

boards, shopping carts and other script modules. We analyzed the CVE vulnerability database and found close to 3, 000 entries that fall into this category. Some common and well-known types are shown in Table 4.

Table 4. Vulnerabilities in web script modules

Vulnerability Types	Number of entries	Percentage
Cross-site scripting	714	24.7%
SQL injection	669	23.1%
PHP remote file inclusion	634	21.9%
Directory/Path traversal	267	9.2%
Cross-site request forgery	50	1.7%
Others	559	19.3%
Total	2893	100%

An interesting finding is that most of the vulnerable software in this category is operating system independent. For example, most PHP modules are deployed on Apache web servers, which can run on all common operating systems. This means that we could use diverse operating systems to introduce software diversity. However, it is different from the application software we analyzed in Section 4, since many of the web script modules operate on top of a web server, and seldom interact with the operating system. If the vulnerable software does not interact with the operating system, then constructing replicas using diverse operating systems is not an effective way of introducing diversity because the exploit code is likely to be the same on different replicas. Therefore, we shift our focus of analysis to using software substitutes for introducing diversity.

Cross-site scripting (XSS) vulnerabilities. Cross-site scripting (XSS) is one of the most common web script module vulnerabilities in the CVE database. Attackers exploit this vulnerability by injecting malicious scripts into the output of an application (usually a web page) which is sent to the client's web browser. This script is then executed on the client's web browser and used to transfer sensitive data to a third party (i.e., the attacker) [24]. Unlike other types of web vulnerabilities, XSS vulnerabilities exist and are exploited on the server side but take effects on the client side. Thus, the protection and prevention mechanisms are carried out both on the server side [25] and the client side [24].

In most cases, the server-side scripts are vulnerable no matter what operating systems or web servers on which the scripts run (see an example in Fig 7, the attack payload is usually some malicious HTML/JavaScript, which is first posted to the server and then downloaded and run at the client side), thus introducing diversity on the server side is not effective. However, introducing diversity on the client side by utilizing diverse browsers is possible. Fig 8 shows two examples of XSS attack payload in the exploit code as shown in Fig 7.

Description	Cross-site scripting vulnerability in `picture.php` in Advanced Guest-book 2.4.2 allows remote attackers to inject arbitrary web script or HTML via the picture parameter.
Exploit code	`http://www.site.com/picture.php?picture=[attack payload]`

Fig. 7. CVE entry CVE-2007-0605 and the corresponding exploit code

[Payload 1] Works for Internet Explorer 6.0 but not Opera 9.0 or Firefox 2.0

```
<IMG SRC=javascript:location.replace('http://
evil.com/steal/index.asp?cookies='+encodeURI(document.cookie))>
```

[Payload 2] Works for Opera 9.0 but not Internet Explorer 6.0 or Firefox 2.0

```
<IMG SRC=javascript:document.createElement('IMG').setAttribute('src',
'http://evil.com/steal/index.asp?cookies='+encodeURI(document.cookie))>
```

Fig. 8. XSS attacks that have different impact on browsers

Both XSS attack payloads shown in Fig 8 utilize the HTML tag `<IMG>` and are used for stealing cookies from client machines that access the vulnerable web site. The exploit codes do not have the same effect on the contemporary browsers because of the implementation difference. The evidences that XSS attack codes have different effects on different browsers can also be found from other resources. For example, 68 out of the 110 XSS attack vectors on the XSS Cheat Sheet (`http://ha.ckers.org/xss.html`) have different impacts on diverse web browsers. Note that the application scenario here is slightly different from the example shown in Fig 1: utilizing diverse browsers to construct the replicated system is a client-side solution instead of the server-side example shown in Fig 1. Our results show that by comparing the different impacts on different browsers when given the same input, many XSS attacks could be detected. Analyzing the detection rate of such a system is out of the scope of this paper.

SQL injection. SQL injection arises when a user input is not correctly or sufficiently filtered. SQL injection attacks are usually launched through specially crafted user inputs on web applications that use strings to construct SQL queries [1]. Although simple SQL statements are constructed exactly the same for different databases, they are different in constructing sophisticated SQL Injection exploits. Consider Blind SQL Injection in CVE-2007-1166, CVE-2007-3051, and many other vulnerable products. The exploit code utilizes the following SQL statements (simplified version).

$$IF\ ((SELECT\ user)\ =\ 'Alice')\ SELECT\ 1\ ELSE\ SELECT\ 1/0$$

After receiving this request, the SQL Server will throw a divide-by-zero error if the current user is not Alice, while the MySQL server will report a *parsing error.*[6] There has also been research on utilizing diverse off-the-shelf databases to obtain fault tolerance [11].

Directory traversal. Directory traversal (or path traversal) vulnerabilities appear when web applications do not sufficiently validate or sanitize the user-supplied file names. It may allow attackers to gain access to directories and files that reside outside of the directory of web documents.

A notable difference in traversing directories on diverse operating systems is that Unix and Unix-like systems use "../", while Windows systems use "..\". Not only that, the root directory on Windows uses the "<drive letter>:\" format, which limits directory traversal to a single partition (e.g., C:\). There are other differences, e.g., the file organization also varies a lot on different operating systems.

Remote File Inclusion (RFI). RFI vulnerabilities allow an attacker to include his own malicious PHP code on a vulnerable web application. RFI attacks are possible because of several PHP configuration flags that are not carefully set. This vulnerability could be avoided easily by disabling two global flags in PHP [6]. Thus, RFI vulnerabilities are not the focus of our study in this paper.

Cross-site Request Forgery (CSRF). By launching a successful CSRF attack to a user, an adversary is able to initiate arbitrary HTTP requests from that user to the vulnerable web application [13]. CSRF attacks are usually executed by causing the victim's web browsers to create hidden HTTP requests to restricted resources. Therefore, similar to XSS vulnerabilities, using diverse browsers is a possible way of detecting CSRF vulnerabilities.

5.2   Operating Systems, Languages and Libraries

For operating system vulnerabilities, we try to find out if diverse operating systems have the same vulnerability. We find that Mac OS X has some common vulnerabilities with BSD (e.g., CVE-2007-0229), mainly because the implementation of Mac OS X kernel shares part of the code of BSD kernel [20]. However, these common vulnerabilities only constitute 2% (2 out of 98) of all the vulnerabilities on Mac OS, which indicates that utilizing Unix/Unix-like OS and Mac OS to construct replicas is effective.

Another observation we have is that different Linux operating systems have many common vulnerabilities, since they share the same kernel (e.g. CVE-2007-3104, CVE-2007-6206 and others). These vulnerabilities contribute 64% (71 out of 111) of all the Linux OS vulnerabilities, which shows that different Linux OS are not diverse enough. Finally, by examining all the 438 OS vulnerabilities, no evidence has been found that the same OS vulnerability exists in both Windows and Unix/Unix-like or in both Windows and Mac operating systems.

---

[6] Example statement here was tested on SQL Server 2005 and MySQL 5.0. More resources on different syntax for constructing SQL Injection attacks to different databases can be found on SQL Injection Cheat Sheet at http://ferruh.mavituna.com/sql-injection-cheatsheet-oku/

Many programming languages and libraries (e.g., Java, PHP, Perl, and etc.) support multiple operating systems. However, our analysis in the CVE vulnerability database shows that many of the vulnerabilities in these products are platform dependent. For example, CVE-2007-5862 (a Java vulnerability that exists only in Mac OS X) and CVE-2007-1411 (a PHP buffer overflow vulnerability that allows local, and possibly remote, attackers to execute arbitrary code via several vulnerable PHP functions that exists only in Windows[7]).

5.3 Summary

Although in general, software diversity is not very effective in web applications, it is successful in detecting exploits of some web script module vulnerabilities by, for example, utilizing diverse browsers to defend against XSS and CSRF attacks and utilizing diverse databases to detect SQL Injection attacks.

Most OS vulnerabilities only exist in one OS family, which indicates that diversity is useful when utilizing diverse operating systems of different OS families. Although most language and library vulnerabilities are platform independent, there are cases in which they exist in only one particular OS version.

6 Conclusion

In this paper, we analyzed the vulnerabilities published in 2007 to evaluate the effectiveness of two ways of introducing software diversity utilizing off-the-shelf software: one is by utilizing different software products that provide the same service, and the other is by utilizing the same software product on different operating systems.

The results show that more than 98.5% of the vulnerable application software products have substitutes and the chance that these software substitutes be compromised by the same attack is very low. Nearly half of the application software products are officially supported to run on multiple operating systems. Although the different OS distributions of the same product have more than 80% of a chance to suffer from the same vulnerability, their attack code is quite different. For the web script modules and other types of software, although software diversity is less effective than that in the application software, some evidence has been found that there are possible ways to benefit from software diversity in these categories.

The limitation of our work mainly includes two parts. The first is that a large amount of manual work has been spent in order to get the accurate statistical

---

[7] This result is obtained by analyzing NVD/CVE, SecurityFocus and the PHP Buglists. SecurityFocus gives misleading information which indicates that this vulnerability exists on Unix/Unix-like systems (see http://www.securityfocus.com/bid/22893/info). However, the PHP Bug Info (Bug #40746) shows that it is a problem with the function dbopen() in the Microsoft ntdblib library, and does not exist when compiled with FreeTDS version of the dblib library that is used by Unix/Unix-like systems.

results, which is too costly and time consuming. Other information retrieval and artificial intelligence techniques could be applied in our future work to speed up the analysis process. The other limitation is that we have not yet obtained the statistics for some categories due to the large information search space and the lack of closely related resources, which is a challenging task that remains to be done in the future.

References

1. Bandhakavi, S., Bisht, P., Madhusudan, P., Venkatakrishnan, V.N.: Candid: preventing sql injection attacks using dynamic candidate evaluations. In: CCS 2007: Proceedings of the 14th ACM conference on Computer and communications security, pp. 12–24. ACM, New York (2007)
2. Barrantes, E.G., Ackley, D.H., Palmer, T.S., Stefanovic, D., Zovi, D.D.: Randomized instruction set emulation to disrupt binary code injection attacks. In: CCS 2003: Proceedings of the 10th ACM conference on Computer and communications security, pp. 281–289. ACM, New York (2003)
3. Bhatkar, S., DuVarney, D.C., Sekar, R.: Address obfuscation: an efficient approach to combat a board range of memory error exploits. In: SSYM 2003: Proceedings of the 12th conference on USENIX Security Symposium, Berkeley, CA, USA, p. 8 (2003), USENIX Association
4. Cox, B., Evans, D., Filipi, A., Rowanhill, J., Hu, W., Davidson, J., Knight, J., Nguyen-Tuong, A., Hiser, J.: N-variant systems – A secretless framework for security through diversity. In: Proceedings of the 15th USENIX Security Symposium (August 2006)
5. Dhamankar, R.: SANS Top-20 Security Risks (2007),
   http://www.sans.org/top20/2007/
6. Edge, J.: Remote file inclusion vulnerabilities (Octobor 2006),
   http://lwn.net/Articles/203904/
7. Fyodor, G.L.: Remote os detection via tcp/ip stack fingerprinting. Technical report, INSECURE.ORG (October 1998)
8. Gao, D., Reiter, M.K., Song, D.: Behavioral distance for intrusion detection. In: Valdes, A., Zamboni, D. (eds.) RAID 2005. LNCS, vol. 3858, pp. 63–81. Springer, Heidelberg (2006)
9. Gao, D., Reiter, M.K., Song, D.: Behavioral distance measurement using hidden markov models. In: Zamboni, D., Krügel, C. (eds.) RAID 2006. LNCS, vol. 4219, pp. 19–40. Springer, Heidelberg (2006)
10. Gao, D., Reiter, M.K., Song, D.: Beyond output voting: Detecting compromised replicas using HMM-based behavioral distance. IEEE Transactions on Dependable and Secure Computing (TDSC) (July 2008)
11. Gashi, I., Popov, P.: Fault tolerance via diversity for off-the-shelf products: A study with sql database servers. IEEE Transactions on Dependable Secure Computing 4(4), 280–294 (2007); Member-Lorenzo Strigini
12. Geer, D., Bace, R., Gutmann, P., Metzger, P., Pfleeger, C.P., Quarterman, J.S., Schneier, B.: Cybersecurity: The cost of monopoly. Technical report, CCIA (2003)
13. Jovanovic, N., Kirda, E., Kruegel, C.: Preventing Cross Site Request Forgery Attacks. In: IEEE International Conference on Security and Privacy for Emerging Areas in Communication Networks, Securecomm (2006)

14. Just, J.E., Reynolds, J.C., Clough, L.A., Danforth, M., Levitt, K.N., Maglich, R., Rowe, J.: Learning unknown attacks - A start. In: Wespi, A., Vigna, G., Deri, L. (eds.) RAID 2002. LNCS, vol. 2516, pp. 158–176. Springer, Heidelberg (2002)
15. Kc, G.S., Keromytis, A.D., Prevelakis, V.: Countering code-injection attacks with instruction-set randomization. In: CCS 2003: Proceedings of the 10th ACM conference on Computer and communications security, pp. 272–280. ACM Press, New York (2003)
16. Linger, R.C.: Systematic generation of stochastic diversity as an intrusion barrier in survivable systems software. In: HICSS 1999: Proceedings of the Thirty-Second Annual Hawaii International Conference on System Sciences, Washington, DC, USA, 1999, vol. 3, p. 3062. IEEE Computer Society, Los Alamitos (1999)
17. O'Donnell, A.J., Sethu, H.: On achieving software diversity for improved network security using distributed coloring algorithms. In: CCS 2004: Proceedings of the 11th ACM conference on Computer and communications security, pp. 121–131. ACM, New York (2004)
18. Reynolds, J., Just, J., Lawson, E., Clough, L., Maglich, R.: The design and implementation of an intrusion tolerant system. In: Proceedings of the 2002 International Conference on Dependable Systems and Networks (DSN 2002) (2002)
19. Salton, G., Wong, A., Yang, C.S.: A vector space model for automatic indexing. Communications of the ACM 18(11), 613–620 (1975)
20. Singh, A.: Mac OS X Internals: A Systems Approach. Addison-Wesley, Reading (2006)
21. Stamp, M.: Risks of monoculture. Communications of the ACM 47(3), 120 (2004)
22. Totel, E., Majorczyk, F., Me, L.: COTS diversity based intrusion detection and application to web servers. In: Valdes, A., Zamboni, D. (eds.) RAID 2005. LNCS, vol. 3858, pp. 43–62. Springer, Heidelberg (2006)
23. Trowbridge, C.: An overview of remote operating system fingerprinting. Technical report, The SANS Institute (July 2003)
24. Vogt, P., Nentwich, F., Jovanovic, N., Kirda, E., Kruegel, C., Vigna, G.: Cross-site scripting prevention with dynamic data tainting and static analysis. In: Proceeding of the Network and Distributed System Security Symposium (NDSS) (February 2007)
25. Wassermann, G., Su, Z.: Static detection of cross-site scripting vulnerabilities. In: ICSE 2008: Proceedings of the 30th international conference on Software engineering, pp. 171–180. ACM, New York (2008)

Using Contextual Information for IDS Alarm Classification (Extended Abstract)

François Gagnon[1], Frédéric Massicotte[2], and Babak Esfandiari[1]

[1] Carleton University, Canada
{fgagnon,babak}@sce.carleton.ca
[2] Communications Research Centre Canada
frederic.massicotte@crc.ca

Abstract. Signature-based intrusion detection systems are known to generate many noncritical alarms (alarms not related to a successful attack). Adding contextual information to IDSes is a promising avenue to identify noncritical alarms. Several approaches using contextual information have been suggested. However, it is not clear what are the benefits of using a specific approach. This paper establishes the effectiveness of using target configuration (i.e. operating system and applications) as contextual information for identifying noncritical alarms. Moreover, it demonstrates that current tools for OS discovery are not adequate for IDS context gathering.

1 Introduction

It has been pointed out in [6, 8] that one of the main drawbacks of signature-based intrusion detection systems (IDSes) is the large amount of *noncritical alarms* they produce.

Definition 1 (Noncritical Alarm). *An alarm is* noncritical *when it is not related to a successful attack. That is, a noncritical alarm is either a false positive (an alarm related to a normal packet) or a non-relevant positive (an alarm related to a failed attack attempt). See shaded area of Figure 1.*

Noncritical alarms pose two problems. First, a security officer might spend all of his time discarding noncritical alarms instead of investigating real threats. Second, in order to automatically prevent attacks based on an IDS alarms, one must be confident that this will not disrupt the normal activities of the network; that is, legitimate traffic should not be dropped due to false positives.

In order to reduce the number of noncritical alarms, researchers have proposed to consider the context of an attack to establish whether it has any chance to succeed. However, little has been done to assess the effectiveness of a given piece of information as context for identifying noncritical alarms.

In this paper, we evaluate, using a large scale experiment, the effectiveness of target configuration information for identifying noncritical alarms. The elements of target configuration we consider are the target operating system (OS)

U. Flegel and D. Bruschi (Eds.): DIMVA 2009, LNCS 5587, pp. 147–156, 2009.

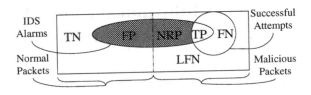

Fig. 1. Alarm Types

version and the version of the applications (App) offering the services available on the target's open ports. Moreover, we demonstrate that current tools for OS discovery are not adequate for IDS context gathering.

The paper is structured as follows. Section 2 discusses IDS context and more specifically target configuration information. Section 3 describes the experimental setup used in this paper. Section 4 presents the experiment results and establishes the effectiveness of target configuration information for identifying noncritical alarms. Section 5 measures the accuracy of current tools for operating system and application discovery for the task of IDS context gathering. Finally, a discussion and some pointers for future work will serve as a conclusion.

2   Contextual Information

There are four main types of IDS contextual information: networking features, target configuration, vulnerability assessment, and attack side effects.

Network-related context contains basic networking information (e.g. network topology, communication protocol specifications, etc). This type of contextual information is (partially) implemented directly in most IDSes. For instance, it helps to prevent squealing [11].

Target configuration considers the operating system and applications of the target to establish, using vulnerability databases such as Security Focus [12], whether an attack has succeeded. The work presented in [3] uses OS information as context directly in Snort rules. However, it only considers the target operating system (not the applications). [3] relies on a Snort plugin to detect the operating systems and a modified rule set to raise an alarm only when the target has a vulnerable OS. A problem with this approach is that when the information about the target configuration is unavailable, the IDS rule does not match and no alarm is triggered. As mentioned in [7] this implies that the upgraded IDS could miss some successful attacks. In this paper, we adopt a more general approach, separating the context gathering process from the IDS engine.

Vulnerability assessment typically relies on an active scanner to determine whether the target is immune to the security flaw exploited by the current attack, see [5]. While vulnerability assessment is possibly very accurate, it usually requires the repeated use of a scanner which creates traffic on the network. This traffic can interact in an inconvenient way with network monitoring tools and a vulnerability scan might unintentionally compromise the scanned computer.

Considering the attack side effects means inspecting the target behavior for evidences that the attack was successful. [16] (using Bro) and [19] (using Snort) propose to specify the target reaction directly in the IDS rules. For a given attack, an alarm should be raised only when a predefined target reaction is observed. As mentioned in [7], this implies that the upgraded IDS could miss some successful attacks, mainly when the reaction cannot be observed because the attempt crashed the system. [5] proposes a different use of the attack side effect: remotely accessing the target after an attempt in order to gather evidences of the attack success (log files, host-based IDSes, etc). In both cases, the attack must actually occur for the information to be available. Thus, this technique cannot help preventing attacks.

3   Experiment Setup

The main goal of this paper is to evaluate the effectiveness of target configuration information for identifying noncritical alarms. We present our experiment environment in two parts: the dataset we used (Section 3.1) and the algorithms we tested to classify the alarms (Section 3.2).

3.1   Dataset

To have a fully automated evaluation process, we rely on three sources of information:

- A well-documented attack dataset containing, at least, the outcome of each attack and the configuration of the targets.
- IDS alarms from Snort (with references to Security Focus).
- The vulnerability description on Security Focus.

Figure 2 illustrates how this information is used in the evaluation process; it works as follows:

1) First, based on an alarm from Snort we know the host targeted by the attack. Then, from the dataset information, we can obtain the complete configuration of that target[1].
2) Second, based on Snort's reference to Security Focus we can obtain the list of products that are vulnerable to the underlying attack.
3) Based on the two pieces of information above, an algorithm can decide whether the alarm is critical or not (see Section 3.2).
4) Finally, using the outcome of the attack (from the dataset documentation), it is possible to validate the choice made by the algorithm.

For our experiment, we used the freely available dataset presented in [7][2]. Every traffic trace contained in this dataset is the result of launching one of 92

---

[1] In Section 5 we rely on external tools to obtain the target configuration.
[2] We are currently unaware of another freely available dataset satisfying the documentation requirements mentioned above.

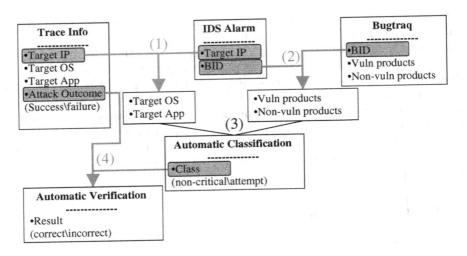

Fig. 2. Automatic Evaluation Process

Vulnerability Exploitation Program (VEP) against a target. Each VEP corresponds to one of 47 Bugtraq ID (BID) referring to the vulnerability database of Security Focus. These VEP are launched against each of 95 targets with different operating systems and/or applications, resulting in a total of 5,761 attack attempts (4,575 failures and 1,186 successes). Each trace contains exactly one attack attempt.

The main limitations of our experiment are:

- The absence of normal (background) traffic in the dataset. Snort does not produce false positives. Thus, we can only measure the capacity to identify non-relevant positives.
- The unbalanced distribution of failed vs successful attempts (an attempt has 80% chances to fail). Although we did not use this information in our decision algorithms, it has to be considered when interpreting the results.
- The unrealistic network diversity. The dataset is not representative of an usual corporate network, since it contains several different types of OSes. However, for evaluation purpose, we believe this is good; it forces OSD tools to provide accurate information.
- The use of a single dataset. The results obtained are not necessarily statistically significant and they are, a priori, only valid with for our dataset.

3.2 Alarm Classification Algorithms

Our goal is to identify, among all the alarms, those that are noncritical. The idea is that alarms should not be deleted, but classified. This allows a security officer to select which classes of alarms he wants to see in real-time and still give him the opportunity to check the lower priority alarms for further forensics.

We implemented four algorithms; each classifying an alarm as noncritical (NC) or attempt (A). This section briefly presents those algorithms: ContextOS (resp. ContextApp) relies only on the OS (resp. App) information of the target, ContextOSApp relies on both the OS and App information, and ContextOSDeduction uses the OS information with a static database to deduce which popular application cannot run on a specific OS (e.g., Microsoft IIS FTP Server 5.0 cannot run on port 21/tcp of a Linux Red Hat 7.0 machine[3]). More details about these algorithms can be found in [2].

ContextOS(alarm a)
(1) if the target OS is listed as non-vulnerable for this exploit, return NC.
(2) if the target OS is not listed as vulnerable
    (2.1) if all the products listed as vulnerable are OSes, return NC.
(3) return A.

ContextApp(alarm a)
(1) if the target App is listed as non-vulnerable for this exploit, return NC.
(2) if the target App is not listed as vulnerable
    (2.1) if all the products listed as vulnerable are Apps, return NC.
(3) return A.

ContextOSApp(alarm a)
(1) if the target OS is listed as non-vulnerable for this exploit, return NC.
(2) if the target App is listed as non-vulnerable for this exploit, return NC.
(3) if the target OS is not listed as vulnerable
    (3.1) if the target App is not listed as vulnerable, return NC.
(4) return A.

ContextOSDeduction(alarm a)
(1) if ContextOS(a) = NC, return NC
(2) if the target OS is not listed as vulnerable
    (2.1) if none of the applications listed a vulnerable can run on the target, return NC.
(3) return A.

4   Results Analysis

The goal of the classification algorithms presented in Section 3.2 is to identify the noncritical alarms among all available alarms. This can be viewed as an information retrieval task [14]. For this reason, we use the classical measures of information retrieval to assess the accuracy of the algorithms. We mainly use precision and recall:

$$Precision = \frac{\text{\# of noncritical alarms classified as NC}}{\text{\# of alarms classified as NC}}$$

---

[3] Application level virtualization, like Wine [17], might disable such static deductions.

$$Recall = \frac{\text{\# of noncritical alarms classified as NC}}{\text{\# of noncritical alarms}}$$

The perfect algorithm would have a recall of 100% (it is able to classify every noncritical alarm as NC) and a precision of 100% (it does not classify any critical alarm as NC). When interpreting the results, it is important to consider that a decrease of precision (i.e., critical alarms begin classified as NC) is more harmful than a decrease of recall (i.e., non-critical alarms being classified as A).

4.1 Precision

There are 5 vulnerabilities for which at least one classification algorithm has a precision less than 100%, making a mistake by classifying some true positives as NC (precision summary is shown in Table 1). At first this is surprising since the algorithms of Section 3.2 should not make such mistakes. However, after further investigation, it turned out that all those mistakes can be explained by the fact that some vulnerable products are not listed as such on Security Focus. For instance, we have an exploit for BID 9633 which successfully compromised a Windows 2000 sp4 target; however, Security Focus does no list this product as vulnerable for BID 9633.

4.2 Recall

Table 1 presents the recall summary for each algorithm on the whole dataset. ContextApp (identifying 23% of noncritical alarms) performs better than ContextOS (15%). ContextOSDeduction (41%) performs much better than ContextApp. ContextOSApp (73%) has the best results.

Table 1. Precision/Recall Summary

Algorithm	Precision	Recall
ContextOS	98.2%	15.3%
ContextApp	100%	22.9%
ContextOSDeduction	99.3%	40.7%
ContextOSApp	99.6%	73.1%

We conclude that target configuration is a valuable piece of information for IDS context as it can identify nearly 75% of noncritical alarms on our dataset. Even if the target configuration is vulnerable, the attack might fail for other reasons, e.g., the string used for buffer overflow is inadequate, the attack requires special target conditions (an application running with admin rights). This accounts for the 25% of unsuccessful attack attempts that do not get tagged as NC when using the complete target configuration information.

5   Using Existing Tools for Context Gathering

Section 4 established the effectiveness of target configuration as contextual information for identifying non-relevant alarms in the ideal case; that is, when we have access to the configuration of each target. However, such an assumption is unrealistic as networks are growing larger and more dynamic (users typically have a lot of freedom with their workstation: installing new applications and even changing or updating their OS). This section relaxes the above assumption and uses existing tools to gather contextual information. Section 5.1 presents how existing tools for operating system discovery (OSD) perform; while Section 5.2 discusses the performance of application discovery (AppD) tools.

5.1   Operating System Discovery Tools

We tested several passive OSD tools (Siphon 0.666beta [15], the passive mode of SinFP 2.00-8 [13], and the 4 modes of p0f 2.0.8 [10], as well as three active tools (Xprobe 2.0.3 [18], Nmap 4.20 [9], and ettercap NG-0.7.3 [4]). We used the ContextOSDeduction algorithm, but now considering a set of possible OSes (as provided by the OSD tools) instead of the actual OS. For the passive tools, the set of possible OSes is the set of OSes guessed by the tool when using the corresponding attack trace as input. For the active tools, we ran the tool once for each target and used the results for every attack against that target.

5.1.1   Precision

Most tools allowed to achieve a reasonable precision, see Table 2. Some errors are still explained by the fact that some vulnerable products are not listed as such on Security Focus. However, another source of errors here is that the tool can provide the wrong OS. This could result in a critical alarm being misclassified as NC. For instance, assume an attack succeeded against a Windows target but the OSD tool wrongly identifies the target as a Linux machine which is not vulnerable to the ongoing attack. The alarm ends up being erroneously classified as NC.

Table 2. Precision/Recall Summary for OSD Tools (ContextOSDeduction algorithm)

OSD Tools	Precision	Recall
p0f (StrayAck)	93.6%	0.6%
SinFP	100%	1.6%
p0f (Syn)	100%	2.2%
Siphon	96.5%	2.4%
p0f(RstAck)	100%	3.4%
Nmap*	98.3%	5.1%
ettercap*	98.7%	8.5%
p0f (SynAck)	96.4%	8.7%
Xprobe*	99.0%	12.7%

*Active tool

5.1.2   Recall

Table 2 also gives the recall summary for each OSD tool. It is clear that OSD tools are not adequate to gather IDS context, identifying at most 12.7% of noncritical alarms. This is only 1/3 of the potential of OS information as ContextOSDeduction scored 40.7% when knowing the exact OS, see Table 1.

5.2   Application Discovery Tools

We tested one active tool (Nmap 4.20 [9]) and one passive tool (the passive module of ettercap NG-0.7.3 [4]) for application discovery. Here, we used the ContextApp algorithm considering the set of possible applications for the target as given by the tools.

5.2.1   Precision

The ContextApp algorithm did not make any classification mistakes when knowing the exact target configuration, see Table 1. Thus, any mistake reported by the AppD tools is the result of a wrong application guess. Surprisingly, both tools have a precision close to 100%. However, application information can only identify noncritical alarms on 12 BIDs. Moreover, out of those 12 BIDs only 7 have successful attacks. Thus, only for those 7 can a precision decrease occur. We believe that on a larger dataset, application discovery tools would have a significantly lower precision. Our intuition is supported by the fact that for 3 BIDs Nmap is "better" (classifies more non-relevant positives as NC) than when we know the exact application. This means that Nmap guessed wrong, but it turned out that the guessed application is not vulnerable (while the actual one is vulnerable). Luckily for Nmap, the attack failed for some other reasons (e.g., the attack requires the application to run as root and this was not the case) where it guessed wrong. One would normally expect to see a decrease in precision for those BIDs, but none of them has a single successful attack.

5.2.2   Recall

Both tools performed well, as shown by the recall of Table 3. The fact that Nmap (27.1%) has a better recall than when we know the exact target application (22.9%) is explained by the observation that some failed attack attempts were luckily classified as NC due to a wrong guess from Nmap, see discussion in Section 5.2.1 above.

Table 3. Precision/Recall Summary for AppD Tools (ContextApp algorithm)

AppD Tools	Precision	Recall
ettercap	99.8%	18.9%
Nmap*	99.8%	27.1%

*Active tool

6   Discussion

The experiment could be conducted on another dataset provided that it is properly documented. Unfortunately, we are not aware of other adequate datasets.

One limitation of using target configuration information to identify noncritical alarms lies in the possibility that an intruder could manipulate the context gathering system to enhance his chances of evading detection. If the intruder can fool the context gathering system into thinking that a specific Windows machine is running Linux (e.g., by injecting carefully crafted packets into the network), then successful attacks against that machine might be classified as NC. However, this requires substantial work from the intruder. Designing context gathering systems specifically tailored for intrusion detection could help prevent this kind of evasion.

Existing attempts towards evaluating contextual approaches for intrusion detection include: [3], [5], and [19]. The former presents results in terms of alarm reduction percentages. Thus, it is not clear whether the suppressed alarms were all noncritical (precision) nor whether the remaining alarms were all critical (recall). [5, 19] rely entirely on manual experiments. Consequently, they were not performed on a large scale and are hard to reproduce.

7   Conclusion and Future Work

Results of Section 4.2 indicate that target configuration information is relevant for IDS context. We also conclude that operating system and application are complementary pieces of information since we get better results when combining them (73% instead of 41% and 23%). However, the results of Section 5.1 demonstrate that existing operating discovery tools are not adequate for IDS context gathering; achieving only 1/3 of their potential.

We are currently working to measure the effectiveness of the other contextual approaches (see Section 2), e.g., using Nessus to obtain vulnerability assessments.

When comparing different contextual approaches, their accuracy is indeed an important criterion, but not the only one. There is also the cost of gathering the information (e.g., number of packet sent). Further work in this direction is needed to establish a list of criteria on which to compare different approaches.

We are also working on a new approach to operating system discovery designed especially for IDS context gathering, see [1]. We expect that it will fill most of the gap between the effectiveness of current OSD tools and the potential of OS information to identify noncritical alarms.

References

[1] Gagnon, F., Esfandiari, B., Bertossi, L.: A Hybrid Approach to Operating System Discovery Using Answer Set Programming. In: Proceedings of the 10th IFIP/IEEE Symposium on Integrated Management (IM 2007), pp. 391–400 (2007)

[2] Gagnon, F., Massicotte, F., Esfandiari, B.: On the Effectiveness of Target Configuration as Contextual Information for IDS Alarm Classification. Technical Report SCE-08-08, Department of Systems and Computer Engineering - Carleton University (2008),
http://www.sce.carleton.ca/~fgagnon/Publications/context.pdf

[3] Dayioglu, B., Ozgit, A.: Use of Passive Network Mapping to Enhance Signature Quality of Misuse Network Intrusion Detection Systems. In: Proceedings of the 16th International Symposium on Computer and Information Science, ISCIS 2001 (2001)

[4] Ettercap, http://ettercap.sourceforge.net

[5] Kruegel, C., Robertson, W.: Alert Verification: Determining the Success of Intrusion Attempts. In: Proceedings of the 1st Workshop on Detection of Intrusions and Malware and Vulnerability Assessment, DIMVA 2004 (2004)

[6] Lippmann, R.P., Fried, D.J., Graf, I., Haines, J.W., Kendall, K.R., McClung, D., Weber, D., Webster, S.E., Wyschogrod, D., Cunnigham, R.K., Zissman, M.A.: Evaluating Intrusion Detection Systems: The 1998 DARPA Off-line Intrusion Detection Evaluation. In: Proceedings of the 2000 DARPA Information Survivability Conference and Exposition (DISCEX 2000), vol. 2, pp. 12–26 (2000)

[7] Massicotte, F., Gagnon, F., Couture, M., Labiche, Y., Briand, L.: Automatic Evaluation of Intrusion Detection Systems. In: Proceedings of the 2006 Annual Computer Security Applications Conference (ACSAC 2006) (2006)

[8] McHugh, J.: Testing Intrusion Detection Systems: A critique of the 1998 and 1999 DARPA Intrusion Detection System Evaluation as Performed by Lincoln Laboratory. ACM Transactions on Information and System Security 3(4), 262–294 (2000)

[9] Nmap, http://www.insecure.org/nmap/

[10] p0f, http://lcamtuf.coredump.cx/p0f.shtml

[11] Patton, S., Yurcik, W., Doss, D.: An Achilles' Heel in Signature-Based IDS: Squealing False Positives in SNORT. In: Lee, W., Mé, L., Wespi, A. (eds.) RAID 2001. LNCS, vol. 2212, Springer, Heidelberg (2001)

[12] Security Focus, http://www.securityfocus.org/

[13] SinFP, http://www.gomor.org/cgi-bin/sinfp.pl

[14] Singhal, A.: Modern Information Retrieval: A Brief Overview. Bulletin of the IEEE Computer Society Technical Committee on Data Engineering 24(4), 35–43 (2001)

[15] Siphon, http://siphon.datanerds.net/

[16] Sommer, R., Paxson, V.: Enhancing Byte-Level Network Intrusion Detection Signatures with Context. In: Proceedings of the 10th ACM Conference on Computer and Communications Security (CCS 2003), pp. 262–271 (2003)

[17] Wine, http://www.winehq.org

[18] Xprobe, http://xprobe.sourceforge.net

[19] Zhou, J., Carlson, A., Bishop, M.: Verify Results of Network Intrusion Alerts Using Lightweight Protocol Analysis. In: Proceedings of the 21st Annual Computer Security Applications Conference, ACSAC 2005 (2005)

Browser Fingerprinting from Coarse Traffic Summaries: Techniques and Implications

Ting-Fang Yen[1], Xin Huang[2], Fabian Monrose[2], and Michael K. Reiter[2]

[1] Carnegie Mellon University, Pittsburgh, PA
[2] University of North Carolina, Chapel Hill, NC

Abstract. We demonstrate that the browser implementation used at a host can be passively identified with significant precision and recall, using only coarse summaries of web traffic to and from that host. Our techniques utilize connection records containing only the source and destination addresses and ports, packet and byte counts, and the start and end times of each connection. We additionally provide two applications of browser identification. First, we show how to extend a network intrusion detection system to detect a broader range of malware. Second, we demonstrate the consequences of web browser identification to the deanonymization of web *sites* in flow records that have been anonymized.

Keywords: Application fingerprinting, traffic deanonymization, malware detection, machine learning.

1   Introduction

On many large networks, the most fine-grained representation of network traffic that is feasible to collect is a coarse summary of each network flow or connection, e.g., flow formats as produced by CISCO NetFlow. Such formats typically include only source and destination addresses and ports, flow start and end times, and packet and byte counts. Limiting the data collected to this information can dramatically reduce the reporting bandwidth and storage requirements by orders of magnitude in comparison to full packet capture, and is widely supported today in commodity routers. Additionally, due to privacy concerns, network administrators are generally reluctant to share packet traces containing payload information, and so flow data presents a good compromise between privacy and utility. For these reasons, flow logging for traffic volume estimation is now common practice, and applications of flow logs for network intrusion detection are increasingly being studied[1].

In this paper we examine a novel use of flow logs, namely to infer the application software running on hosts whose traffic is represented in a flow log. We demonstrate this by focusing on a particular software application, namely web browsers, and show that the browser implementation on a host (e.g., Internet

---

[1] For example, the annual FloCon workshop is devoted to this topic (http://www.cert.org/flocon/).

U. Flegel and D. Bruschi (Eds.): DIMVA 2009, LNCS 5587, pp. 157–175, 2009.

Explorer (IE), Firefox, Opera, or Safari) can be determined given its web traffic in flow records, *without* access to payload information. More importantly, our techniques do not rely upon observing web retrievals that are unique to a single browser platform, e.g., Firefox checking for updates at the Firefox update server. We eschew such telltale events both because they tend to be relatively rare (e.g., Opera checks for updates only once per week) and so might not be represented in a flow log under consideration, but also because in the case of anonymized network data, such events may not be evident.

Rather, our techniques infer the browser implementation by applying machine-learning techniques to the behavioral features of the traffic in which it is involved when interacting with regular sites, as observed even in coarse flow records. It is arguably surprising that browser implementations could be discerned in this way, since a browser's network behavior is primarily determined by the content and structure of the pages it accesses. Moreover, classification could be complicated by various factors that are inherent in traffic, including variations in the users' browsing behavior or browser configuration, differences in the web page content being retrieved (both across different websites and in the same website over time), the client hardware configuration, and the different geographic locations from which the content is retrieved.

One of the contributions of this work is to evaluate the impact of the above factors on the classification accuracy of the browser type. We do so on the basis of web traffic induced by the four most popular browsers, as measured in retrievals of the main pages of the top 150 websites on the Internet[2] over the course of two months, and on the basis of web retrievals recorded at the border of the Carnegie Mellon University network. Our results show that even when the training and testing datasets are from different time frames, to different websites, and collected at different geographic locations, we were still able to achieve 75% classification precision and 60% recall (see Section 4).

Our focus of web browsers for this study is partly due to their relative importance among applications today, but is also due to the implications of their identification. A second contribution of our work is the demonstration of these implications, in two contexts. First, because of their widespread use, attacks that exploit vulnerabilities in specific browser implementations have also emerged. In this context, inferring the type of browser from traffic traces is beneficial for network intrusion detection systems that identify hosts infected by platform-dependent malware by observing suspicious traffic from hosts with similar software configurations. We describe an application of this in the TĀMD system [1], which previously classified hosts as similar on the basis of only their operating systems. Our techniques enable TĀMD to incorporate browser similarity into this evaluation.

Second, we demonstrate the consequences of web browser identification to the deanonymization of web *sites* in flow records that have been anonymized. We show that the identification of the web browser in flow records enables the application of per-browser website classifiers to yield a more precise deanonymization

---

[2] According to Alexa, `http://www.alexa.com/`

of the websites represented in the traffic than has previously been achievable from flow records. Specifically, we show that we can deanonymize websites visited by a host using a per-browser classifier with up to a 17% improvement in precision over the case in which we use a similarly trained generic classifier.

To summarize, our contributions include (i) techniques to identify the web browser represented in flow records of web page accesses; (ii) quantification of the impact of various factors on browser classification accuracy; (iii) the application of this technique to improve network intrusion detection systems; and (iv) the application of this technique to more accurately deanonymize the websites represented in anonymized network traffic.

2   Related Work

Many fingerprinting tools are *active* in nature, probing services with carefully crafted queries (e.g., those produced by Nmap and Nessus) to detect implementation-specific characteristics [2,3]. More relevant to our work are *passive* fingerprinting techniques that infer the implementations of network applications or operating systems based solely on observing the traffic they send. Passive fingerprinting tools and techniques are numerous, though most focus on identifying TCP/IP implementations and utilize specific information [4,5,6] that is unavailable in coarse flow records. While passive techniques have more recently been proposed to identify the *application* (e.g., peer-to-peer file transfers versus web retrievals) or the class of application (e.g., interactive sessions versus bulk-data transfers) reflected in packet traces [7,8,9,10,11], few proposals (e.g., [12,13,14,15]) have done so from coarse flow records. Moreover, to the best of our knowledge, none of these proposed techniques attempt to identify particular *implementations* of an application (e.g., the browser) from passive observations of flow records alone.

We explore in this paper the implications of browser identification for the problem of deanonymizing web *sites* in anonymized flow records. Several works have examined the susceptibility of anonymized traffic traces to deanonymization, e.g., [16,17,18]. Similar to our work, these approaches re-identify hosts or websites on the basis of their behaviors as exhibited in the anonymized traffic traces. However, none of these earlier works have taken into consideration the fact that on-the-wire behaviors are influenced by the particular implementation of their protocol peers. As we show later, first classifying the browser involved in a web retrieval can improve the fidelity with which one can deanonymize websites present in anonymized network flows.

We also demonstrate how reliable identification of the browser can be used to detect platform-dependent malware by identifying suspicious traffic coming from hosts with similar software configurations [1]. Like TĀMD, other network intrusion-detection systems employ fingerprints of host software platforms when detecting intrusions, though most generate these fingerprints actively (e.g., [19]). As far as we are aware, none do so passively on the basis of coarse flow information, however, and so our techniques might enhance a range of network intrusion-detection systems when flow information is all that is available.

3   Data Sets

The empirical analysis in this paper takes advantage of several sources of data recorded in the Argus (Audit Record Generation and Utilization System [20]) flow format. Argus is a real time flow monitor based on the RTFM flow model [21,22]. Argus inspects each packet and groups together those with the same attribute values into one bi-directional record. In particular, TCP flows are identified by the 5-tuple (source IP address, destination IP address, source port, destination port, protocol)[3], and packets in both directions are summarized into a single Argus flow record. The browser fingerprinting techniques we propose in this paper require only that each flow record include the source and destination IP addresses and ports, the protocol, and the total bytes and packets sent in each direction. In our data collection, however, we extend this basic flow record format with additional information — notably, the first 64 bytes of payload on the connection, and time-to-live (TTL) values in IP packet headers — for the sole purpose of determining ground truth of certain attributes to use in our evaluation. To be clear, this additional information is not used by our classifiers, and is only taken into consideration when determining the accuracy of our techniques and for extracting testing instances from live network data.

We use the following data sources in our evaluations:

The CMU dataset. This dataset consists of anonymized traffic from the edge routers of the wired CMU campus network, which includes one /16 subnet. We do not consider hosts (that is, IP addresses) from the wireless network, since those hosts typically have short-lived DHCP-assigned IP addresses, such that hosts using different browsers may be associated with the same address, leading to inconsistencies in the data. The rate of the traffic in the CMU dataset is about 5000 flow records per second, and was collected over six weeks from October to December 2007. We are interested in reducing this dataset only to web retrievals for the purposes of this paper, but one of the challenges in processing live network data is in accurately identifying the boundaries that separate website retrievals (c.f., [18,23]). In this work, we leverage the first 64 bytes of each flow to identify the start boundary of a website retrieval from a host internal to the CMU network. More specifically, we define a web retrieval to begin with a port-80 connection comprised of an HTTP request of the form "GET / ", as such a connection would be highly unlikely to be part of another retrieval. The web retrieval is then comprised of this flow and all subsequent flows originating from the same host in the next 10 seconds. Our choice of 10 seconds is based on empirical evaluations. The use of the flow payload for parsing web retrievals can be replaced, for example, by checking for a certain amount of idle time before a burst of web traffic [16], though we do not explore this alternative here. Incomplete retrievals, or those with less than three flows, do not carry enough information about the browser implementation in order for the

---

[3] Since Argus records are bi-directional, the source and destination IP addresses are swappable in the logic that matches packets to flows. However, the source IP address in the record is set to the IP address of the host that initiated the connection.

classifier to make a well-grounded decision, and so we only consider retrievals with more than three flows in our analysis.

As mentioned earlier, we examine the 64 bytes of available payload in each flow to infer the browser involved in the retrieval. Specifically, for the purposes of ground-truth, a host is identified to be using the Opera browser if the user-agent string in its HTTP request starts with the string "Opera". Firefox hosts are identified by the special "safe-browsing" requests issued by the browser to check the validity of the website being contacted (https://wiki.mozilla.org/Phishing_Protection). Due to the 64-byte restriction in the available payload length, we were not able to reliably identify hosts using IE and Safari in the CMU data set.

The PlanetLab-Native dataset. In order to perform our evaluations in which the CMU dataset serves as the testing data, we would like a training dataset from hosts that are diverse in terms of geography and hardware platform. Planet-Lab [24] offers a platform that is generally available and that enables the retrieval of web pages from a wide range of hosts with different hardware configurations and geographic locations. To collect this dataset, we deployed a program to fourteen hosts across five PlanetLab networks; this program sequentially retrieved the front page (i.e., generating "GET / " HTTP requests) of the top 150 most popular websites in the U.S. (according to Alexa) repeatedly over the course of one month. Each web retrieval was comprised of the flows observed in the thirty seconds since the start of the retrieval. Machines on PlanetLab are required to run a Linux operating system, so we performed retrievals from Linux-compatible browsers, namely Firefox and Opera[4]. Recall that these two browsers are also the only ones reliably identifiable in the CMU dataset, and so the PlanetLab-Native dataset can serve well as training data for testing with the CMU dataset.

The PlanetLab-QEMU dataset. In an effort to develop a dataset that includes traffic for all of the major browsers (IE, Firefox, Opera and Safari), we utilized a processor emulator, QEMU [25], to run an emulated Windows operating system on PlanetLab hosts. As in the PlanetLab-Native dataset, we ran an automated program to sequentially retrieve the front page of the top 150 most popular websites repeatedly over the course of one month. Each web retrieval was comprised of the flows observed in the thirty seconds since the start of the retrieval. We deployed this emulated version of Windows on seven hosts across three PlanetLab networks[5].

Arguably, the PlanetLab datasets may not accurately represent website retrievals generated by actual user activities, where frequent visits to a particular website may result in much of the content being cached. To compensate for this effect, we set the browser cache sizes to be sufficiently large (400MB) so that objects would not be evicted from cache.

---

[4] To generate our PlanetLab-Native dataset, we used Firefox 2.0.0.16 and Opera 9.51.

[5] To generate our PlanetLab-QEMU dataset, we used IE 7.0, Firefox 2.0.0.13, Opera 9.51 and Safari 3.1.

Feature Selection

To capture browser-specific characteristics in network traffic, we extracted nine main features from each website retrieval, listed in Table 1. The mean, standard deviation, maximum, minimum, median, first and third quartile, inter-quartile range, and the cumulative sum, are also calculated for each flow statistic. Our feature selection strategy is based on examining the information gain associated with each of the statistics for the aforementioned nine main features. More specifically, using the PlanetLab-Native dataset, we select the top statistics whose cumulative information gain accounts for at least 90% of the overall information gain. These selected statistics are combined into a feature vector F_r for website retrieval r. Among the most important features are those associated with the byte and packet counts in each direction, the cumulative flow duration, and the retrieval duration. While we have not fully explored the root cause for all of these differences, they are related to the different orders in which the browsers retrieve objects on a given page, different numbers of objects retrieved in one connection, and the numbers of connections that can be active simultaneously. Of course, while these features play an important role in distinguishing different browser implementations in our tests, we acknowledge that they may not be optimal for distinguishing browsers not included in the training data, or future browser versions that behave fundamentally differently from the ones covered in this study. That said, the methodology outlined in this paper can be easily applied to incorporate new browser types into the classifier.

Table 1. Main features extracted for each retrieval

Flow Statistics	Byte count (in each direction)
	Packet count (in each direction)
	Flow duration
	Number of flows active simultaneously to this one
	Start time minus most closely preceding flow start time
Retrieval Statistics	Total number of flows
	Cumulative byte count from destination
	Cumulative flow duration
	Retrieval duration

4   Browser Identification from Flow Records

As discussed in Section 1, our first goal is to develop techniques for inferring the browser implementation that is participating in recorded flows that represent web retrievals from that browser. At first, it might seem that distinguishing the browser should be difficult, since a browser primarily serves to interpret and render the HTML and other types of content it receives. As such, its behavior should be primarily dictated by the content it is accessing.

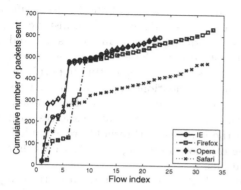
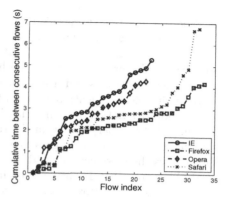

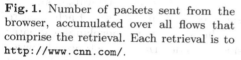

Fig. 1. Number of packets sent from the browser, accumulated over all flows that comprise the retrieval. Each retrieval is to http://www.cnn.com/.

Fig. 2. Cumulative time between consecutive flows that comprise the retrieval. Each retrieval is to http://www.cnn.com/.

An example of why this intuition might not be true is shown in Figure 1, which shows just one feature (see Table 1) for the four most popular browsers (IE, Firefox, Opera, and Safari) when each retrieved http://www.cnn.com/ at nearly the same time and from a host in the University of North Carolina campus network. The feature pictured is the number of packets sent from the browser, accumulated over all flows that comprise the retrieval. It is evident that in these retrievals, Firefox initiates more flows than the other browsers, Opera sends more packets in earlier flows, and Safari sends fewer packets overall. Figure 2 shows the start time of each flow minus the most closely preceding flow start time, accumulated over all flows in the retrieval. This feature clearly shows that certain browsers (e.g., Firefox) try to improve response time by multiplexing the retrieval of content across substantially more flows than other browsers.

However, using these differences to reliably determine the browser from flow records is not as straightforward as it may seem, and in particular is not as easy to automate as Figures 1–2 might suggest. Aside from the content and structure of the websites, users' browsing behavior, browser configuration, geographic location, and the client hardware configuration can also affect browser network behavior. As such, in the remainder of this section we test with what precision and recall an automatic classifier can distinguish among browsers in different scenarios.

More specifically, the classifier type that we utilize is Support Vector Machines (SVM)[6], which have been widely applied to many supervised learning problems [27,28]. Given two sets of labeled data, the SVM finds a hyperplane that separates the data and maximizes the distance to each data set. When multiple classes are involved, the SVM generates a group of pair-wise binary

---

[6] We utilize the SVM implementation included in the Weka machine learning package [26].

classifiers. Each binary classifier gives a vote to a class, and the final classification is the class with the highest vote. Loosely speaking, since an instance is classified depending on which side of the separating hyperplane it lies on, and not necessarily on how far from the hyperplane it is, there can be cases where an instance is misclassified if it is located "close" to the separating hyperplane.

To aid in our classification, we modify the aforementioned application of SVMs to incorporate a notion of "confidence". The confidence threshold is the minimum distance of the hyperplane from the testing instance, where only instances with distance to the hyperplane greater than the confidence threshold are classified. This allows the classifier to avoid making decisions in ambiguous situations that would likely result in incorrect classifications.

The general structure of each test described below is that we first train a browser classifier on one dataset and then classify each retrieval in another dataset to obtain a guess of the browser used in that retrieval. Each website retrieval is classified only if its distance to the separating hyperplanes is greater than the confidence threshold. The classifier then determines the type of browser used by host h to be the browser classified most often in h's retrievals. To avoid errors due to a host having a small number of retrievals, we only consider hosts with more than thirty classified retrievals in our analysis. Our choice of thirty retrievals was determined empirically, and provides a good balance between precision and the number of hosts classified from the dataset.

We denote the classification for host h to be browserguess(h), and the actual browser used by host h to be browser(h). Note that browser(h) $= \perp$ if the actual browser for h could not be determined, which occurred in the CMU dataset in some cases; see Section 3. Also, browserguess(h) $= \perp$ can result if the classifier makes no classification for h, since no overwhelming choice arises for h's retrievals. The precision and recall across all hosts in the test dataset is defined as follows:

$$\text{Precision} = \Pr[\text{browser}(h) = b \mid \text{browserguess}(h) = b \neq \perp]$$
$$= \frac{|\{h : \text{browserguess}(h) = \text{browser}(h)\}|}{|\{h : \text{browserguess}(h) \neq \perp\}|}$$
$$\text{Recall} = \Pr[\text{browserguess}(h) = b \mid \text{browser}(h) = b \neq \perp]$$
$$= \frac{|\{h : \text{browserguess}(h) = \text{browser}(h)\}|}{|\{h : \text{browser}(h) \neq \perp\}|}$$

Keep in mind that a classifier that makes random guesses, i.e., classifying each host as a particular browser with $\frac{1}{n}$ probability, where n is the number of browsers, and a network where the browsers are distributed evenly among the hosts, the precision can only be expected to be $\frac{1}{n^2}$.

4.1   Tests on PlanetLab-QEMU Dataset

In an ideal web browsing scenario, only one website retrieval is taking place at any time, such that boundaries between consecutive retrievals are clearly delineated, and each webpage is allowed to fully download before the next one. While this idealistic scenario will be compounded by many other issues in practice, we argue that tests in a controlled environment are valuable in that they enable us to better understand what factors influence classification the most.

We evaluate the results of browser identification under this setting using the PlanetLab-QEMU dataset. To simulate multiple hosts, each running a specific browser implementation, data from each host is separated by the browser that generated the traffic. This traffic pertaining to a specific browser from one host serves as testing data, while the classifier is trained on traffic from all other hosts, for each experiment. Since in some applications it will not be possible to obtain retrievals from every website that may be present in the testing data, we set the training data to be traffic from the top 100 websites, and use traffic from the remaining 50 websites (from top 100 to 150) for testing.

The precision and recall are shown in Figure 3, for confidence thresholds set to one of {0.35, 0.65, 0.95, 1.15, 1.30, 1.50}. The rise in precision is likely due to incorrect classifications being filtered out as a result of the increase in confidence threshold, to the point that most of a host's classified retrievals are then correct. On the other hand, recall decreases with the confidence since more hosts are unclassified (i.e., $\{h : \mathsf{browserguess}(h) = \perp\}$). In all cases the correct browser can be identified with at least 71% precision and recall, and the precision grows to 100% with recall at 43% as the confidence threshold is increased. These results show that browser implementations exhibit different traffic behaviors that can be accurately identified even in coarse flow records.

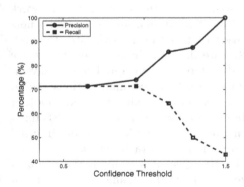

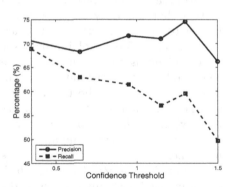

Fig. 3. Precision and recall for browser classification on the PlanetLab-QEMU dataset

Fig. 4. Precision and recall for browser classification on the CMU dataset (Train: PlanetLab-Native, Test: CMU)

4.2   Tests on CMU Dataset

Unlike the controlled setting of the PlanetLab experiments, the CMU dataset provides a setting for evaluating our techniques on traffic recorded in the real world. That said, we remind the reader that for purposes of ground truth, we could only reliably identify hosts using Firefox and Opera in the CMU dataset, and consequently, our analysis here is restricted to these cases. Out of those hosts, the vast majority of them used Firefox, and to not bias our results to that of a single-browser evaluation, we randomly select Firefox hosts in the CMU dataset but ensure that we have an equal number of Firefox and Opera hosts. The PlanetLab-Native dataset is used in this case for training a browser classifier.

Figure 4 shows the precision and recall for the CMU dataset, for confidence thresholds set to one of {0.35, 0.65, 0.95, 1.15, 1.30, 1.50}. The precision generally increases slightly with the confidence threshold, as instances that were incorrectly classified are now filtered out (because they were too close to the separating hyperplane), while recall decreases as a higher threshold leads to more unclassified instances (i.e., $\{h : \mathsf{browserguess}(h) = \bot\}$). As the confidence threshold increases, some hosts whose majority of retrievals were correctly classified now have those correct classifications filtered out, so that these hosts are left with more misclassified retrievals that cause the browser to be identified incorrectly; this results in a decrease in precision at the end of the curve. The peak in precision is 74.56%, when the confidence threshold is 1.30. We note that in this test (where the number of Firefox and Opera hosts are balanced) our precision is substantially greater than that of random guessing (i.e., 25%).

5   Applications to Network Intrusion Detection

TĀMD (Traffic Aggregation for Malware Detection) [1] is an intrusion detection system that passively observes traffic passing through an enterprise network border to identify internal hosts infected by stealthy malware, such as botnets and spyware. TĀMD exploits the observation that, however subtle, stealthy malware still needs to communicate to exfiltrate data to the attacker, to receive commands, or to carry out the commands. Moreover, since malware rarely infiltrates only a single host in a large enterprise, these communications should emerge from multiple hosts within coarse temporal proximity to one another (e.g., within an hour of one another). Based on these observations, TĀMD functions by finding new communication "aggregates" involving multiple internal hosts, i.e., communication flows that share common characteristics.

One of the characteristics on which TĀMD aggregates traffic is the *platform* of the internal hosts involved in sending or receiving that traffic, which is useful for identifying platform-dependent malware infections. That is, suspicious traffic common to a collection of hosts becomes even more suspicious if the hosts share a common software platform. Previously, forming platform aggregates in TĀMD was based solely on the hosts' operating systems. As such, malware that is application-dependent, such as malware that exploits Firefox only[7], might span multiple aggregates formed by O/S fingerprinting alone (if the exploit works on

---

[7] Examples of such application-dependent malware are the `Infostealer.Snifula` trojan that exploits Mozilla Firefox, the `MSIL.Yakizake` worm that exploits Mozilla Thunderbird, the `Imspam` trojan that sends spam through MSN or AOL Messenger, among others.

Malware traces [1]	Homogeneity threshold		
	70%	80%	90%
Bagle	0.25 (±4.95)	0.09 (±3.05)	0.09 (±3.05)
IRCbot	0.05 (±2.18)	0.01 (±0.99)	0.01 (±0.99)
Mybot	0.03 (±1.39)	0.00 (±0.00)	0.00 (±0.00)
SDbot	0.06 (±1.94)	0.00 (±0.00)	0.00 (±0.00)
Spybot	0.02 (±1.40)	0.00 (±0.00)	0.00 (±0.00)
HTTP bot	0.03 (±1.39)	0.00 (±0.00)	0.00 (±0.00)
Large IRC bot	0.19 (±3.05)	0.06 (±2.19)	0.06 (±2.19)

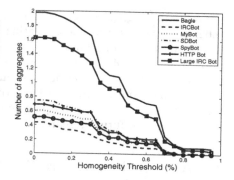

Fig. 5. Average number of aggregates per hour (± standard deviation) due to browser similarity, in addition to the identified malware cluster and to O/S aggregates. For descriptions of the malware, please refer to [1].

multiple operating systems) or might represent a small subset of an O/S aggregate (e.g., all Windows machines). In either case, the mismatch between the software fingerprinted (the O/S) and the software exploited (the browser) can cause platform aggregation to fail to detect an exploit.

Here we consider the impact of reliable *browser* fingerprinting on TĀMD. Specifically, we modified its platform aggregation function so that a platform aggregate is identified when the largest fraction of hosts sharing the same O/S *or* the same web browser is above a given threshold. In doing so, we are able to detect both platform-dependent and browser-dependent malware, while incurring only slight overhead.

To quantify this overhead, we followed the same experiments that were performed in that earlier work [1], which involved seven types of O/S-specific (but not browser-specific) malware. Briefly, the experiment consisted of overlaying recordings of malware traffic onto the CMU dataset, which was done by assigning malware traffic to originate from randomly selected internal hosts. More specifically, we assigned malware traffic to random internal hosts running the O/S that the malware exploits, as determined by the time-to-live (TTL) field in packets.

This combined data, consisting of the CMU dataset overlaid with malware traffic, is then given to TĀMD — configured to identify common host platforms based on their O/S or browsers, but otherwise configured identically as in [1] — in hourly batches, where the goal is to identify the single aggregate consisting of the malware traffic. The same experiment is repeated for each hour over three weeks in November and December 2007, for each of the seven different malware.

Figure 5 shows the number of browser aggregates, in addition to the malware aggregate and other O/S aggregates, that is identified by this new version of TĀMD that incorporates our browser classifier from Section 4, for different thresholds on the homogeneity of the platform aggregate, for each malware experiment. When the threshold is set to 90% (as it was for the original O/S-based platform aggregation in [1]), meaning that at least 90% of the hosts in the aggregate are required to share a common browser (which cannot be ⊥), the number of additional aggregates reported due to browser similarity on average per hour is 0.0229. This shows that incorporating browser fingerprinting into TĀMD induces a limited amount of additional cost, while giving TĀMD the ability to detect a wider range of malware, i.e., browser-dependent malware.

Other intrusion detection systems that operate on flow records (e.g., [29,30,31,32]) and approaches for profiling network traffic (e.g., [7,33,34]), can also potentially benefit from passive application fingerprinting. We plan to investigate this in future research.

6   Applications to Traffic Deanonymization

Website deanonymization techniques attempt to infer the actual web *sites* contacted in anonymized traffic traces, without examining the contents of the communication. In order to retain the utility of these datasets for networking research, IP addresses are typically anonymized in a consistent fashion, i.e., so that the same real IP address is mapped consistently to the same pseudonym in the anonymized dataset. This enables the behaviors of the anonymous web servers to be examined, however, which can sometimes lead to their deanonymization. As a trivial example, the larger number of bytes typically transmitted from the main page of cnn.com would enable it to be differentiated from google.com. Moreover, since a page retrieval can involve connections to multiple physical servers (e.g., image servers or content distribution networks), Coull et al. [18] also found that the sequential order of the servers contacted to retrieve objects on a webpage can enable websites to be differentiated. While previous works placed emphasis on observing traffic behaviors of the websites, to our knowledge, no study has accounted for this behavior as influenced by the particular implementation of their protocol peers, i.e., the browser. In what follows, we show that classifying the browser first can yield a more precise deanonymization of websites.

6.1   Feature Selection

As described in Section 3, we extract nine main flow features from each web page retrieval. While previously these features were calculated over all flows in a retrieval, in the case of website classification, we calculate these features for all flows *per physical server*, for each of the first five servers contacted. The features are then arranged according to the order that the server was contacted, i.e., for retrieval r, the feature vector is $\{F_{r1}, ..., F_{r5}\}$, where F_{rj} refers to the features derived from the flows to physical server j, for website retrieval r. Breaking down the retrieval features by physical server provides a finer-grained representation of the retrieval and an order to the physical servers, both of which have been utilized in previous website deanonymization efforts (e.g., [18]). Furthermore, to eliminate redundancies and reduce dimensionality, we selected a subset of those features that are most consistent across datasets, specifically by computing the correlation of each feature from one day of retrievals to http://www.cnn.com/ in the PlanetLab-Native dataset to one day of such retrievals in the CMU dataset.

This yielded nine features: the byte and packet counts to/from the first server contacted, and the number of flows to each of the first five servers contacted.

We focus on deanonymizing those websites that are "stable", as judged by their standard deviation for the total number of flows, bytes, and packets, and also those websites that are complex enough, as judged by the total number of flows. It has been previously established [18] that websites with a high variability in their contents (e.g., espn.com) or those that are too simple (e.g., google.com, orkut.com) will typically not be identified accurately. Specifically, we determine a website as "stable" if the average number of flows from the first five servers contacted is greater than one, and the byte and packet counts to/from the first server has a small standard deviation, i.e., within twice the average value. In this way, we narrow down the list of websites that we will attempt to deanonymize in traffic traces to the front pages of 52 of the top 100 websites according to alexa.com.

6.2 Website Classifier

We build our website classifiers using Bayesian belief networks, which have been shown to yield good results [18]. Given a test instance, the classifier outputs a probability for each class, which is the likelihood of the instance belonging to that class, according to the model built from training data. The class with the highest probability is taken as the classification of the test instance. This may not always yield optimal classification, for example, in cases where the probabilities for several classes are close to each other, or when all of the probabilities are small.

To establish some notion of "confidence" on the classification, one way is to let the classifier make a decision only from classes with probabilities greater than a cutoff value, and only when there exist probabilities above the cutoff. Although this has limited impact when multiple classes have similar probabilities, it allows the classifier to provide answers based on more confident results, avoiding cases where uncertainty (small probabilities) are likely to cause incorrect classifications. The higher the cutoff parameter, the higher the probability of the test instance belonging to its class must be.

For the PlanetLab-QEMU dataset, we group the data by the browser that generated the traffic, as well as a combined group with traffic from all four browsers. This allows us to build four per-browser website classifiers (IE, Firefox, Opera, Safari), and one generic website classifier. The former are trained on traffic from a single browser type, while the latter is trained on combined browser traffic. In the following, we quantify the benefits of first classifying the browser in website deanonymization by applying these two types of classifier models separately and comparing their results. When testing with the CMU dataset, the browser type for each host is determined by our browser classifier developed in Section 4, using a confidence threshold set at 1.30. The per-browser website classifier is then applied to a website retrieval based on the browser determined for the host that performed the retrieval.

For each testing instance, i.e., each website retrieval, the classifier returns the class with the highest probability above the cutoff. If no probability larger than the cutoff exists, the instance is unclassified. Let the classification for retrieval r be websiteguess(r), and its actual website be website(r), where website$(r) = \perp$ if the ground-truth website for retrieval r cannot be determined in the dataset (which only happens in the case of the CMU dataset). Then, the precision and recall are

$$\text{Precision} = \Pr[\text{website}(r) = s \mid \text{websiteguess}(r) = s \neq \perp]$$
$$= \frac{|\{r : \text{websiteguess}(r) = \text{website}(r)\}|}{|\{r : \text{websiteguess}(r) \neq \perp\}|}$$
$$\text{Recall} = \Pr[\text{websiteguess}(r) = s \mid \text{website}(r) = s \neq \perp]$$
$$= \frac{|\{r : \text{websiteguess}(r) = \text{website}(r)\}|}{|\{r : \text{website}(r) \neq \perp\}|}$$

In the following tests, we only report results for cutoff values where the classifier is able to make at least thirty classifications. This is to avoid cases where not enough classifications can be made for the results to be representative.

6.3   Tests on PlanetLab-QEMU Dataset

Similar to the experiments described in Section 4.1, we first evaluate the results of website deanonymization under an ideal setting using the PlanetLab-QEMU dataset. In each experiment, the testing data consists of retrievals from one host, while the training data is from all other hosts. We apply each per-browser website classifier to retrievals determined to have been performed with that browser by our classifier in Section 4, to generate the per-browser results. We generate results for the generic website classifier by applying that classifier to all retrievals. Our tests are "closed-world", in the sense that only retrievals of the 52 selected websites (see Section 6.1) are tested.

Figure 6 and 7 show the precision and recall from the per-browser and generic website classifiers. Cutoff values range from 0.01 to 0.99, in steps of 0.01. The precision increases with the cutoff, but the recall decreases since some instances are not classified at higher cutoff values. The drops in precision are due to cases where correct classifications that do not have a high probability are filtered out by the cutoff value. The generic classifier was not able to classify more than thirty retrievals after the cutoff reaches 0.78, so we do not plot its results for cutoff values greater than 0.78. To present an alternate view depicting our overall accuracy, let Precision(c) and Recall(c) be the precision and recall, respectively, when the cutoff is set to be c. We then define the precision "integral", over the range $[c_{\min}, c_{\max}]$, to be

$$\sum_{c=c_{\min}}^{c_{\max}} \text{Precision}(c)$$

and we define the recall "integral" similarly. $c_{\min}$ and $c_{\max}$ are defined as the endpoints of the range where both the per-browser and generic classifiers were

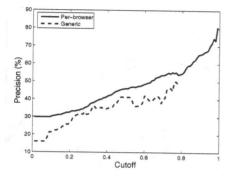 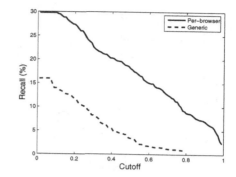

Fig. 6. Website classification precision on the PlanetLab-QEMU dataset

Fig. 7. Website classification recall on the PlanetLab-QEMU dataset

able to make enough classifications. The integral is a measure of how the classifier performs across different cutoff values, in that larger integrals show higher precision (or recall) overall. The integral of precision and recall over $[0.01, 0.78]$, in steps of 0.01, are shown in Table 2, with the generic case serving as baseline. The maximum difference in precision for per-browser and generic classifiers is 15.61%. While website deanonymization remains a challenging problem in practice, we note that the improvement in recall between per-browser and generic classifiers remains significant, across all cutoff values, where the average difference is 14.01% and the maximum difference is 16.11%.

Table 2. Comparing the precision and recall integrals on website classification on the PlanetLab-QEMU dataset

Classifier	Precision	Recall
Generic	26.16	5.34
Per-browser	+6.01	+10.93

6.4   Tests on CMU Dataset

To evaluate the impact of first classifying the browser on website deanonymization in a more realistic setting, we turn to the CMU dataset, with the PlanetLab-Native dataset serving as training data. Since the IP addresses are anonymized in the CMU data, we have no direct knowledge of the websites contacted. So, to build ground truth for the classification, we examined information available in the first 64 bytes of each flow payload. Specifically, the "Host" field in HTTP requests are extracted to identify the domain name of the websites. Of the 52 websites targeted for identification, we found only 23 in the CMU dataset in this way, and so used only these retrievals for testing (while the training data still

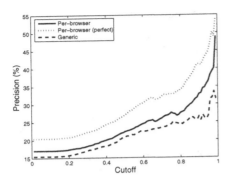
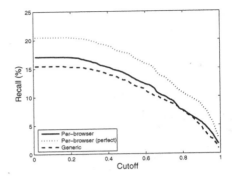

Fig. 8. Website classification precision on the CMU dataset (Train: PlanetLab-Native, Test: CMU)

Fig. 9. Website classification recall on the CMU dataset (Train: PlanetLab-Native, Test: CMU)

Table 3. The integral of precision and recall on website classification in the CMU dataset (Train: PlanetLab-Native, Test: CMU)

Classifier	Precision	Recall
Generic	20.53	11.30
Per-browser	+2.73	+1.07
Per-browser (perfect)	+7.93	+4.38

consists of traffic to the 52 websites). Only retrievals from hosts whose ground-truth browser type could be determined were used (see Section 4).

For each retrieval to one of the chosen 52 websites (see Section 6.1) in the CMU dataset from a Firefox or Opera browser, we classify it using both the appropriate per-browser classifier (i.e., for the browser identified using the classifier of Section 4) and the generic website classifier, built using the PlanetLab-Native dataset. The results are shown in Figures 8 and 9, for the two cases when (i) our browser classifier from Section 4 is applied first, and (ii) when we assume perfect browser classification, i.e., the per-browser website classifier applied to a website retrieval is based on the actual browser that performed that retrieval, as opposed to the browser determined by our classifier. When our browser classifier is applied, the difference in precision between the per-browser and generic classifiers can reach close to 17% at high cutoff values. Table 3 shows the integral of precision and recall over cutoff values from 0.01 to 0.99, in steps of 0.01. The results in Figures 8 and 9 are calculated across all 52 websites.

However, for an attacker who is only interested in deanonymizing certain websites, such as those listed in Table 4, a classifier that is able to classify those websites well would be more useful than a general website classifier. For example, the per-browser classifier has a 84.62% precision for `dailymotion.com`, a 27.57% improvement to the generic classifier. These results point out that in live network

Table 4. The precision and recall for the per-browser classifier on some of the websites in the CMU dataset, when our browser classifier from Section 4 is applied first (Train: PlanetLab-Native, Test: CMU)

Website	Precision (%)		Recall (%)	
	Per-browser	Generic	Per-browser	Generic
adobe.com	17.59	0.00	9.55	0.00
aol.com	9.15	8.03	5.67	4.73
dailymotion.com	84.62	57.05	50.00	44.95
myspace.com	19.32	18.57	12.40	11.65
nytimes.com	21.15	16.26	12.26	9.13
wordpress.com	13.98	0.00	7.15	0.00
yahoo.com	45.52	29.60	29.81	19.78

traffic, classifying the browser first can bring a non-trivial advantage to website deanonymization.

7 Conclusion

In this paper we have explored the passive identification of browser implementations from coarse flow records. We have shown that browser implementations can be identified with substantial precision and recall, even using flow records from real traffic recorded at a different time and on a different network from the traffic used to train the classifier.

We have also demonstrated two applications of browser fingerprinting. In the first, we demonstrated how browser identification can be used to improve a network intrusion-detection system called TĀMD, by permitting the intrusion-detection system to identify aggregates of hosts on the network that share the same browser. Suspicious traffic is even more suspect when coming from such an aggregate, since this may indicate that these hosts have succumbed to a browser-specific exploit. Our browser fingerprinting techniques would enable TĀMD to detect more types of malware, i.e., those that are browser-dependent, while incurring slight overhead.

The second application of browser fingerprinting that we explored is deanonymization of network traffic. Our techniques assume that the traffic is anonymized using consistent pseudonyms, which is a common practice today; this enables traffic trace deanonymization by examining the trace for the retrieval characteristics of websites of interest. We demonstrated that improvements in deanonymizing retrieved websites can be achieved by first classifying the browser in use.

References

1. Yen, T.-F., Reiter, M.K.: Traffic aggregation for malware detection. In: Zamboni, D. (ed.) DIMVA 2008. LNCS, vol. 5137, pp. 207–227. Springer, Heidelberg (2008)
2. Comer, D.E., Lin, J.C.: Probing TCP implementations. In: Proceedings of the USENIX Summer 1994 Technical Conference (June 1994)

3. Padhye, J., Floyd, S.: On inferring TCP behavior. In: Proceedings of ACM SIG-COMM, August 2001, pp. 287–298 (2001)
4. Paxson, V.: Automated packet trace analysis of TCP implementations. In: Proceedings of ACM SIGCOMM, pp. 167–179 (1997)
5. Lippmann, R., Fried, D., Piwowarski, K., Streilein, W.: Passive operating system identification from TCP/IP packet headers. In: Proceedings of the ICDM Workshop on Data Mining for Computer Security (2003)
6. Beverly, R.: A robust classifier for passive TCP/IP fingerprinting. In: Barakat, C., Pratt, I. (eds.) PAM 2004. LNCS, vol. 3015, pp. 158–167. Springer, Heidelberg (2004)
7. Karagiannis, T., Papagiannaki, K., Faloutsos, M.: BLINC: multilevel traffic classification in the dark. In: Proceedings of ACM SIGCOMM, August 2005, pp. 229–240 (2005)
8. Bernaille, L., Teixeira, R., Akodkenou, I., Soule, A., Salamatian, K.: Traffic classification on the fly. ACM SIGCOMM Computer Communication Review 36(2), 23–26 (2006)
9. Hernandez-Campos, F., Nobel, A.B., Smith, F.D., Jeffay, K.: Understanding patterns of TCP connection usage with statistical clustering. In: Proceedings of 13th Symposium on Modeling, Analysis, and Simulation of Computer and Telecommunication Systems, September 2005, pp. 35–44 (2005)
10. Roughan, M., Sen, S., Spatscheck, O., Duffield, N.: Class-of-service mapping for QoS: A statistical signature-based approach to IP traffic classification. In: Proceedings of the 4th ACM SIGCOMM conference on Internet measurement, October 2004, pp. 135–148 (2004)
11. Crotti, M., Dusi, M., Gringoli, F., Salgarelli, L.: Traffic classification through simple statistical fingerprinting. ACM SIGCOMM Computer Communication Review 37(1) (2007)
12. Collins, M.P., Reiter, M.K.: Finding peer-to-peer file-sharing using coarse network behaviors. In: Gollmann, D., Meier, J., Sabelfeld, A. (eds.) ESORICS 2006. LNCS, vol. 4189, pp. 1–17. Springer, Heidelberg (2006)
13. Zander, S., Nguyen, T., Armitage, G.: Automated traffic classification and application identification using machine learning. In: Proceedings of the 2005 IEEE Conference on Local Computer Networks (2005)
14. Moore, A.W., Papagiannaki, K.: Toward the accurate identification of network applications. In: Dovrolis, C. (ed.) PAM 2005. LNCS, vol. 3431, pp. 41–54. Springer, Heidelberg (2005)
15. Erman, J., Mahanti, A., Arlitt, M., Williamson, C.: Identifying and discriminating between web and peer-to-peer traffic in the network core. In: Proceedings of the 16th International World Wide Web Conference (May 2007)
16. Koukis, D., Antonatos, S., Anagnostakis, K.: On the privacy risks of publishing anonymized IP network traces. In: Proceedings of Communications and Multimedia Security, October 2006, pp. 22–32 (2006)
17. Coull, S.E., Wright, C.V., Monrose, F., Collins, M.P., Reiter, M.K.: Playing devil's advocate: Inferring sensitive information from anonymized network traces. In: Proceedings of the 2007 ISOC Network and Distributed System Security Symposium (February 2007)
18. Coull, S.E., Collins, M.P., Wright, C.V., Monrose, F., Reiter, M.K.: On web browsing privacy in anonymized NetFlows. In: Proceedings of the 16th USENIX Security Symposium, August 2007, pp. 339–352 (2007)

19. Shankar, U., Paxson, V.: Active mapping: Resisting NIDS evasion without altering traffic. In: Proceedings of the 2003 IEEE Symposium on Security and Privacy (May 2003)
20. QoSient LLC: Argus - auditing network activity, http://qosient.com/argus/
21. Brownlee, N., Mills, C., Ruth, G.: Traffic flow measurement: Architecture. RFC 2722 (1999)
22. Handelman, S., Stibler, S., Brownlee, N., Ruth, G.: New attributes for traffic flow measurement. RFC 2724 (1999)
23. Spiliopoulou, M., Mobasher, B., Berendt, B.: A framework for the evaluation of session reconstruction heuristics in web-usage analysis. INFORMS Journal on Computing 15(2) (2003)
24. Chun, B., Culler, D., Roscoe, T., Bavier, A., Peterson, L., Wawrzoniak, M., Bowman, M.: PlanetLab: an overlay testbed for broad-coverage services. ACM SIG-COMM Computer Communication Review 33(3), 3–12 (2003)
25. Bellard, F.: QEMU, a fast and portable dynamic translator. In: USENIX Annual Technical Conference, FREENIX Track (2005)
26. Witten, I., Frank, E.: Data Mining: Practical machine learning tools and techniques. Morgan Kaufmann, San Francisco (2005)
27. Joachims, T.: Text categorization with support vector machines: Learning with many relevant features. In: Nédellec, C., Rouveirol, C. (eds.) ECML 1998. LNCS, vol. 1398. Springer, Heidelberg (1998)
28. Osuna, E., Freund, R., Girosit, F.: Training support vector machines: an application to face detection. In: Proceedings of the IEEE Computer Society Conference on Computer Vision and Pattern Recognition (June 1997)
29. Karasaridis, A., Rexroad, B., Hoeflin, D.: Wide-scale botnet detection and characterization. In: Proceedings of the 1st Workshop on Hot Topics in Understanding Botnets (April 2007)
30. Gates, C., Becknel, B.: Host anomalies from network data. In: Proceedings of the 6th IEEE Systems, Man and Cybernetics Information Assurance Workshop (June 2005)
31. Gu, G., Perdisci, R., Zhang, J., Lee, W.: Botminer: Clustering analysis of network traffic for protocol- and structure-independent botnet detection. In: Proceedings of the USENIX Security Symposium (August 2008)
32. Collins, M.P., Reiter, M.K.: Hit-list worm detection and bot identification in large networks using protocol graphs. In: Kruegel, C., Lippmann, R., Clark, A. (eds.) RAID 2007. LNCS, vol. 4637, pp. 276–295. Springer, Heidelberg (2007)
33. Xu, K., Zhang, Z., Bhattacharyya, S.: Profiling internet backbone traffic: Behavior models and applications. In: Proceedings of ACM SIGCOMM (August 2005)
34. Aiello, W., Kalmanek, C., McDaniel, P., Sen, S., Spatscheck, O., Van der Merwe, J.E.: Analysis of communities of interest in data networks. In: Dovrolis, C. (ed.) PAM 2005. LNCS, vol. 3431, pp. 83–96. Springer, Heidelberg (2005)

A Service Dependency Modeling Framework for Policy-Based Response Enforcement

Nizar Kheir[1,2], Hervé Debar[1], Frédéric Cuppens[2], Nora Cuppens-Boulahia[2], and Jouni Viinikka[1]

[1] France Télécom R&D Caen, 42 Rue des Coutures BP 6243, 14066 CAEN, France
{nizar.kheir,herve.debar,jouni.viinikka}@orange-ftgroup.com
[2] Télécom Bretagne, 2 rue de la Chataigneraie, 35512 Cesson Sévigné Cedex, France
{frederic.cuppens,nora.cuppens}@telecom-bretagne.eu

Abstract. The use of dynamic access control policies for threat response adapts local response decisions to high level system constraints. However, security policies are often carefully tightened during system design-time, and the large number of service dependencies in a system architecture makes their dynamic adaptation difficult. The enforcement of a single response rule requires performing multiple configuration changes on multiple services. This paper formally describes a Service Dependency Framework (SDF) in order to assist the response process in selecting the policy enforcement points (PEPs) capable of applying a dynamic response rule. It automatically derives elementary access rules from the generic access control, either allowed or denied by the dynamic response policy, so they can be locally managed by local PEPs. SDF introduces a *requires/provides* model of service dependencies. It models the service architecture in a modular way, and thus provides both extensibility and reusability of model components. SDF is defined using the Architecture Analysis and Design Language, which provides formal concepts for modeling system architectures. This paper presents a systematic treatment of the dependency model which aims to apply policy rules while minimizing configuration changes and reducing resource consumption.

1 Introduction

Intrusion Detection Systems (IDSes) have been recently superseded by Intrusion Prevention Systems (IPS), which add the capability to passivate the threat in addition to detecting and reporting. IPSes are widely used as local control points which take only limited actions (e.g. closing a connection, killing a process, etc.). The major weakness of those IPSes is their static behavior, which relies on pre-defined mappings between intrusive behaviors and suitable response actions. The taxonomy in [1] thus confirms the need for more complex and dynamic response mechanisms. Cuppens et al. propose in [2] a reaction workflow which links the local response decisions to the higher level of security policy. They state that local response decisions should be assisted by global decisions managed at the policy level. In [3], Debar et al. provide a comprehensive approach for managing intrusion response at the policy level using contextual security policies.

U. Flegel and D. Bruschi (Eds.): DIMVA 2009, LNCS 5587, pp. 176–195, 2009.

Intrusion response is specified using contextual access control rules which are triggered when their associated threat contexts are activated. The policy-based response architecture in [3] separates the response instantiation process which triggers response rules from the response decision process. While the instantiation process is sufficiently detailed in [3], contributions for the decision process remain sparse. This paper completes the architecture in [3] by defining a service modeling framework which enables the decision process to automatically select local enforcement points able to apply a dynamic response rule.

The decision process maps policy instances into concrete actions applicable on local Policy Enforcement Points (PEPs). [4] proposes a derivation process which translates high level policies into local firewall actions, but it only manages network policies. The use of application services provides more granularity for the specification and application of response policies. A service may be configured with accurate access control rules to the data it manages. It thus enables accurate response applications not always possible at the network layer. Moreover, service dependencies may provide several alternatives for the application of response policies. The access to a dependent service may be modified through the reconfiguration of the access to its antecedent service. Unfortunately, the use of service dependencies for automated response is still, at the best of our knowledge, restrained to static mappings. The lack of a formal representation of those services and their dependencies is a major reason. This paper combines policy-based response with topological information about services and their dependencies. Services endowed with access control capabilities (ACLs, Application Firewalls, configuration files, etc.) are considered as PEPs. The Service Dependency Framework (SDF), a formal framework for modeling services and their dependencies, is defined in this paper. It assists the decision process in deriving local accesses to antecedent services from the generic access to the dependent service which is either allowed or denied by the response policy. The decision process analyzes those accesses with respect to PEPs capabilities. It selects the optimal set of PEPs capable of applying the security rule.

The paper is structured as follows. Section 2 summarizes the state of the art, including the presentation of the policy-based response process, the need for a SDF and description of related work. Section 3 presents the service dependency model. Section 4 defines the framework for building the dependency model. Section 5 provides a systematic treatment of the SDF by the decision process. Section 6 concretely implements the SDF on a mail delivery testbed.

2   State of the Art

2.1   Policy-Based Intrusion Response

Access control policies include permission and/or prohibition rules which apply to subjects when they intend to perform actions on objects. Some rules specify requirements which apply during normal operation, they form the *operational* policy. Others apply in case of security threats, they form the *threat* policy. The switching between operational and threat policies is driven by contextual constraints. We specify contextual policies using the Organization Based Access Control (OrBAC) Model [5]. This paragraph recalls the OrBAC concepts we need in this paper (see [6] for details).

The OrBAC Model uses the abstract triplet *(Role, Activity, View)* instead of the concrete triplet *(subject, action, object)* when defining access control policies. The concept of *Role* was first introduced by the RBAC model [7]. A *Role* is a set of subjects which have the same permissions. OrBAC adds *Activities* and *Views* as abstractions of *actions* and *objects* respectively. An Activity (e.g. access data) is an operation implemented by some actions (e.g. *get* and *retr* commands for http and pop3 protocols respectively). These can be grouped within the same activity for which we may define a single rule. A *View* is a set of objects that possess the same security-related properties so they can be accessed in the same way. Abstracting *objects* into *Views* avoids the need for writing one rule for each of them. OrBAC introduces contexts [5] which add conditions under which a certain rule can be applied. OrBAC uses four predicates:

- *empower (subj, Role)*: subject *subj* is empowered in the role *Role*.
- *consider (act, Activity)*: action *act* is implemented in the activity *Activity*.
- *Use (obj, View)*: object *obj* is used in the view *View*.
- *hold (ctxt, subj, act, obj)*: context *ctxt* is active for the triplet $(subj, act, obj)$.

A security rule is expressed as *Sr (Decision, R, A, V, Context)*[1]. When *context* is active, *R*'s request to perform the activity *A* on the View *V* is submitted to the decision *Decision*. An example of an OrBAC security rule is: *Sr (Prohibition, User, login, internal_Host, not_working_Hours)*. *User* is a role for any system user; *login* is the activity of connecting to a host; *internal_Host* is any host connected to the internal network and the context *not_working_Hours* is true outside working hours. *Sr* states that such an operation is prohibited outside working hours.

Reaction Policies in the OrBAC model are associated with threat contexts. A threat context is assigned to an intrusion class. It is activated when the associated intrusion is detected (e.g. DoS, Buffer overflow). As in [3], threat contexts are only activated for the concrete triplets described in alerts. For instance, a brute force attack from a certain address *addr* against an account *Acc* using the *login* service activates the *Brute_Force* context as follows:

Hold (addr, login, Acc, Brute_Force) ← alert (Source, Target, Classification),
Classification (Brute_Force), service (Target, login), Account (Target, Acc)

The context activation may trigger policy rules associated with this context. These rules specify new security requirements appropriate for countering the detected threat. Threat contexts activation uses mappings from IDMEF alert attributes [8] onto concrete policy components. While the mappings are deliberately simplified in our example, they may introduce different granularities in order to consider different attack classes (e.g. a DDoS attack is managed differently than a targeted buffer overflow attack)[3].

---

[1] OrBAC associates organizations with security rules. To simplify, these are not made visible in this paper since we consider only a single organization.

2.2   Policy Decision Models

The decision process contains two steps [4]. The first is architecture-dependent. It segments a response into elementary actions. The second step is component-dependent. It translates elementary actions into concrete configurations. [9] proposes a formal approach for the specification and deployment of network security policies. Unfortunately, it does not consider the overlying service architecture. The modeling of services and their dependencies provides means for a fine grained response application, which it is not always applicable on the network layer. Let's check for instance the following concrete response policy:

Prohibition (IP, HTTP/Get, retail_Appli), Permission (IP, HTTP/Get, mail_Appli)
where both applications are hosted on the same server. Applying this policy at the network layer is tedious since firewalls are less likely to have visibility over application data. While application layer firewalls are more appropriate, they are not always available on the server. A model-based analysis of service architectures may provide more suited alternatives for the application of such response policies. For instance, when the web server is accessible through traffic redirection from a remote proxy, a SDF links between the web service and the proxy service so that the decision process automatically selects the proxy for applying this policy.

A formal dependency framework which establishes the link between the access to an antecedent service and the access to its dependent service does not seem to exist. This paper provides a *requires/provides* model framework for service dependencies. This framework assists the Policy Decision Process (PDP) in tracing all the elementary accesses in order to access a certain data. As such, and when this access is prohibited, the PDP alters some elementary accesses in order to deny the prohibited access. Moreover, when the access is allowed, the PDP satisfies at least one single access path to the data. The decision process in this paper is different from the approach described in [10] in that it aims at finding the best suitable set of PEPs capable of applying a response, after and only after this response is selected. We first briefly describe existing dependency models and their usages before presenting our dependency model and its use.

2.3   Service Dependency Models and Applications

Existing dependency models. An XML based dependency model is presented in [11]. This model provides a backend for building a dependency database, without providing a formal specification of service dependencies. [12] defines a dependency algebra for modeling dependency strengths. It separates the *Dependency* relation from the *Use* relation. It states that critical components should only use and not depend on non-critical components. In [13], a UML-based dependency model describes service dependencies in ad hoc systems. It focuses on the dependencies relevant to ad hoc collaborative environments. Moreover, a service dependency classification for system management analysis is provided in [14]. It separates between functional (implementation-independent) and structural dependencies (implementation-dependent).

Service Dependency Usages. A cost-sensitive approach for balancing between intrusion and response costs is provided in [15]. A system map holding dependency information is used as a basis for deciding on response strategy. [16] proposes a function which evaluates intrusion response impacts using dependency trees. It allows a cost-sensitive selection of intrusion responses. Another cost-sensitive analysis of intrusion responses is presented in [17]. It uses dependency graphs instead of dependency trees. Service dependencies are also used for fault analysis [18], dependability analysis [19] and many other applications. The existing dependency models such as graph [15,17,16] or class-based [13] models classify service dependencies using static attributes. These are often informally defined, and adapted to only specific system implementations. The adoption of those models still confronted to their expressiveness and the dependency characteristics they deal with. The decision process needs more than to know about the existence of a certain dependency and its strength. In order to derive elementary accesses to antecedent services, and to do it automatically, the decision process must be able to discern the access to the antecedent service through the access to its dependent services. In other terms, it must be aware of what data is required from the antecedent service, how, when and why is it accessed.

On the other hand, the SDF must enable the regrouping of elementary services into dependency blocks with well-defined interfaces. Those blocks can be implemented in other dependency blocks, and thus providing reusability of the dependency model. The SDF must also allow the abstraction of certain dependencies, and thus representing only the dependencies relevant for the application purposes. We have choosen to define the SDF using the Architecture Analysis and Design Language (AADL)[20]. AADL fulfills those requirements through the modeling of service architectures. In the following section, we summarize the main AADL concepts we use in this paper and present our SDF.

3   The Service Dependency Model

3.1   Using AADL to Model the SDF

AADL has been released and standardized by the Society of Automotive Engineers. AADL provides formal modeling concepts for the description and analysis of application system architectures in terms of distinct components and their interactions. We privileged AADL over common modeling languages like UML because AADL provides more powerful features for modeling system runtime behaviors. AADL provides standardized textual and graphical notations for modeling systems and their functional interfaces. It has been designed to be extensible so that analyses that the core language does not support can be supplied. The extensibility in AADL is provided through the *Annex* extension construct.

SDF models user runtime behaviors when accessing the data provided by dependent services. It contrasts with most functional dependency models since it focuses on the data flows associated with the access to a dependent service rather than modeling its functional dependencies. This is a main concept in our approach since policy-driven responses require PEPs to deny some of these data flows. We thus model services as abstractions, and these are decoupled from the concrete components which realize them. Our decision can be best motivated by the fact that concrete components only introduce functional dependencies which are not relevant in our approach. For instance, a web service is defined through its dependencies, independently whether it is implemented by apache2 server or windows web server. We use for this purpose AADL system abstractions (see section 3.2). AADL models dependencies using inter-component connections. AADL connnections reproduce the service topology. They allow modeling multiple service paths through the use of multiple connection paths to the same data. We also use AADL operational modes in order to represent the dependency sequencing during the workflow of the dependent service. We use the *AADL Error Model Annex* [21] which has also been standardized to add features for modeling the system behavior in the presence of faults. We use faults as model constructs in order to represent the behavior of a dependent service when it can not access to the antecedent service due to a response application. In the remaining of this section, we describe the main elements of our AADL dependency model.

3.2   Service and Service Dependency Definition

We define a service as the implementation of an interface which *provides* data access to its users (e.g. Web service, IP service). A service often *requires* access to subsidiary data during its normal behavior. It is thus identified through the specification of its required and provided data accesses. We model an elementary service in AADL as a black box with specific *requires/provides* interfaces. Each interface enables a specific data access, either required or provided by the service (see Figure 1). We may add constraints between data required and provided by a service (e.g. the required account is the owner of the provided data). These are expressed as predicates assigned, when necessary, to the corresponding interfaces.

Service A depends on service B when A requires data access which is provided by B. A is the *dependent* service, and B is the *antecedent* service. The failure of B, due to an attack or a response, prevents it from providing the data required by A. The proper behavior of A is thus conditioned by the proper behavior of B. Required data accesses enable dependency compliance check: A may never depend on a B if the data access provided by B is not required by A. However, a required data access does not necessarily imply the need for a dependency,

```
1     -- Implementation of elementary service --
2     system Service_Name
3       features
4         RF1: requires data access data_Set_r1;
5         ...
6         RFn: requires data access data_Set_rn;
7         PF1: provides data access data_Set_p1;
8         ...
9         PFm: provides data access data_Set_pm;
10    end Service_Name;
```

Requires data access

RF1 RF2   RFn

Service_name

PF1 PF2   PFm

Provides data access

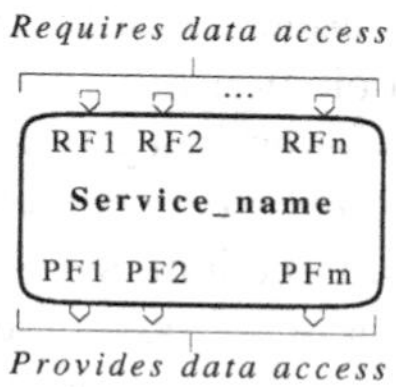

Fig. 1. Elementary Service definition

```
1    system implementation Dependency_Model.A
2      subcomponents
3        A: system dependent;
4        B: system antecedent;
5      connections
6        const_AB: data access B.PF1 -> A.RF1;
7    end Dependency_Model.A;
```

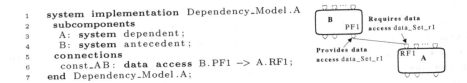

Fig. 2. Explicit Service Dependency Representation

because this access can be managed by the service itself. For instance, a mail delivery service requires access to user accounts. These can be managed locally by the service (passwords file), or remotely accessed through a directory service. Only the latter case implies a dependency for the directory service.

We model the dependency of service A to service B by connecting the *provides* interface of B to its complementary *requires* interface of A. The AADL model checks the compliance of this dependency by verifying that the access required by A corresponds to the access provided by B (see Figure 2).

3.3   Service Dependency Specification

The SDF specifies dependencies by modeling: the data exchanged in each dependency, the paths followed by these data, the sequencing of dependencies during the operation of the dependent service and the impact due to the unfulfillment of each dependency. We thus define the following dependency characteristics.

- *Dependency type* defines the path of the network flow, and describes the data assets exchanged between the dependent and the antecedent service.

- *Dependency mode* makes precise the occurrence of a dependency within the lifecycle and workflow of the dependent service.

- *Dependency Impact* evaluates the influence of the insatisfaction or degradation of the relation between antecedent and dependent services.

While these characteristics may be completed at a later time, we believe that they are the most relevant for our purpose of using the dependency model for assisting the decision process as described in section 2. In the remainder of this section, we discuss each attribute, and we show how it is modeled in AADL.

Service Dependency Types describe elementary paths followed by the data provided by the antecedent service. They only describe access paths for the direct dependencies of a service. Complete data paths, due to indirect dependencies (dependencies of the direct antecedents of a service), are automatically inferred from elementary access paths for each service as explained later in section 4.

A dependency type may be either *service-side*, *user-side* or *proxy* dependency.
- *Service-side dependency:* the dependent service initiates the interaction with the antecedent service. The user connects to the dependent service as if no dependency exists (see Figure 3-a).

- *User-side dependency:* the user obtain credentials from the antecedent service and present them to the dependent service. The connection is transparent for the dependent service (see Figure 3-b).

a- Service-side   **b-** User-side   **c-** Proxy

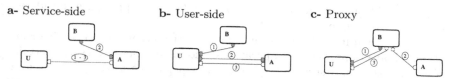

White interfaces represent the data flow provided by the dependent service for its users.
Gray interfaces represent data flow provided by the antecedent service.
A is the dependent service, *B* is the antecedent service, and *U* is the user of the dependent service.

Fig. 3. Service Dependency Types

- *Proxy dependency:* the access path to the dependent service is intercepted by the antecedent service. No access path explicitly exists between the dependent service and its user during the dependency (see Figure 3-c).

Service Dependency Modes describe the sequencing of dependencies within the lifecycle and workflow of the dependent service. We use AADL operational *modes* for modeling dependency sequencing. AADL *modes* are constructs which represent operational states of a component. Each mode illustrates an operational phase for the dependent service which is characterized by the need for a certain dependency. As such, the dependent service does not notice the failure and/or inaccessibility of the antecedent service unless the former reaches an operational mode where it requires the access to the data provided by the antecedent service. The transition into a dependency mode means that the dependent service has reached an operational phase where it requires access to the data provided by the antecedent service. The transition out of this mode means that the dependency is no longer required.

A service has four operational modes. These modes describe the lifecycle of this service. Every dependency mode exists necessarily in at least one of these operational modes. We shall first describe service lifecycle in AADL, and later we describe dependency sequencing during this lifecycle.

Service lifecycle holds four operational modes: Start, Idle, Request and Stop modes (see the associated AADL model in Figure 4). They are defined as follows:

- *start Mode* characterizes the launching period of a service. The process realizing the service is loading configurations and assets. The transition out of this mode occurs when the process is ready to receive user requests. Dependencies in start mode are one-time dependencies only required during service start-up.
- *Idle Mode* characterizes the period during which a service is waiting for incoming user requests. The transition out of this mode is initiated by a user request, or by a decision to stop the service. The dependencies in this phase are mainly functional dependencies not relevant for the purpose of this paper, but which can be further investigated as for impact evaluations (see section 7).
- *Request Mode* starts when the service receives a user request. It characterizes the in-line dependencies required in order to process this request. The transition from this mode occurs after the user connection is closed.

- *Stop mode* All the actions a service may take before stopping are considered as part of the stop mode.

The sojourn time in each operational mode varies according to service configurations. Transitions between operational modes may also vary for certain services. For instance, a service may start on a per-request basis. It therefore directly switches to the stop mode at the end of the request mode.

Dependency sequencing. Dependencies in each operational mode are invoked in a certain sequence related to the service behavior. These are defined as AADL operational sub-modes assigned to the components of each operational mode (lines 2-6 in Figure 4). We thus state dependencies within the lifecycle of the dependent service, and we determine the dependency sequencing within the same lifecycle phase. We obtain a Dependency Finite State Machine (DFSM) with sub-states. Dependencies appear in three possible sequences described as follows.

- *Stateless sequencing*: the satisfaction of the parent dependency is an obligation prior to the access to the child dependency. However, the former does not need to remain satisfied once the latter is accessed (Figure 5-a).

- *Statefull sequencing*: the parent dependency must remain satisfied as long as the child dependency is not satisfied yet (Figure 5-b).

- *Alternative sequencing*: characterizes redundant dependencies. The transition from the parent dependency leads to one child dependency (Figure 5-c).

Stateless and statefull sequencings express conjuctive dependencies. Alternative sequencing expresses disjunctive dependencies where only one alternative dependency is required. Each dependency mode is associated with a specific *require* interface (see Figure 1) which is connected to a specific antecedent service.

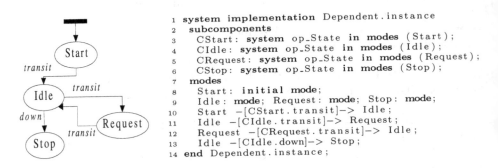

```
1  system implementation Dependent.instance
2    subcomponents
3      CStart: system op_State in modes (Start);
4      CIdle: system op_State in modes (Idle);
5      CRequest: system op_State in modes (Request);
6      CStop: system op_State in modes (Stop);
7    modes
8      Start: initial mode;
9      Idle: mode; Request: mode; Stop: mode;
10     Start -[CStart.transit]-> Idle;
11     Idle -[CIdle.transit]-> Request;
12     Request -[CRequest.transit]-> Idle;
13     Idle -[CIdle.down]-> Stop;
14 end Dependent.instance;
```

Fig. 4. Dependent Service Modes

a- Stateless sequencing   **b-** Statefull sequencing   **c-** Alternative sequencing

Fig. 5. Service Dependency Sequencing

Service Dependency Impacts express the consequence of any degradation of the antecedent service, which alters the access to data required by the dependent service. The failure of a dependency alters the transitions between operational modes. This alteration is motivated by the fact that the failure of a dependency denies reaching its subsequent dependencies in case of no alternative dependency.

Dependency failure does not only alter the normal transition out of the failed dependency. It may also restrain the service to switch to another operational mode. For instance, a web server may switch to unsecure connections when the SSL service does not respond. We use the AADL error model annex to represent the impact of a dependency failure. Each service is attributed at least two AADL error states, which are normal and failure states. The impact of a dependency is expressed by constraining the transition out of a dependency to occur depending on the error state of the antecedent service. This is done by defining *Guard_Transition* properties which use error propagations. Error propagations are AADL constructs which notify the component at the remote end of a connection about the error state of the other component. We use *Error_Free* and *Failed* propagations which notify respectively an error free and a failed dependency states. Each dependency state may dispose of two transitions. The first is the normal transition, constrained by the satisfaction of the dependency. The second transition is optional. It is constrained by the unsatisfaction of the dependency.

The following example of a Mail Delivery Service (MDS) illustrates these specifications. MDS authenticates its users using LDAP service. Authenticated users are granted access to their remote mailboxes mounted using the NFS service. The accounts of connected users are locked in order to prevent simultaneous sessions. MDS unlocks an LDAP account after its corresponding user closes his/her opened session. The normal behavior of MDS is modeled in lines 1-6 of Figure 6.

The impact of the second LDAP dependency is stated as follows. Firstly, authenticated users cannot disconnect if the MDS cannot access to the LDAP service. The *Guard_Transition* in lines 11-12 states that the transition to the Idle phase (line 6) only occurs if the dependency is in the *Error_Free* state. Secondly, authenticated users remain blocked in the NFS dependency state as long as the second LDAP dependency is not restored (lines 7-10 of Figure 6).

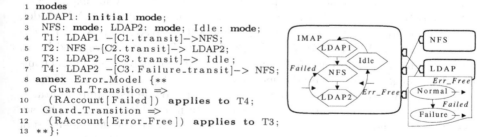

```
1  modes
2  LDAP1: initial mode;
3  NFS: mode; LDAP2: mode; Idle: mode;
4  T1: LDAP1 -[C1.transit]->NFS;
5  T2: NFS -[C2.transit]-> LDAP2;
6  T3: LDAP2 -[C3.transit]-> Idle;
7  T4: LDAP2 -[C3.Failure_transit]-> NFS;
8  annex Error_Model {**
9     Guard_Transition =>
10    (RAccount[Failed]) applies to T4;
11    Guard_Transition =>
12    (RAccount[Error_Free]) applies to T3;
13 **};
```

Fig. 6. Service dependency Impact

4   Dependency Model Framework

Section 3 has defined the service dependency characteristics managed using our approach. This section describes the steps for building a dependency model using our framework summarized in Figure 7. We use the Open Source AADL Tool Environment (OSATE)[2] which is a set of Eclipse plug-ins. OSATE maintains AADL models as XML-based files, which allows the reusability of the model.

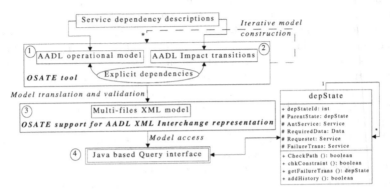

Fig. 7. Dependency Model Framework

The modeling framework is split into four steps. The user is intended to do the first two steps. The last two steps are automatically generated.

Step 1 consists of modeling the explicit dependencies of a service. Each service has a dedicated dependency model defined in an AADL package. Only explicit dependencies are represented. Antecedent services are considered as independent services, and therefore indirect dependencies are not represented.

Step 2 consists of modeling the dependency impacts. Failure impacts are specified as in section 3.3. Only the impacts of explicit dependencies are modeled. Indirect dependency impacts are infered from those of explicit dependencies.

The iteration over the first two steps consists of replacing antecedent services by the implementation of their composite dependency models. Antecedent services, previously used as abstract independent components, are replaced by instantiations of their dependency packages (see the case study for examples).

In **Step 3**, OSATE translates the AADL model into a multi-file XML model. Each package (i.e. elementary dependency model) is saved as an XML file expressed using the AADL XML Interchange format. This step is preceded by an automated model validation. OSATE checks the connections between model components. It flags inappropriate dependencies where a dependent service is made dependent of an antecedent service which does not provide its required data.

Step 4 is the implementation of a query interface which manages the access to the dependency model. This interface is queried for the dependencies of a specific service. We use the Java-based Document Object Model to explore

---

[2] http://la.sei.cmu.edu/aadlinfosite/OpenSourceAADLToolEnvironment.html

the AADL/XML model. The query interface builds a Dependency Finite State Machine (DFSM) with substates in order to represent service dependencies.

The DFSM schema is illustrated in Figure 7. It summarizes all the dependency characteristics modeled in the first two steps. The attributes of a dependency state are (1) the antecedent service, (2) the required data (section 3.2), (3) the requester (dependency type), (4) the dependency impact, (5) the parent dependency and (6) the next dependency (dependency modes). Cyclic dependencies are discarded, and thus a dependency state cannot be a parent for another dependency state which points to the same service.

5   Service Dependencies: Application to Security

5.1   Using Services as Policy Enforcement Points

Deriving Concrete DFSM from Abstract DFSM. Policy-based responses are expressed as (s, a, o) triplets. The SDF is queried for the DFSM of the service which implements the action a. It thus provides a DFSM which holds abstract components while the PDP receives concrete rules (see section 2.1). We thus need to derive a concrete DFSM using the abstract DFSM provided by the query interface. We associate abstract services with the concrete components which realize them using the predicate $realize(component, Service)$. It states that the service $Service$ is realized by the component $component$. The derivation process replaces the abstract service with its concrete implementation. It also derives concrete data instances from abstract data interfaces through the application of their associated constraints to the object o in the security rule (see section 3.2). A service may be realized by several component instances. The single abstract dependency is thus instantiated into several disjunctive concrete dependencies.

The derivation process follows the dependency sequencing in the abstract DFSM. It substitutes abstract components with concrete implementations. The

```
input  : Sr(s, a, o), DFSM
output : DFSM
curState = DFSM.start;
repeat
    if curState == DFSM.start then
        Only in the first iteration
        curState.Requester = Sr.s;
        curState.AntService = Sr.a;
        curState.RequiredData = Sr.o;
    else
        if curState.Requester == User then curState.Requester = Sr.s;
        else curState.Requester = subject.realize(subject, curState.Requester);
        curState.RequiredData = curState.RequiredData.chkConstraint(Sr.o);
        auxSr.s = curState.Requester; auxSr.a = curState.AntService;
        aurSr.o = curState.RequiredData;
        MakeTransClosure(auxSr, curState.getChilds());
        getChilds() Returns the sub state machine for the current state
    curState = curState.getNext();
until curState = DFSM.end ;
```

Algorithm 1. Transitive Closure

initial concrete components are provided by the concrete response rule. Subsequent concrete accesses are derived from the abstract DFSM and the concrete response rule. We use for this purpose the `MakeTransClosure` function of algorithm 1. It iteratively substitutes the abstract DFSM with a concrete DFSM using the concrete security rule delivered by the policy instantiation process.

Modeling Policy Enforcement Points. The derivation of concrete elementary accesses is followed by a decision process. It aims to reconfigure elementary accesses so that the initial response access rule could be applied. In case of permission, the decision process satisfies at least a minimal set of dependencies. In case of a prohibition, it checks that no dependency path enables the prohibited data access. Access permissions are modified through the reconfiguration of PEPs which are modules associated with services. We therefore consider each service as a PEP having limited access control capabilities. This capability, when it exists, is limited to a specific class of subjects. It thus restrains the PEP capability to apply elementary access rules. For instance, firewall visibility is limited to network level information, it is not able to monitor user-level credentials.

A PEP is able to apply a security rule when (1) the subject in this rule belongs to the capability set of the PEP, (2) the service pointed by the action is managed by the PEP and (3) the object is a data provided by the service (this constraint is satisfied by the derivation process of algorithm 1)). The capability of a PEP depends on its concrete implementation (see examples in the case study). It is defined as a constraint which must be satisfied by the subject in the security rule. Services which do not have access control capabilities are assigned null capability sets. The PDP may select a certain PEP if the subject within the elementary concrete rule derived for this PEP belongs to its capability class. The PDP selects the optimal response set according to two criteria.

- A prohibition is applied the closer possible to the start state of the DFSM, in order to reduce resource consumption. This is motivated by the fact that when the access is denied at the beginning of the DFSM, subsequent dependency accesses are denied, which contributes in reducing resource consumption.

- The PDP minimizes the configuration changes required for the application of a security rule by minimizing the services which need to be reconfigured.

Section 5.2 describes how we fulfill those requirements using our approach.

5.2   Selecting Policy Enforcement Points

S is the set of services obtained from the AADL model. We model the DFSM for the service s_{Dep} as $DFSM_{s_{Dep}} = \{S_a, T_a\}$ where $s_i \in S_a \subset S$ is an antecedent for s_{Dep} and $a_{ij} \in T_a \subset S \times S$ is a transition. A path p_{ij} is a sequence of adjacent transitions which lead from the dependency state s_i to the dependency state s_j. If this path does not exist then $p_{ij} = \phi$. For an input security rule, the PDP crosses $DFSM_{s_{Dep}}$. It searches the minimal set of dependencies which applies the security rule and reduces superfluous resource transactions. Algorithm 2 illustrates the behavior of the PDP. In case of a permission, the PDP searches for the dependency path which requires the least modifications (i.e. reconfigurations)

```
input  : Sr(Type, s, a, o)
output: List < s_i, Sr_i > Resp with s_i ∈ S
FSM_a = makeTransClosure(getDFSM(a), Sr);
dStart = FSM_a.start; dEnd = FSM_a.end;
if Type = Prohibition then
    foreach p_ij in FSM_a with (i=dStart) & (j=dEnd) do
        if chkRespHistory(p_ij) (returns False if the path has beed already intercepted)
        then
            curState = dStart;
            repeat
                curState = curState.getNext(p_ij); returns the next state on the path p_ij
                if chkCapability(curState) then
                    Resp.add(curState.AntService, curState.Sr);
                    curState.addHistory(curState.Sr); add Sr to the resp. history
                    auxPath = FSM_a.getPath(curState.getFailureTrans(), dEnd);
                    if (auxPath ≠ φ)∧(curState.getFailureTrans().parent ≠ Idle) then
                        p_ij ← auxPath;
            until curState = dEnd ;
else
    In case of permission, the PDP allows the path requiring minimum modifications
    minPath = null; minLength = Infinity;
    foreach p_ij in FSM_a with (i=dStart) & (j=dEnd) do
        curLength = 0;
        repeat
            curState = curState.getNext(p_ij);
            if !chkRespHistory(curState) then curLength ++;
        until curState = dEnd ;
        if curLength < minLength then {minLength = curLength; minPath = p_ij;}
    allow(minPath); Liberates the path in parameter
```

Algorithm 2. Evaluation of the resulting impact transfer matrices

in order to allow the access. The selected path is liberated in order to apply the input permission. In case of a prohibition, the PDP denies all dependency paths. When altering a dependency state, the PDP switches to the failure transition of this state and checks that it does not belong to a permissible path.

6 Case Study: E-Mail Service

6.1 Testbed Description

This section implements our dependency model for the example of an email service. The email testbed manages mailboxes using the NFS service. Local mail access is granted by both IMAP and POP services. Remote mail access is granted by a webmail service. The webmail application connects directly to the POP server, and indirectly to the IMAP server through an IMAP proxy which caches IMAP connections. Users are authenticated using the LDAP service.

The available PEPs are ModSecurity[3] which monitors the access to the webmail application, the super daemon XInetd which monitors access to the IMAP Proxy. The LDAP server monitors the access to user accounts and the NFS service

---

[3] http://www.modsecurity.org/

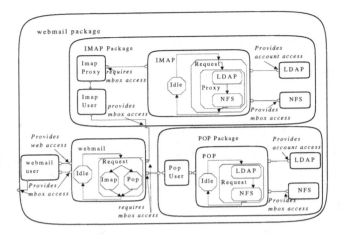

Fig. 8. TestBed AADL model

monitors the access to the shared files using the /etc/exports file. The visibility of XInetd and NFS is limited to internal IP addresses. ModSecurity only manages external IP addresses. Finally LDAP manages its internal accounts.

6.2   Description of the Testbed AADL Model

Figure 8 illustrates the graphical AADL reprentation of the testbed dependency model. The main parts of the AADL textual representation are described in appendix A. We interpret in this paragraph the AADL code in appendix A.

The serviceDB package (lines 1-13) contains the modeled services. POP service requires access to user accounts (line 4). It provides access to mailboxes (line 6) which are remotely accessed by the POP service (line 5). The webmail service is granted by a webmail application which must be accessible for webmail users (line 10). The webmail service recuperates mailboxes (line 9) and provides them to its users (line 11). The POP package (lines 14-35) provides mailbox access (lines 15-17). The LDAP and NFS (line 20-21) services are extracted from the serviceDB package. LDAP and NFS dependencies are service-side dependencies; they are both connected to the POP service (lines 23-24). They are in the request mode (lines 27-28) since they are accessed by the POP service while processing user requests. LDAP dependency is stateless because the access to user accounts is not required after authentication (line 29). Its failure alters the transition to the NFS dependency (lines 29&32). The failure of the NFS dependency initiates a transition to the Idle mode (lines 30&33). The modeling of POP and IMAP dependencies (The IMAP package is omitted for space limitations) gives two packages which provide mailbox access. We use these packages in order to model the webmail service (lines 40-41). The latter is granted by a webmail application. We model the access for webmail users to the webmail application through the connection in line 46. The

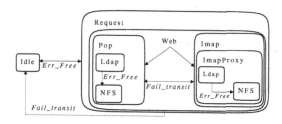

Fig. 9. Webmail Dependency FSM

webmail application provides access to mailboxes recuperated from the mail delivery services (lines 44-45). Lines 53-56 model the multiple access paths to the mail boxes using both POP and IMAP services. The access to the web service must be maintained as long as the connection to the mail delivery services is still required. The web dependency is thus a statefull dependency. POP and IMAP dependencies are modeled as substates of the web dependency (line 49).

The query interface generates a webmail DFSM (see Figure 9) which summarizes all dependency states and transitions (both normal and failure transitions).

6.3   The Use of Service Dependencies for Response Application

We demonstrate in this section the use of the SDF. We adopt the same mappings provided in [3], and we show that for the same abstract rule, the selected PEPs vary according to the mapping outcome. We prefer to use the simple response policy shown in listing 1.1 in order to show the use of our dependency model. This response policy requires that the attacker must be forbidden from accessing to the threatened data through the victim service.

Listing 1.1. Testbed Response Policy

```
1  -- The abstract response rule --
2  Sr (prohibition, att_Source, victim_Serv, target_Data, attack_Threat)
3  -- The Or-Bac Hold fact which transforms alerts into contexts --
4  Hold (Subject, Action, Object, Th_Context) :-
5      alert (Source, Target, description) &
6      map_Subject (Source, Subject) &
7      map_Action (Target.Service, Action) &
8      map_Object (Target, Object) &
9      map_Context (description, Th_Context).
```

The mapping functions in listing 1.1 are XSLTs which extract data from IDMEF alerts [8]. We implemented a prototype for algorithm 2. We simulated several attack instances and we observed the subsequent behavior of the PDP. In the remaining, we give four attack examples and the associated responses fired by the Policy Instantiation Engine and managed by the PDP using our prototype. Figure 10 summarizes the alerts received, the PDP behavior and the selected PEPs. It also shows the configurations automatically generated for each selected PEP

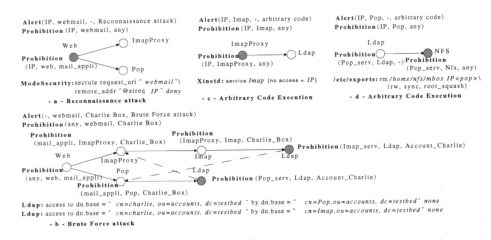

Fig. 10. Attack and Response Samples managed by the Testbed

according to its appropriate elementary access rule derived by the PDP. The attributes in italic are simple mappings from the associated access rules. These are generated by component-specific agents interfacing with each PEP.

Reconnaissance attack is generated by an external user who tries to find valid user IDs. The attacker does not have a valid account. The alert source thus lacks information about a known user. The response module is alerted about an IP address performing a reconnaissance attack against the webmail application. As in Figure 10-a, the PDP selects the first dependency state since the source specified in the elementary rule belongs to the PEP capability set.

Brute Force attack is account centric. The attacker has already acquired a valid account ID. He now tries to break the associated password. The alert notifies a brute force attack from a spoofed address against Charlie's mailbox. The dependency selected in the former example can not be used since no IP address is selected. The PDP chooses to deny the access for both POP and IMAP servers to Charlie's account. The dashed arrows (Figure 10-b) are failure transitions followed by the PDP after it has altered their source dependency nodes.

Arbitrary Code Execution allows an intruder to execute arbitrary code on the target machine on the behalf of the exploited service. The threatened services are IMAP and POP respectively. The alerts respectively notify an IMAP and a POP threat. The selected DFSMs are those of POP and IMAP services. In case of IMAP service (Figure 10-c), the first dependency is selected since the source IP address belongs to the capability set of Xinetd. The LDAP dependency for the POP service can not be used since no LDAP account was instantiated by the transitive closure (Figure 10-d). The NFS service is found to be able to apply its elementary access control rule. It consists of unmounting mailboxes in the /etc/exports file. It is true that the decision process did not provide a solution which protects the POP server. However, a close look to the PEPs capabilities shows that such a solution at least protects the mailbox alteration following a successful attack.

7   Discussion and Conclusion

In this paper, we have presented a modeling framework for the services and their dependencies. The novelty of this framework resides in its ability to formally define dependency attributes, rather than assigning static dependency parameters as in most of the existing class-based models. The formal definition of dependency parameters provides a strong platform for the use of those dependencies for security management. This paper demonstrates that service dependencies can be used for more than only *a-posteriori* evaluation of intrusion response impacts, after these have been selected (although being an important challenge for the security research community). It describes an *a-priori* use of service dependencies, notably for the selection of suitable means to apply an intrusion response, if any. The efficiency of a response application is measured through its ability to satisfy the security requirements while pushing the response closer to the attacker and minimizing the configuration changes.

Limitations of this work include the separated treatment of responses and dependencies search. Firstly, the separated treatment of each response will be extended in order to consider the overall response policy. The optimal application of each response apart does not necessarily provide an optimal application of the response policy, as certain rules may overlap. However, since new response rules may be generated continuously, other problems must be considered such as the stability of the system. Secondly, the upward search for dependencies can be extended with a downward search (i.e. searching for dependents of a service) of dependencies in order to evaluate the impact of selected responses. Future work will focus on adding a third criterion for the selection of a candidate response, being its impact on other services. This will be seen as collateral damages since an antecedent service may have several dependent services other than the service explicitly designated in the intrusion response.

References

1. Stakhanova, N., Basu, S., Wong, J.: A taxonomy of intrusion response systems. Int. Journal of Information and Computer Security 1 (2007)
2. Cuppens, F., Cuppens-Boulahia, N., Bouzida, Y., Kanoun, W., Croissant, A.: Expression and deployment of reaction policies. In: SITIS Wkshp. Web-Based Information Technologies & Distributed Systems (2008)
3. Debar, H., Thomas, Y., Cuppens, F., Cuppens-Boulahia, N.: Enabling automated threat response through the use of a dynamic security policy. Journal in Computer Virology 3 (2007)
4. Cuppens, F., Cuppens-Boulahia, N., Sans, T., Miège, A.: A formal approach to specify and deploy a network security policy. In: Wkshp. Formal Aspects in Security and Trust (2004)
5. Cuppens, F., Miège, A.: Modeling contexts in the or-bac model. In: Proc. Int. Annual Computer Sercurity Application Conf. (2003)
6. Kalam, A.A.E., Baida, R.E., Balbiani, P., Benferhat, S., Cuppens, F., Deswarte, Y., Miège, A., Saurel, C., Trouessin, G.: Organization based access control. In: IEEE Int. Wkshp. Policies for Distributed Systems and Networks (2003)

7. Sandhu, R.S., Coynek, E.J., Feinsteink, H.L., Youmank, C.E.: Role-based access control models. IEEE Computer 28, 38–47 (1996)

8. Debar, H., Curry, D., Feinstein, B.: The intrusion detection message exchange format. Internet Draft, RFC 4765 (March 2007)

9. Preda, S., Cuppens-Boulahia, N., Cuppens, F., Alfaro, J.G., Toutain, L.: Reliable process for security policy deployment. In: Int. conf. Security and Cryptography (2007)

10. Papadaki, M., Furnell, S.M.: Informing the decision process in an automated intrusion response system. Information Security Technical Report 10 (2005)

11. Ensel, C., Keller, A.: Managing application service dependencies with xml and the resource description framework. In: Proc. Int. IEEE Symp. Integrated Management, pp. 661–674 (2001)

12. Ding, H., Sha, L.: Dependency algebra: A tool for designing robust real-time systems. In: Proc. IEEE Int. Real-Time Systems Symp. (2005)

13. Randic, M., Blaskovic, B., Knezevic, P.: Modeling service dependencies in ad hoc collaborative systems. In: Proc. Int. conf. EUROCON (2005)

14. Keller, A., Kar, G.: Dynamic dependencies in application service management. In: Proc. Int. conf. Parallel and Distributed Processing Techniques and Applications (2000)

15. Balepin, I., Maltsev, S., Rowe, J., Levitt, K.N.: Using specification-based intrusion detection for automated response. In: Vigna, G., Krügel, C., Jonsson, E. (eds.) RAID 2003. LNCS, vol. 2820, pp. 136–154. Springer, Heidelberg (2003)

16. Toth, T., Kruegel, C.: Evaluation the impact of automated intrusion response mechanisms. In: Proc. Int. Annual Computer Sercurity Application Conf. (2002)

17. Jahnke, M., Thul, C., Martini, P.: Graph based metrics for intrusion response measures in computer networks. In: IEEE Conf. Local Computer Networks (2007)

18. Gruschke, B.: Integrated event management: Event correlation using dependency graphs. In: Proc. Int. Wkshp. Distributed Systems (1999)

19. Rugina, A.E., Kanoun, K., Kaâniche, M.: A system dependability modeling framework using aadl and gspns. In: de Lemos, R., Gacek, C., Romanovsky, A. (eds.) Architecting Dependable Systems IV. LNCS, vol. 4615, pp. 14–38. Springer, Heidelberg (2007)

20. SAE-AS5506: Sae architecture analysis and design language. Int. Society of Automotive Engineers (November 2004)

21. SAE-AS5506/1: Sae architecture analysis and design language, error model annex. Int. Society of Automotive Engineers (June 2006)

Appendix A

This section summarizes the AADL textual representation for the email testbed.

```
 1 package serviceDB -- Service database --
 2    public -- Only two sample services are presented --
 3       system POP   -- Implementation of the Pop service --
 4          features mb_Owner: requires data access dataDB::Account;
 5                   R_mb: requires data access dataDB::mBox;
 6                   P_mb: provides data access dataDB::mBox;
 7          end POP;
 8       system WEBMAIL -- Implementation of the webmail service --
 9          features R_mb: requires data access dataDB::mBox;
10                   R_api: requires data access dataDB::mailAPI;
11                   P_mb: provides data access dataDB::mBox;
12       end WEBMAIL;
13 end serviceDB;
14 package Pop -- The implementation of the Pop dependency model --
15    public System POP
16             features P_mb: provides data access dataDB::mbox;
17          end POP;
18    private system implementation POP.instance
19          subcomponents PopUser: system user;
20                        Ldap: system serviceDB::Ldap;
21                        NFS: system serviceDB::NFS;
22                        Pop: system dependent.instance;
23          connections data access Ldap.P_a-> Pop.mb_Owner;
24                      data access NFS.P_mb-> Pop.R_mb;
25                      data access Pop.P_mb-> PopUser.R_mb;
26          end POP.instance;
27          system implementation op_State.Request
28             modes LDAP: initial mode; NFS: mode; Idle: mode;
29                   T1: LDAP-[C1.transit]-> NFS;
30                   T2: NFS-[C2.Fail_transit]-> Idle;
31             annex Error_Model {**
32                Guard_Transition => (mb_Owner[Error_Free]) applies to T1;
33                Guard_Transition => (R_mb[Failed]) applies to T2; **};
34             end op_State.Request;
35 end Pop;
36 package webmail
37    public -- same as the Pop public interface --
38    private system implementation webmail.instance
39             subcomponents webmailUser: system user;
40                           Imap: system Imap::IMAP;
41                           Pop: system Pop::POP;
42                           web: system serviceDB::Web;
43                           webmail: system dependent.instance;
44             connections data access Imap.P_mb -> webmail.R_mb1;
45                         data access Pop.P_mb -> webmail.R_mb2;
46                         data access web.P_api -> webmailUser.R_api;
47                         data access webmail.P_mb -> webmailUser.R_mb1;
48          end webmail.instance;
49          system implementation op_State.web
50          subcomponents C1: system op_State in modes (Idle);
51                        C2: system op_State in modes (Pop);
52                        C3: system op_State in modes (Imap);
53          modes Idle: initial mode; Pop: mode; Imap: mode;
54                T1:Idle -[C1.transit]->Pop;T2:Idle -[C1.transit]->Imap;
55                T3:Pop-[C2.Fail_transit]->Imap;T4:Imap-[C3.Fail_transit]->Pop;
56                T5:Pop-[C2.transit]->Idle;T6:Imap-[C3.transit]->Idle;
57          annex Error_Model {**
58                Guard_Transition => (R_mb2[Failed]) applies to T3;
59                Guard_Transition => (R_mb1[Failed]) applies to T4;
60                Guard_Transition => (R_mb2[Error_Free]) applies to T5;
61                Guard_Transition => (R_mb1[Error_Free]) applies to T6; **};
62          end op_State.web;
63 end webmail;
```

Learning SQL for Database Intrusion Detection Using Context-Sensitive Modelling
(Extended Abstract)

Christian Bockermann[1], Martin Apel[2], and Michael Meier[2]

[1] Artificial Intelligence Group
`christian.bockermann@udo.edu`
[2] Information Systems and Security Group
{`martin.apel`,`michael.meier`}`@udo.edu`

Department of Computer Science
Technische Universität Dortmund

Abstract. Modern multi-tier application systems are generally based on high performance database systems in order to process and store business information. Containing valuable business information, these systems are highly interesting to attackers and special care needs to be taken to prevent any malicious access to this database layer. In this work we propose a novel approach for modelling SQL statements to apply machine learning techniques, such as clustering or outlier detection, in order to detect malicious behaviour at the database transaction level. The approach incorporates the parse tree structure of SQL queries as characteristic e.g. for correlating SQL queries with applications and distinguishing benign and malicious queries. We demonstrate the usefulness of our approach on real-world data.

1 Introduction

The majority of today's web-based applications does rely on high performance data storage for business processing. A lot of attacks on web-applications are aimed at injecting commands into database systems or try to otherwise trigger transactions to gain unprivileged access to records stored in these systems. See [1] for a list of popular attacks on web applications.

Traditional network-based firewall systems offer no protection against these attacks, as the malicious (fractions of) SQL or tampered requests are located at the application layer and thus are not visible to most of these systems.

The usual way of protecting modern application systems is by introducing detection models on the network layer or by the use of web application firewall systems. These systems often employ a misuse detection approach and try to detect attacks by matching network traffic or HTTP request against a list of known attack patterns. A very popular system based on pattern matching is for instance the Snort IDS [2]. Another project aiming at the detection of tampered HTTP requests is the ModSecurity module, which provides a rule-engine for employing pattern based rules within a Web-Server [3].

U. Flegel and D. Bruschi (Eds.): DIMVA 2009, LNCS 5587, pp. 196–205, 2009.

Instead of using pattern based approaches, there exists a variety of papers on employing anomaly-based methods for detecting web-based intrusions [4,5,6]. These either try to analyze log-files or protocol-level information to detect anomalies based on heuristics or data-mining techniques. We earlier proposed a rule based learning approach using the ModSecurity module in [7].

These approaches are rooted at the network or application protocol layer. In this work we focus on the detection at the database layer, i.e. the detection of anomalous SQL statements, that are either malicious in the sense that they include parts of injected code or differ from the set of queries usually issued within an application. The main contribution of our work is the use of a grammar based analysis, namely tree-kernel based learning, which became popular within the field of natural language processing (NLP). Our approach incorporates the parse tree structure of SQL queries as characteristic e.g. for correlating SQL queries with applications and distinguishing benign and malicious queries. By determining a context sensitive similarity measure we can locate the nearest legal query for an malicious statements which tremendously helps in root cause analysis.

The remainder of this paper is organized as follows: Section 2 states the problem in detail and gives an overview of related work regarding intrusion detection in databases. In Section 3 we give a short introduction to kernel-based learning algorithms in general and their application on structured data in detail. Following this overview we define our tree-kernel based method and describe its application to learning SQL for intrusion detection in databases in Section 4. Finally we present our results on real-world data in Section 5 and summarize our experiments.

2   Problem and Related Work

Executing malicious statements on a database may result in severe problems, which can range from exposure of sensitive information to loosing records or broken integrity. Once an attacker manages to inject code into a database this will likely not only affect specific records, but may lead to a compromise of the complete application environment. This in turn can cause severe outages with respect to data records and a company's public reputation.

Although the risk may seem low on a first glance, given the database layer is separated from the public interface (web/presentation layer) and not directly accessible from the outside, anomalous queries caused by e.g. SQL injection attacks are a widespread problem. The *Web Hacking Incident Database* provides a listing of recent web hacks, a lot of them relying on SQL injections [8].

There have been approaches to apply data-mining and machine learning methods to detect intrusions in databases. Lee et al [9] suggest learning fingerprints of access patterns of genuine database transactions (e.g. read/write sequences) and using them to identify potential intrusions. Typically there are many possible SQL queries, but most of them only differ in constants that represent the user's input. SQL queries are summarized in fingerprints (regular expressions) by replacing the constants with variables or wild-cards. Such fingerprints capture some structure of the SQL queries. Following the approach of [9], queries

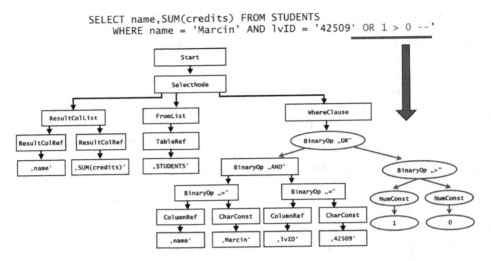

Fig. 1. SQL parse tree of an SQL injection

not matching any of the existing fingerprints are reported as malicious. A drawback of this approach is its inability to correlate and identify fingerprints with applications.

In [10] the authors also try to detect SQL injections by a kind of fingerprints. They use parse trees of queries as fingerprints for the queries structure. The main idea here is to compare the parse tree of an SQL statement before and after user-variables have been inserted. Injected SQL fragments will typically significantly change the trees structure. An example of such structural changes in the parse tree of a query is shown in figure 1. In this figure, the rounded nodes of the tree indicate the additional parts that have been added due to the injection SQL fragment ' OR 1 > 0 --. As this work only uses a one-to-one comparison on parse-trees it is missing any generalization capabilities and thus not applicable for machine learning methods, such as clustering and outlier detection.

A similar grammar-based approach has been used in [11], which studied the use of syntax-aware analysis of the FTP protocol using tree-kernel methods on protocol parse-trees. A slightly different approach was taken in [12] where the parse tokens are used along with their values to detect anomalies in HTTP-traffic. The latter approach does not use the full parse tree but its leaves. Our work is similar to [11,12] in the sense that it employs machine learning methods on syntax trees derived from a protocol parser.

Also approaches on investigating data dependencies have been proposed in [13] and [14]. Data dependencies refer to access correlations among sensitive data items. Data dependencies are generated in form of classification rules like *before an update of item1 a read of item2 is likely*. Transactions not compliant to these rules are flagged as malicious. Srivastava et al [14] further distinguish different levels of sensitivity of data items which need to be specified by hand.

Both approaches ignore the structure of SQL queries and are unable to correlate SQL queries with applications. A more recent work has been presented in[15], focusing on the sequential nature of SQL queries. These studies also make use of a smart modelling technique to easily apply data mining methods on their SQL representations.

3   A Grammar-Based Modelling

Since most learning approaches work on vectorized data, a key issue when using machine learning for intrusion detection is the representation of monitored data to apply any learning algorithm. A popular technique in IDS is the exhaustive creation of n-grams, yielding histogram vectors for observed input data. These do not maintain any syntactical information of SQL. A little more syntax is regarded by creating *term-vectors* of a query. A *term-vector* can be obtained by splitting the query in a "proper way", i.e. by splitting on whitespace characters (optionally maintaining quoted strings).

As in this work we are dealing with the detection of malicious database queries, we choose a grammar based approach to represent SQL queries. We propose two alternative modelling approaches for making SQL queries suitable for machine learning.

3.1   Parsing SQL

The basic idea of [10] is to detect SQL injection attacks by means of changes in a queries syntax tree. An example of such a tree has been shown before (see figure 1). In order to obtain such a parse tree, a parser for the SQL dialect is required. Usually complex parsers are automatically generated based on a given grammar description using tools such as *yacc*, *antlr* or *javacc*. Unfortunately, the availability of proper grammar descriptions for SQL is pretty sparse and most existing parser implementations are tightly wired into the corresponding DBMS, making it laborious to extract a standalone parser.

We therefore decided to modify an existing open-source DBMS, in our case the Apache Derby database, which provides a standalone deployment. The Derby parser is itself generated off a grammar file using *javacc*, but does not explicitly output a syntax tree suitable for our decomposition. Using the tree-interface of the parser, we derived a tree-inspection tool which traverses the tree object of a query and writes out the corresponding node information.

3.2   Vectorization of SQL Queries

To incorporate more syntax, we determine the parse tree of a query. As we are interested in the detection of abnormal queries within our database application, we are looking for a similarity measure for the space of structured objects, i.e. the space of valid SQL parse trees. Thus, we are faced with the problem of having to create a distance function for matching trees.

Definition: Let q be an SQL query and τ_q the parse tree of q, identifying with τ_q the root node of the tree. Each node n within that tree is labeled with an identifier type(n), *reflecting the node type.*

For a node n within τ_q we denote by succ(n) *the ordered set of successors of n and by* $\mathrm{succ}_i(n)$ *the ith child of n.*

This definition is basically just a formalization of a query's syntax tree. It allows us to enlist the production or grammar rules, which generate a given SQL query q. This list of production rules will be defined as follows:

Definition: For a node n within the parse tree τ_q of a query q, the list of production rules P(n) is given by

$$P(n) = \biguplus_{c \in \mathrm{succ}(n)} \{\mathrm{type}(n) \to \mathrm{type}(c)\} \ \uplus \ \biguplus_{c \in \mathrm{succ}(n)} P(c).$$

Given P(n), denote by $|P(n)|_r$ the number of times the rule r occurs in P(n).

Please note that we use the $\uplus$ notation here for list concatenation, thus, the resulting list may contain the same rule more than once. Now, denoting with Q the set of all valid trees for a given SQL dialect, these simple definitions allow us to define a mapping $\varphi : Q \to \mathbb{R}^n$, by following the *bag of words* approach known from text classification tasks like *spam detection* as proposed in [16].

Definition: Let R be the sorted set of all possible production rules, defined by some SQL grammar and r_i the ith rule of R. For an SQL query q with the associated parse tree τ_q the rule vector $\mathbf{v} \in \mathbb{R}^{|R|}$ is given by $v_i = |P(\tau_q)|_{r_i}$. The function φ maps an SQL query q to the vector space $\mathbb{R}^{|R|}$ by $\varphi(q) = \mathbf{v}$.

Since an SQL query usually consists of only a small fraction of the complete SQL grammar, these rule vectors are typically very sparse. Based on this mapping we can now define a distance measure on SQL queries using any distance function Δ in the vector space $\mathbb{R}^{|R|}$ by defining the corresponding distance function Δ_{SQL} using

$$\Delta_{SQL}(q_1, q_2) := \Delta(\varphi(q_1), \varphi(q_2)), \tag{1}$$

where q_1, q_2 are any two SQL statements of a common dialect. This allows for the application of a wide range of distance based learning algorithms such as clustering or outlier detection.

4   Using Tree-Kernels for SQL Grammars

The simple vectorization of SQL queries defined above includes a weak context based reasoning to be used within the distance measure in $\mathbb{R}^{|R|}$. It can be seen as an an *explicit feature extraction* approach, as it explicitly creates feature vectors from SQL statements. Unfortunately, the rule counting does only incorporate direct antecessor relationships, limiting the contextual scope.

4.1 Introduction to Tree-Kernels

To overcome these limitations the natural language processing community makes use of context based tree-kernels, which provide a so-called *kernel-function* over trees. In the machine learning community kernel-based methods have received a lot of attention not ultimately owing to the well-known *support vector machine* method, which has also been used for intrusion detection [17,12]. These methods make use of a kernel-function to measure the similarity between instances of some input space $\mathcal{X}$, i.e. a kernel k is symmetric and positive (semi-) definite function

$$k : \mathcal{X} \times \mathcal{X} \rightarrow \mathbb{R}$$

which implicitly computes an inner product in a reproducing kernel Hilbert space. There exists kernel functions for complex structures like trees or graphs, which are often defined as convolution kernels [18]. For these kernels one defines a kernel over atomic structures and defines the convolution kernel for complex objects by combining the kernel function of its sub structures.

In [19] Collins and Duffy propose a simple kernel over trees for use in natural language processing. The basic idea is to capture structural information over trees in the kernel function by incorporating all sub-trees occuring within the trees of interest. Let $\mathcal{T}$ be the space of all trees in question and denote with T the ordered set of all possible sub-trees in $\mathcal{T}$. For a tree $\tau \in \mathcal{T}$ denote by $h_i(\tau)$ the number of occurrences of the i-th sub-tree of T in τ and with $N(\tau)$ the set of all nodes in τ. For two trees τ_1, τ_2 the tree-kernel in [19] is defined by

$$K_C(\tau_1, \tau_2) = h_i(\tau_1)h_i(\tau_2) = \sum_{n_1 \in N(\tau_1), n_2 \in N(\tau_2)} \Delta(n_1, n_2).$$

The function Δ is defined as follows

$$\Delta(n_1, n_2) = \begin{cases} 0 & \text{if } P(n_1) \neq P(n_2) \\ \lambda & \text{if } \text{height}(n_1) = \text{height}(n_2) = 1 \\ \Delta^*(n_1, n_2) & \text{otherwise,} \end{cases}$$

where $\Delta^*(n_1, n_2)$ is recursively defined as

$$\Delta^*(n_1, n_2) = \lambda \prod_{k=1}^{|\operatorname{succ}(n_1)|} [1 + \Delta(\operatorname{succ}_k(n_1), \operatorname{succ}_k(n_2))]$$

Roughly speaking, this kernel measures the similarity of two trees by the set of common sub trees. As it does not consider the context of a sub tree, Zhou et al [20] designed a *context-sensitive convolution* tree-kernel, by taking into account a sub trees' context by means of its ancestors.

Starting with a tree τ, a root node path of length l in τ is a path from the root node τ or any of its successors to a node in τ, which has a length of l. Following the notation of [20], the set of all root node paths for a tree τ_j with a maximal length of m is denoted by $N^m[j]$. Given a maximum length m for the root node paths considered, the context-sensitive tree-kernel is given be

$$K_{CSC}(\tau_1, \tau_2) = \sum_{i=1}^{m} \sum_{n_1^i[1] \in N_1^i[1], n_2^i[2] \in N_1^i[2]} \Delta_{CSC}(n_1^i[1], n_2^i[2]),$$

where $n_1^i[j] = (n_1, n_2, \ldots, n_i)[j]$ denotes a root node path of length i in tree τ_j. This kernel will therefore incorporate the similarity of common sub-trees.

4.2   Using Tree-Kernels for SQL Parse-Trees

As mentioned in the beginning, the use of tree-kernels in intrusion detection has been proven to provide a syntax-oriented analysis in protocols such as FTP or HTTP [11,12]. To exploit the benefit of syntax-level awareness in SQL query-analysis, we derive the distance measure induced by a tree-kernel function to directly measure the similarity of SQL queries by means of their parse-trees.

For a kernel k and examples x_1, x_2, such a distance can be obtained by

$$d(x_1, x_2) = \sqrt{k(x_1, x_2) - 2k(x_1, x_2) + k(x_1, x_2)}. \tag{2}$$

Using a tree-kernel we can therefore use this kernel to directly compute the distance of two SQL parse-trees using (2).

5   Experimental Analysis and Results

For an evaluation of the different modelling approaches we collected data of the popular Typo3 content management system. This application heavily depends on the use of SQL for various tasks beyond page content storage, such as session-persistence, user-management and even page-caching.

We created a set of distinct queries and added synthetic attacks, which closely reflect modifications that would follow from SQL injections, by inserting typical injection vectors such as OR 'a' = 'a' or the like into legal statements. The intention was to observe whether, using different models, the SVM is to distinguish between legal and malicious statements even though the latter were only marginally different. We created two sets with different ratios of normal to malicious queries, one with 200:15, the other with 1000:15 queries.

5.1   Importance of Context

A central question in our work is the importance of contextual information when analyzing SQL queries. We therefore analyzed approaches such as n-grams, term-vector and the SQL vectorization described in section 3.2. In this experiment we did not mean to train a detector, but wanted to explore the expressiveness of the different models and determined the detection rate (TPR) and the false-positive rate (FPR) of the different modelling approaches. As learning algorithm we used an SVM approach within a 10-fold cross-validation.

Table 1. Separation capabilities of the different models based on a 10-fold cross-validation

Model	Ratio 200:15			Ratio 1000:15		
	TPR	FPR	time	TPR	FPR	time
3-gram	0.6667	0.000	71 s	0.6667	0.002	643 s
4-gram	0.3333	0.000	149 s	0.7333	0.002	1055 s
Term vectors	0.6667	0.005	2 s	0.7333	0.002	283 s
SQL vectors	0.8667	0.000	16 s	0.8667	0.001	67 s

As you can see from table 1, the use of context information results in performance gains especially with respect to the detection rate (TPR) and the fraction of false positives (FPR). This supports our thesis on the importance of the context when analyzing SQL queries. It is worth noting, that the variance in TPR/FPR within the 10-fold cross validation proved to be much smaller for the context-sensitive methods. Additionally, the training time using term- or sql-vectorization decreased due to the smaller number of (irrelevant) attributes. The times in table 1 refer to the complete parameter-optimization and 10-fold cross-validation process.

5.2   Query Analysis Using Tree-Kernels

Using the tree-kernel similarity we are interested in analyzing an application's structure by means of different sets of similar statements used. Therefore we used the kernel similarity within an interval self-organizing map (ISOM) to create a visualization of an application's statements. In figure 2 you see the ISOM of 200 regular queries taken from Typo-3 (dots), supplemented by 15 modified "malicious" modifications (squares).

As can be seen in figure 2 the kernel does consolidate similar queries into clusters, an inspection of the clustered regions revealed very reasonable groups, such as "all page-content queries", "all session update queries" and so on. The heaps of dots turned out to be of a very similar structure, only differing in terminal symbols. Further adding edges to the ISOM showed, that the modified queries are consolidated very late, showing that they are highly dissimilar.

Fig. 2. ISOM of 215 Typo-3 queries (200 legal, 15 anomalous), created by the CSC tree-kernel ($\lambda = 0.6, m = 10$)

Fig. 3. Intra-Cluster ISOM of a cluster consisting of 46 legal queries and one single anomalous modification, which resulted from adding SQL injection elements

5.3   Intra-cluster ISOMs

As the ISOM experiments proved to be useful to get a feeling for the similarity measure, we employed a KMedoids clustering algorithm based on the tree-kernel distance and inspected the clusters by creating ISOMs of each cluster separately. Figure 3 shows the ISOM of a cluster containing "attacks" which are similar to the majority of the queries, but differ by injected SQL fragments.

Within this cluster the anomalous queries is the one most dissimilar from all other, resulting in isolation. The queries in the left-hand group are related to selecting language-specific content from the database, whereas the group on the right contains queries selecting page-content related to a user-id UID. The anomalous query contains an additional OR UID > 0, neutralizing the UID check.

This yields a two-way analysis which uses a clustering approach to first group the different kinds of statements and then uses an intra-cluster outlier detection for the detection of malicious queries.

6   Conclusions and Future Work

We presented two approaches for a context sensitive modelling/fingerprinting of SQL queries by use of generic models. Using tree-kernels for analyzing SQL statements brings together the results of natural language processing with a highly structured query language. The results confirm the benefit of incorporation of syntax information of previous works [11,12] in the domain of SQL queries.

The consideration of the SQL structures shows performance gains in both performance and speed, the later due to the fewer but far more meaningful features. Compared to previous approaches the tree-kernels allow for a similarity measure on SQL statements providing flexible generalization capabilities.

However, a drawback in the use of tree-kernels is their computational overhead. Given a set of 1015 queries, the computation of the kernel matrix took about 210 seconds. Use of hierarchical models, such as hierarchical clustering, may lower the impact of this performance decrease for future detection models.

Here, our first Clustering and ISOM experiments in 5 show the usefulness of tree-kernels as a similarity measure in order to visualize SQL queries in applications. However, the tree-kernel approach still offers a lot of optimization possibilities and needs further investigation. In future works we therefore plan on using inter-cluster outlier detection to create hierarchical anomaly detection models based on tree-kernels over SQL parse-trees.

References

1. Open Web Application Security Project. The Top list of most severe web application vulnerabilities (2004)
2. Roesch, M.: Snort: Lightweight intrusion detection for networks. In: Proc. of LISA, pp. 229–238. USENIX (1999)
3. Ristic, I.: ModSecurity - A Filter-Module for the Apache Webserver (1998)
4. Kruegel, C., Vigna, G.: Anomaly Detection of Web-based Attacks. In: Proc. of ACM CCS, pp. 251–261. ACM Press, New York (2003)
5. Kruegel, C., Vigna, G., Robertson, W.: A Multi-model Approach to the Detection of Web-based Attacks. Computer Networks 48(5), 717–738 (2005)
6. Valeur, F., Vigna, G., Kruegel, C., Kirda, E.: An Anomaly-driven Reverse Proxy for Web Applications. In: Proc. of ACM SAC (2006)
7. Bockermann, C., Mierswa, I., Morik, K.: On the automated creation of understandable positive security models for web applications. In: Proc. of IEEE PerCom, pp. 554–559. IEEE Computer Society, Los Alamitos (2008)
8. Shezaf, O., Grossman, J.: Web Hacking Incident Database (2008)
9. Lee, S.-Y., Low, W.L., Wong, P.Y.: Learning fingerprints for a database intrusion detection system. In: Gollmann, D., Karjoth, G., Waidner, M. (eds.) ESORICS 2002. LNCS, vol. 2502, pp. 264–280. Springer, Heidelberg (2002)
10. Buehrer, G., Weide, B.W., Sivilotti, P.A.G.: Using parse tree validation to prevent sql injection attacks. In: Proc. of SEM, pp. 106–113. ACM, New York (2005)
11. Gerstenberger, R.: Anomaliebasierte Angriffserkennung im FTP-Protokoll. Master's thesis, University of Potsdam, Germany (2008)
12. Düssel, P., Gehl, C., Laskov, P., Rieck, K.: Incorporation of application layer protocol syntax into anomaly detection. In: Sekar, R., Pujari, A.K. (eds.) ICISS 2008. LNCS, vol. 5352, pp. 188–202. Springer, Heidelberg (2008)
13. Hu, Y., Panda, B.: A data mining approach for database intrusion detection. In: Proc. of ACM SAC, pp. 711–716. ACM, New York (2004)
14. Srivastava, A., Sural, S., Majumdar, A.K.: Database intrusion detection using weighted sequence mining. JCP 1(4), 8–17 (2006)
15. Roichman, A., Gudes, E.: DIWeDa - detecting intrusions in web databases. In: Atluri, V. (ed.) DAS 2008. LNCS, vol. 5094, pp. 313–329. Springer, Heidelberg (2008)
16. Lewis, D.D.: Naive (bayes) at forty: The independence assumption in information retrieval. In: Nédellec, C., Rouveirol, C. (eds.) ECML 1998. LNCS, vol. 1398, pp. 4–15. Springer, Heidelberg (1998)
17. Rieck, K., Holz, T., Willems, C., Düssel, P., Laskov, P.: Learning and classification of malware behavior. In: Zamboni, D. (ed.) DIMVA 2008. LNCS, vol. 5137, pp. 108–125. Springer, Heidelberg (2008)
18. Haussler, D.: Convolution kernels on discrete structures. Technical report, Dept. of Computer Science, UC Santa Cruz (1999)
19. Collins, M., Duffy, N.: Convolution kernels for natural language. In: Advances in Neural Information Processing Systems 14, pp. 625–632. MIT Press, Cambridge (2001)
20. Zhou, G.D., Zhang, M., Ji, D.H., Zhu, Q.M.: Tree kernel-based relation extraction with context-sensitive structured parse tree information. In: Proc. of Joint Conf. on Empirical Methods in Natural Language Processing and Computational Natural Language Learning, pp. 728–736. Assoc. for Computer Linguistics (2007)

Selecting and Improving System Call Models for Anomaly Detection

Alessandro Frossi, Federico Maggi, Gian Luigi Rizzo, and Stefano Zanero

Politecnico di Milano, Dipartimento di Elettronica e Informazione
{alessandro.frossi,gian.rizzo}@mail.polimi.it,
{fmaggi,zanero}@elet.polimi.it

Abstract. We propose a syscall-based anomaly detection system that incorporates both deterministic and stochastic models. We analyze in detail two alternative approaches for anomaly detection over system call sequences and arguments, and propose a number of modifications that significantly improve their performance. We begin by comparing them and analyzing their respective performance in terms of detection accuracy. Then, we outline their major shortcomings, and propose various changes in the models that can address them: we show how targeted modifications of their anomaly models, as opposed to the redesign of the global system, can noticeably improve the overall detection accuracy. Finally, the impact of these modifications are discussed by comparing the performance of the two original implementations with two modified versions complemented with our models.

Keywords: Anomaly Detection, System Call Models, Deterministic Models, Stochastic Models, Self Organizing Map.

1   Introduction

Since the seminal work of Forrest et al. [1], system call-based anomaly detection enjoyed immense popularity. The core of any anomaly detection system consists of a *composition* of effective *models* to *accurately* capture the observed system *behavior*.

While usually the approach is to re-design the whole system, we propose a much more effective way of improving over previous results. We selectively identify well-performing models, and compose them in novel ways to create improved detectors. To demonstrate our point, two alternative and quite *complementary* techniques [2,3] are chosen, in order to have a rich set of models to analyze and improve. In particular, we focus on incremental models improvements, and on cross-pollination among different approaches. We show how this process of analysis and improvement leads to globally improved detection accuracy with minimal efforts, as opposed to the re-design of the global system structure. We concentrate on the use of unsupervised learning algorithms, because this type of learning uses rather complex models and representations, creating an ideal testing ground for model improvement. Also, while most models are only based

U. Flegel and D. Bruschi (Eds.): DIMVA 2009, LNCS 5587, pp. 206–223, 2009.

on the program control flow, we deem it important to analyze also the content of the calls, as many attacks today are not exclusively based on control flow deviations.

The first prototype we analyze is based on a *Finite State Automaton* (FSA) augmented with dataflow information. We show that its promising capabilities (e.g., precise modeling of the control flow and solid relationship) are paid dearly in terms of low robustness. Indeed, several false detections are triggered by slight differences between the actual parameters and the learned, crisp models. On the opposite hand, we examine a model based on Markov chain modeling augmented by statistical anomaly models. It is able to capture frequency information and to infer relationships between different arguments of same system call, but has a number of shortcomings in terms of false positives and negatives.

We propose a set of modifications that can address some of the shortcomings of these prototypes. The impact of these modifications is analyzed by comparing performance and detection accuracy of the two original prototypes versus two modified, hybrid versions complemented with the new models. Without taking into account arguments values, hybrid systems based on both syscall sequences and control/data flows are not more accurate than pure control flow based ones [4]. On the other hand, we empirically show how the accuracy of a data flow IDS increases if call arguments are included in the models.

The remainder of this paper is organized as follows. In Section 2 we describe the two different prototypes implemented in previous works, along with the improvements we describe in Section 3. In Section 4 we evaluate the *Detection Rate* (DR), the *False Positive Rate* (FPR), and speed of the original and modified systems. In Section 5 we review the most relevant, recent host-based anomaly detection proposed in the literature.

2   Two Existing Approaches to System Call Anomaly Detection

In this section we describe the results of the analysis we conducted on the chosen anomaly detection systems.

2.1   FSA-Based Implementation

The first prototype we analyzed is a deterministic IDS which builds an FSA model of each monitored program [2], on top of which it creates a network of relations (or *properties*) among the system call *arguments* encountered during training. In the following, we call it "FSA-DF" as a shorthand. Such a network of properties is the main difference w.r.t. other FSA based IDSes. Instead of a pure *control flow* check, which focuses on the behavior of the software in terms of sequences of system calls, it also performs a so called *data flow* check on the internal variables of the program along their existing cycles.

This knowledge is exploited in terms of *unary* and *binary* relationships. For instance, if an **open** system call always uses the same filename at the same point,

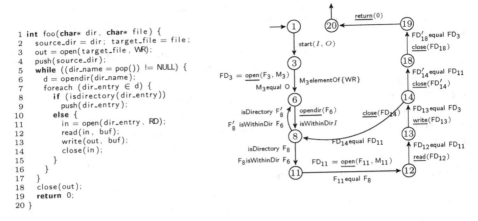

```
1  int foo(char* dir, char* file) {
2    source_dir = dir; target_file = file;
3    out = open(target_file, WR);
4    push(source_dir);
5    while ((dir_name = pop()) != NULL) {
6      d = opendir(dir_name);
7      foreach (dir_entry ∈ d) {
8        if (isdirectory(dir_entry))
9          push(dir_entry);
10       else {
11         in = open(dir_entry, RD);
12         read(in, buf);
13         write(out, buf);
14         close(in);
15       }
16     }
17   }
18   close(out);
19   return 0;
20 }
```

Fig. 1. A data flow example with both unary and binary relations

a unary property can be derived. Similarly, relationships among two arguments are supported, by inference over the observed sequences of system calls, creating constraints for the detection phase. Unary relationships include equal (the value of a given argument is always constant), elementOf (an argument can take a limited set of values), subsetOf (a generalization of elementOf, indicating that an argument can take multiple values, all of which drawn from a set), range (specifies boundaries for numeric arguments), isWithinDir (a file argument is always contained within a specified directory), hasExtension (file extensions). Binary relationships include: equal (equality between system call operands), isWithinDir (file located in a specified directory; contains is the opposite), hasSameDirAs, hasSameBaseAs, hasSameExtensionAs (two arguments have a common directory, base directory or extension, respectively).

The behavior of each application is logged by storing *Process IDentifier* (PID), *Program Counter* (PC), along with the system calls invoked, their arguments and returned value. The use of the PC to identify the states in the FSA stands out as an important difference from other approaches. The PC of each system call is determined through *stack unwinding* (i.e., going back through the activation records of the process stack until a valid PC is found). FSA-DF obviously handles process cloning and forking.

The learning algorithm is rather simple: each time a new value is found, it is checked against all the known values of the same type. Relations are inferred for each execution of the monitored program and then pruned on a "set intersection" basis. For instance, if relations R_1 and R_2 are learned from an execution trace T_1 but R_1 only is satisfied in trace T_2, the resulting model will not contain R_2. Such a process is obviously prone to false positives if the training phase is not exhaustive, because invalid relations would be kept instead of being discarded. Figure 1 shows an example (due to [2]) of the final result of this process. During detection, missing transitions or violations of properties are flagged as alerts. The detection engine keeps track of the execution over the learned FSA, comparing

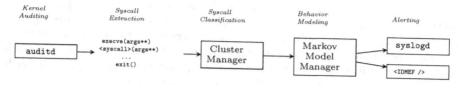

Fig. 2. The high-level architecture of our S^2A^2DE prototype

transitions and relations with what happens, and raising an alert if an edge is missing or a constraint is violated.

The FSA approach is promising and has interesting features especially in terms of detection capabilities. On the other hand, it only takes into account relationships between different types of arguments. Also, the set of properties is limited to pre-defined ones and totally deterministic. This leads to a possibly incomplete detection model potentially prone to false alerts. In Section 3 we detail how our approach improves the original FSA-DF implementation.

2.2 Markov Chains-Based Implementation

The second prototype we analyze is called S^2A^2DE (Syscall Sequence and Argument Anomaly Detection Engine) [3,5]. It exploits Markov chains to describe the behavior of a process. More specifically, S^2A^2DE analyzes processes as sequences of system calls $S = [s_1, s_2, s_3, \ldots]$. Each call s_i is characterized by a *type* (e.g. read, write, exec, etc.), a list of *arguments* (e.g., the resource path passed to open), a *return value*, and a *timestamp*. Neither the return value nor the *absolute* timestamp are taken into account.

S^2A^2DE can be decomposed in the basic blocks shown in Figure 2. During *training*, each application is profiled using a two-phase procedure applied to each type of system call separately. *Firstly*, a single-linkage, bottom-up, agglomerative, hierarchical clustering algorithm [6] is used to find sub-clusters of invocations with similar arguments. Anomaly models are created upon these clusters, and not on the specific system call, in order to better capture normality and deviations on a more compact input space. This is important because some system calls, most notably open, are used in very different ways. By exploiting effective distance models between arguments of the same type, the agglomerate system call is divided into sub-groups that are specific to a single function. For instance, invocations of open in httpd differs from those in, say, login. Afterwards, the system builds anomaly models of the parameters inside each cluster. It is important to note that the models used for computing distance (for clustering) and those used to build the "representation" of the cluster for anomaly detection are not necessarily the same. More details on how the distance are defined, and on the anomaly models used by S^2A^2DE, can be found in [3].

The *second phase* of training takes into account the execution *context* of each call to build a behavioral profile of programs flow. Markov chains are constructed on top of the various clusters output from the first phase: *one cluster* corresponds to *one state* of the chain. For instance, with three clusters for the open syscall, and two of the execve syscall, then the chain is constituted by five states: $open_1$, $open_2$, $open_3$, $execve_1$, $execve_2$. Each transition reflects the probability of passing from one of these groups to another through the program. This approach was investigated in former literature [7,8,1,9,10], but never in conjunction with the handling of parameters and with a clustering approach.

During *training*, each execution of the program in the training set is considered as a sequence of observations. Using the output of the clustering process, each syscall is classified into the correct cluster, by computing the probability value for each model and choosing the cluster whose models give out the maximum composite probability along all known models: $\max(\prod_{i \in M} P_i)$. The other probabilities are then straightforward to compute. S^2A^2DE is resistant to the presence of a limited number of outliers (e.g. abruptly terminated executions or attacks) in the training set, because the resulting transition probabilities will drop near zero. For the same reason, it is also resistant to the presence of any cluster of anomalous invocations created by the clustering phase. Therefore, the presence of a minority of attacks in the training set will not adversely affect the learning phase, which in turn does not require an attack-free training set, and thus it can be performed on the deployment machine.

At *detection* time, the cluster models are once again used to classify each syscall into the correct cluster. The probability value for each model is computed and the stored cluster whose models give out the maximum composite probability $P_c = \max(\prod_{i \in M} P_i)$ is chosen as the correct "system call class". Anomaly thresholds are built upon two probabilities, the *punctual* probability P_p and the *sequence* probability P_s. The former is $P_p = P_c \cdot P_m$, where P_c is the probability of the *system call* to belong to the best-matching cluster and P_m is the *latest transition* probability in the chain. P_s is the probability of the whole *execution sequence* to fit the whole chain. To avoid P_s to quickly reach zero for long sequences of system calls, the probability is scaled as $P_s(l) = \sqrt[2l]{\prod_{i=1}^{l} P_p(i)^i}$, where l is the sequence length).

For both the probabilities, threshold values are equal to the lowest probability over all the training dataset, for each single application, scaled through a user-defined *sensitivity* which allows to trade off between detection rate and false positive rate. A process is flagged as malicious if either P_s or $P_p = P_c \cdot P_m$ are lower than the corresponding thresholds.

3   Enhanced Detection Models

The improvements we made focus on *path* and *execution* arguments. *String length* is now modeled using a Gaussian interval as detailed in Section 3.1. The new *edge frequency* model described in Section 3.2 have been added to detect *Denial of Service* (DoS) attacks. Also, in Section 3.3 we describe how we exploited *Self Organizing Maps* (SOMs) to model the similarity among *path arguments*. The resulting system, Hybrid IDS. incorporates the models of FSA-DF and S^2A^2DE along with the aforementioned enhancements.

3.1   Arguments Length Using Gaussian Intervals

The model for system call execution arguments implemented in S^2A^2DE takes into account the minimum and maximum length of the parameters found during training, and checks whether each string parameter falls into this range (model probability 1) or not (model probability 0). This technique allows to detect common attempts of buffer overflow through the command line, for instance, as well as various other command line exploits. However, such criteria do not model "how different" two arguments are to each others; a smoother function is more desirable. Furthermore, the frequency of each argument in the training set is not taken into account at all. Last but not least, the model is not resilient to the presence of attacks in the training set; just one occurrence of a malicious string would increase the length of the maximum interval allowing argument of almost every length.

The improved version of the interval model uses a Gaussian distribution for modeling the argument length $X_{args} = |args|$, estimated from the data in terms of sample mean and sample variance. The anomaly threshold is a percentile T_{args} centered on the mean. Arguments which length is *outside* the stochastic interval are flagged as anomalous. This model is resilient to the presence of outliers in the dataset. The Gaussian distribution has been chosen since is the natural stochastic extension of a range interval for the length. An example is shown in Figure 3.

Model Validation. During detection the model self-assesses its precision by calculating the kurtosis measure [11], defined as $\gamma_X = \frac{E^4(X)}{Var(X)^2}$. Thin tailed distributions with a low peak around the mean exhibit $\gamma_X < 0$ while positive values are typical of fat tailed distributions with an acute peak. We used $\hat{\gamma}_X = \frac{\mu_{X,4}}{\sigma_X^4} - 3$ to estimate γ_X. Thus, if $\gamma_{X_{args}} < 0$ means that the sample is spread on a big interval, while positive the values indicates a less "fuzzy" set of values. It is indeed straightforward that highly negative values indicates not significant estimations as the interval would include almost all lengths. In this case, the model falls back to a simple interval.

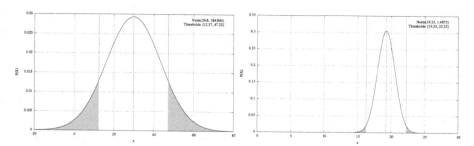

Fig. 3. Estimated Gaussian intervals for string length. Training data of `sudo` (left) and `ftp` (right) was used. $\mathcal{N}(29.8, 184.844)$, thresholds $[12.37, 47.22]$ (left) and $\mathcal{N}(19.25, 1.6875)$, thresholds $[16.25, 22.25]$ (right).

3.2   DoS Detection Using Edge Traversal Frequency

DoS attacks which force the process to get stuck in a legal section of the normal control flow could be detected by S^2A^2DE as violations of the Markov model, but not by FSA-DF. On the other hand, the statistical models implemented in S^2A^2DE are more robust but have higher *False Negative Rates* (FNR) than the deterministic detection implemented in FSA-DF. However, as already stated in Section 2.2, the cumulative probability of the traversed edges works well only with execution traces of similar and fixed length, otherwise even the rescaled score decreases to zero, generating false positives on long traces.

To solve these issues a stochastic model of the edge frequency traversal is used. For each trace of the training set, our algorithm counts the number of edge traversals (i.e., Markov model edge or FSA edge). The number is then normalized w.r.t. all the edges obtaining frequencies. Each edge is then associated to the sample $X_{edge} = x_1, x_2, \ldots$. We show that the random samples X_{edge} is well estimated using a Beta distribution. Figure 4 shows sample plots of this model estimated using the mt-daapd training set; quantiles associated to the thresholds are computed and shown as well. As we did for the Gaussian model (Section 3.1), the detection thresholds are defined at configuration time as a percentile T_{edge} centered on the mean (Figure 4). We chose the Beta for its high flexibility; a Gaussian is unsuitable to model skewed phenomena.

Model Validation. Our implementation is optimized to avoid overfitting and meaningless estimations. A model is valid only if the training set includes a significant $(|\min_i\{x_i\} - \max_i\{x_i\}| \geq \delta x_{min} = 0.04)$ amount $(N^{min}_{edge} = 6)$ of paths. Otherwise it construct a simpler frequency range model. The model exhibits the side effect of discarding the extreme values found in training and leads to erroneous decisions. More precisely, if the sample is $X_{edge} = 1, 1, \ldots, 0.9, 1$, the right boundary will never be exactly 1, and therefore legal values will be discarded. To solve this issue, the quantiles close to 1 are approximated to 1 according to a configuration parameter $\bar{X}_{cut}$. For instance, if $\bar{X}_{cut} = 3$ the quantile $F_X(\cdot) = 0.99\underline{9}$ is approximated to 1.

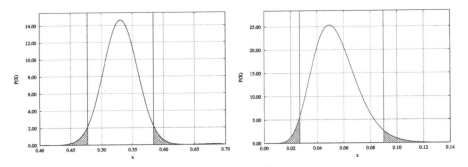

Fig. 4. Two different estimations of the edge frequency distribution. Namely, Beta(178.445,   157.866)   with   thresholds   [0.477199,   0.583649]   (left)   and Beta(10.3529,181.647) with thresholds [0.0266882, 0.0899057] (right).

3.3   Path Similarity Using Self Organizing Maps

Path argument models are already implemented in S^2A^2DE and FSA-DF. Several, general-purpose string comparison techniques have been proposed so far, especially in the field of database systems and data cleansing [12]. We propose a solution based on Symbol-SOMs [13] to define an accurate distance metric between paths. Symbol SOM implements a smooth similarity measure otherwise unachievable using common, crisp distance functions among strings (e.g., edit distance).

The technique exploits *Self Organizing Maps* (SOMs), which are unsupervised neural algorithms. A SOM produces a compressed, multidimensional representation (usually a bi-dimensional *map*) of the input space by preserving the main topological properties. It is initialized randomly, and then adapted via a competitive and cooperative learning process. At each cycle, a new input is compared to the known models, and the *Best Matching Unit* (BMU) node is selected. The BMU and its neighborhood models are then updated to make them better resemble future inputs.

We use the technique described in [14] to map *strings* onto SOMs. Formally, let $S_t = [s_t(1)\cdots s_t(L)]$ denote the t-th string over the alphabet $\mathcal{A}$ of size $|\mathcal{A}|$. Each symbol $s_t(i), i = 1\ldots L$, is then encoded into a vector $\underline{s}_t(i)$ of size $|\mathcal{A}|$ initialized with zeroes except at the w-th position which corresponds to the index of the encoded symbol (e.g., $s_t(i) = $ 'b' would be $\underline{s}_t(i) = [0\ 1\ 0\ 0 \cdots 0]^T$, $w = 2$). Thus, each string S_t is represented with sequence of L vectors like $\underline{s}_t(i)$, i.e. a $L \times |\mathcal{A}|$-matrix: $\underline{\underline{S}}_t$.

Let $\underline{\underline{S}}_t$ and $\underline{\underline{M}}_k$ denote two vector-encoded strings, where $\underline{\underline{M}}_k$ is the model associated with SOM node k. The distance between the two strings is $D'(S_t, M_k) = D(\underline{\underline{S}}_t, \underline{\underline{M}}_k)$. $D(\cdot, \cdot)$ is also defined in the case of $L_{S_t} = |S_t| \neq |M_k| = L_{M_k}$ relying on dynamic time warping techniques to find the best alignment between the two sequences before computing the distance. Without going into details, the algorithm [13] aligns the two sequences $\underline{s}_t(i) \in \underline{\underline{S}}_t, \underline{m}_k(j) \in \underline{\underline{M}}_k$ using a mapping $[\underline{s}_t(i), \underline{m}_k(j)] \mapsto [\underline{s}_t(i(p)), \underline{m}_k(j(p))]$ defined through the warping function $F : [i, j] \mapsto [i(p), j(p)]$: $F = [[i(1), j(1)], \ldots, [i(p), j(p)], \ldots, [i(P), j(P)]]$. The distance function D is defined over the warping alignment of size P, $D(\underline{\underline{S}}_t, \underline{\underline{M}}_k) = \sum_{p=1}^{P} d(i, j)$, which is $P = L_{S_t} = L_{M_k}$ if the two strings have equal lengths. $d(i, j) = d(i(p), j(p)) \| \underline{s}_t(i(p)) - \underline{m}_k(j(p)) \|$.

The distance is defined upon $g_{i,j} = g(i, j)$, the variable which stores the cumulative distance in each trellis point $(i, j) = (i(p), i(p))$. The trellis is first initialized to 0 in $(0, 0)$, to $+\infty$ for both $(0, \cdot)$ and $(\cdot, 0)$, otherwise:

$$g(i, j) = \min \begin{cases} g(i, j - 1) + d(i, j) \\ g(i - 1, j - 1) + d(i, j) \\ g(i - 1, j) + d(i, j) \end{cases}$$

Note that $i \in [1, L_{S_t}]$ and $j \in [1, L_{M_k}]$ thus the total distance is $D(\underline{\underline{S}}_t, \underline{\underline{M}}_k) = g(L_{S_t}, L_{M_k})$. A simple example of distance computation is show in Figure 5 ($\mathcal{A}$ is the English alphabet plus extra characters). The overall distance is $D'(S_t, M_k) = 8.485$. We used a symmetric Gaussian neighborhood function h whose center is

$$D(\underline{\underline{S}}_t, \underline{\underline{M}}_k) = \begin{array}{c} \\ / \\ v \\ a \\ r \\ / \\ l \\ o \\ g \end{array} \begin{pmatrix} 0 & +\infty & +\infty & +\infty & +\infty & +\infty & +\infty & +\infty \\ +\infty & 0 & 1.414 & 2.828 & 4.242 & 4.242 & 5.656 & 7.071 \\ +\infty & 1.414 & 1.414 & 2.828 & 4.242 & 5.656 & 5.656 & 7.071 \\ +\infty & 2.828 & 2.828 & 2.828 & 4.242 & 5.656 & 7.071 & 7.071 \\ +\infty & 4.242 & 5.656 & 5.656 & 5.656 & 4.242 & 5.656 & 7.071 \\ +\infty & 4.242 & 4.242 & 4.242 & 4.242 & 5.656 & 7.071 & 8.485 \\ +\infty & 5.656 & 5.656 & 7.071 & 7.071 & 5.656 & 5.656 & 7.071 \\ +\infty & 7.071 & 7.071 & 7.071 & 8.485 & 7.071 & 7.071 & 7.071 \\ +\infty & 8.485 & 8.485 & 8.485 & 8.485 & 8.485 & 8.485 & \mathbf{8.485} \end{pmatrix} \begin{array}{c} / \ b \ i \ n \ / \ s \ h \end{array}$$

Fig. 5. Distance computation example between `/bin/sh` an `/var/log`

located at the BMU $c(t)$. More precisely, $h(k, c(t), t) = \alpha(t)e^{-\frac{d(c(t),k)}{2\sigma^2(t)}}$, where $\alpha(t)$ controls the learning rate and $\sigma(t)$ is the actual width of the neighborhood function. The SOM algorithm uses *two* training cycles. During (1) *adaptation* the map is more flexible, while during (2) *tuning* the learning rate $\alpha_{(.)}$ and the width of the neighborhood $\sigma_{(.)}$ are decreased. On each phase such parameters are denoted as $\alpha_1, \alpha_2, \sigma_1, \sigma_2$.

Symbol SOMs are "plugged" into FSA-DF by associating each transition with the *set* of BMUs learned during training. At detection, an alert occurs whenever a path argument falls into neighborhood of a non-existing BMU. Similarly, in the case of S^2A^2DE, the neighborhood function is used to decide whether the string is anomalous or not, according to a proper threshold which is the minimum value of the neighborhood function encountered during training, for each node.

4   Experimental Evaluation

In this section we describe our efforts to cope with the lack of reliable testing datasets for intrusion detections. The testing methodology is here detailed along with the experiments we designed. Both detection accuracy and performance overhead are subjects of our tests.

4.1   Testing Methodology and Data Generation

Comparing and benchmarking IDSes is a well known problem [15]. Since the commonly used DARPA evaluation datasets exhibit well known shortcomings, we decided to generate a new dataset. We chose a number of recent exploits from CVE, including different types of vulnerabilities (code injections, file writes, denial of service attacks) as well as attacks that easily evade existing IDSes by slightly modifying the data flows and not the control flows. Clean training data was obtained by collecting benign system calls sequences during the normal execution of the target applications. We used attacks against `sing`, `mt-daapd`, `proftpd`, `sudo`, and `BitchX`. We refer to the vulnerabilities by their *Common Vulnerabilities Exposures* (CVE) ID.

Table 1. Parameters used to train the IDSes. Values includes the number of traces used, the amount of paths encountered and the number of paths per cycle.

	sing	mt-daapd	proftpd	sudo	BitchX	mceject	bsdtar
SOM size	15×15	15×15	15×15	15×15	10×10	15×15	15×15
Traces	18	18	18	18	14	10	240
Syscalls	5808	194879	64640	52034	103148	84	12983
Paths	2700	2700	23632	1316	14921	48	3477
Paths/cycle%	2	2	1	8	1	50	2

Specifically, sing is affected by CVE-2007-6211, a vulnerability which allows to write arbitrary text on arbitrary files by exploiting a combination of parameters. This attack is meaningful because it does not alter the control flow, but just the data flow, with an **open** which writes on unusual files. Training datasets contain traces of regular usage of the program invoked with large sets of command line options.

mt-daapd is affected by a format string vulnerability (CVE-2007-5825) in ws_-addarg(). It allows remote execution of arbitrary code by including the format specifiers in the username or password portion of the base64-encoded data on the Authorization: Basic HTTP header sent to /xml-rpc. The mod_ctrls module of proftpd let local attackers to fully control the integer regarglen (CVE-2006-6563) and exploit a stack overflow to gain root privileges.

sudo does not properly sanitize data supplied through SHELLOPTS and PS4 environment variables, which are passed on to the invoked program (CVE-2005-2959). This leads to the execution of arbitrary commands as privileged user, and it can be exploited by users who have been granted limited superuser privileges. The training set includes a number of execution of programs commonly run through sudo (e.g., passwd, adduser, editing of /etc/ files) by various users with different, limited superuser privileges, along with benign traces similar to the attacks, invoked using several permutations of option flags.

BitchX is affected by CVE-2007-3360, which allows a remote attacker to execute arbitrary commands by overfilling a hash table and injecting an EXEC hook function which receives and executes shell commands. Moreover, failed exploit attempts can cause DoS. The training set includes several IRC client sessions and a legal IRC session to a server having the same address of the malicious one.

In order to evaluate and highlight the impact of each specific model, we performed targeted tests rather than reporting general DRs and FPRs only. Also, we ensured that all possible alerts types are inspected (i.e., true/false positive/negative). In particular, for each IDS, we included one *legal* trace in which file operations are performed on files *never* seen during training but with a similar name (e.g., training on /tmp/log, testing on /tmp/log2); secondly, we inserted a trace which mimics an attack.

4.2   Comparison of Detection Accuracy

The detection accuracy of Hybrid IDS (H), FSA-DF (F) and S^2A^2DE (S) is here analyzed and compared. Both training parameters and detection results are summarized in Table 1. The parameters used to train the SOM are fixed except for $\sigma_1(t)$: $\alpha_1(t) = 0.5 \div 0.01$, $\sigma_2(t) = 3$ and $\alpha_2(t) = 0.1 \div 0.01$. Percentiles for both X_{args} and X_{edge} are detailed. The "paths/cycle%" (paths per cycle) row indicates the amount of paths arguments used for training the SOM. The settings for clustering stage of S^2A^2DE are constant: minimum number of clusters (3, or 2 in the case of the open); maximum merging distance (6, or 10 in the case of the open); the "null" and the "don't care" probability values are fixed at 0.1 and 10, respectively, while 10 is the maximum number of leaf clusters. In order to give a better understanding of how each prototype works, we analyzed by hand the detection results on each target application.

sing: Hybrid IDS is not tricked by the false positive mimic trace inserted. The Symbol SOM model recognizes the similarity of /tmp/log3 with the other paths inserted in the training. Instead, both FSA-DF and S^2A^2DE raise false alarms; the former has never seen the path during training while the latter recognizes the string in the tree path model but an alarm is raised because of threshold violation. S^2A^2DE recognizes the attack containing the longer subsequent invocations of mmap2; FSA-DF also raises a violation in the file name because it has never been trained against /etc/passwd nor /etc/shadow; and Hybrid IDS is triggered because the paths are placed in a different SOM region w.r.t. the training.

mt-daapd: The legit traces violate the binary and unary relations causing several false alarms on FSA-DF. On the other hand, the smoother path similarity model allows Hybrid IDS and S^2A^2DE to pass the test with no false positives. The changes in the control flow caused by the attacks are recognized by all the IDSes. In particular, the DoS attack (special-crafted request sent fifty times) triggers an anomaly in the edge frequency model.

proftpd: The legit trace is correctly handled by all the IDSes as well as the anomalous root shell that causes unexpected calls (setuid, setgid and execve) to be invoked. Howerver, FSA-DF flags more than 1000 benign system calls as anomalous because of temporary files path not present in the training.

sudo: Legit traces are correctly recognized by all the engines and attacks are detected without errors. S^2A^2DE fires an alert because of a missing edge in the Markov model (i.e., the unexpected execution of chown root:root script and chmod +s script). Also, the absence of the script string in the training triggers a unary relation violation in FSA-DF and a SOM violation in Hybrid IDS. The traces which mimic the attack are erroneously flagged as anomalous, because the system call sequences are *strictly* similar to the attack.

BitchX: The exploit is easily detected by all the IDSes as a control flow violation through extra execve system calls are invoked to execute injected commands. Furthermore, the Hybrid IDS anomaly engine is triggered by three edge frequency violations due to paths passed to the FSA when the attack is performed which are different w.r.t. the expected ones.

4.3   Specific Comparison of SOM-S²A²DE and S²A²DE

We also specifically tested how the introduction of a Symbol SOM improves over the original probabilistic tree used for modeling the path arguments in S^2A^2DE. As summarized in right side of Table 2, the FPR decreases in the second test. However, the first test exhibits a lower FNR as detailed in the following.

The mcweject utility is affected by a stack overflow CVE-2007-1719 caused by improper bounds checking. Root privileges can be gained if mcweject is setuid. The exploit is as easy as eject -t illegal_payload, but we performed it through userland exec [16] to make it more silent avoiding the execve that obviously triggers an alert in the S^2A^2DE for a missing edge in the Markov chain. Instead, we are interested in comparing the string models only. SOM-S^2A^2DE detects it with no issues because of the use of different "types" of paths in the opens.

An erroneous computation of a buffer length is exploited to execute code via a specially crafted PAX archives passed to bsdtar (CVE-2007-3641). A heap overflow allows to overwrite a structure pointer containing itself another pointer to a function called right after the overflow. The custom exploit [16] basically redirects that pointer to the injected shellcode. Both the original string model and the Symbol SOM models detect the attack when the unexpected special file /dev/tty is opened. However, the original model raises many false positives when significantly different paths are encountered. This situation is instead handled with no false positives by the smooth Symbol SOM model.

4.4   Performance Evaluation and Complexity Discussion

We performed both empirical measurements and theoretical analysis of the performance of the various proposed prototypes. Detection speed results are summarized in Table 3. The datasets for detection accuracy were reused: we selected

Table 2. Comparison of the FPR of S^2A^2DE vs. FSA-DF vs. Hybrid IDS and S^2A^2DE vs. SOM-S^2A^2DE. Values include the number of traces used. Accurate description of the impact of each *individual* model is in Section 4.2 (first five columns) and 4.3 (last two columns).

	sing	mt-daapd	profdtpd	sudo	BitchX	mcweject	bsdtar	
Traces	22	18	21	22	15	12	2	
Syscalls	1528	9832	18114	3157	107784	75	102	
S²A²DE	10.0%	0%	0%	10.0%	0.0%			
FSA-DS	5.0%	16.7%	28%	15.0%	0.0%	0.0%	8.7%	S²A²DE
Hybrid IDS	0.0%	0%	0%	10.0%	0.0%	0.0%	0.0%	SOM-S²A²DE

Table 3. Detection performance measured in μsec/syscall. The average speed is measured in syscall/sec (last column).

	sing	sudo	BitchX	mcweject	bsdtar	Avg. speed
System calls	3470	15308	12319	97	705	
S^2A^2DE	115.3	52.26	154.2	1030	141.8	8463
FSA-DF	374.6	97.98	97.41	-	-	7713
Hybrid IDS	7492	378.8	2167	-	-	1067
SOM-S^2A^2DE	-	-	-	90721	26950	25

the five test applications on which the IDSes performed worst. Hybrid IDS is slow because the BMU algorithm for the symbol SOM is invoked for each system call with a path argument (opens are quite frequent), slowing down the detection phase. Also, we recall that the current prototype relies on a system call interceptor based on ptrace which *introduces high runtime overheads*, as shown in [2]. To obtain better performance, an in-kernel interceptor could be used. The theoretical performance of each engine can be estimated by analyzing the bottleneck algorithm.

Complexity of FSA-DF. During training, the bottleneck is the binary relation learning algorithm. $T_F^{train} = O(S \cdot M + N)$, where M is the total number of system calls, $S = |Q|$ is the number of states of the automaton, and N is the sum of the length of all the string arguments in the training set. At detection $T_{FSA-DF}^{det} = O(M + N)$.

Assuming that each system call has $O(1)$ arguments, the training algorithm is invoked $O(M)$ times. The time complexity of each i-th iteration is $Y_i + |X_i|$, where Y_i is the time required to compute all the unary and binary relations and $|X_i|$ indicates the time required to process the $i - th$ system call X. Thus, the overall complexity is bounded by $\sum_{i=1}^{M} Y + |X_i| = M \cdot Y + \sum_{i=1}^{M} |X_i|$. The second factor $\sum_{i=1}^{M} |X_i|$ can be simplified to N because strings are represented as a tree; it can be shown [2] that the total time required to keep the longest common prefix information is bounded by the total length of all input strings. Furthermore, Y is bounded by the number of unique arguments, which in turn is bounded by S; thus, $T_F^{train} = O(S \cdot M + N)$. This also prove the time complexity of the detection algorithm which, at each state and for each input, requires unary and binary checks to be performed; thus, its cost is bounded by $M + N$. ∎

Complexity of Hybrid IDS. In the training phase, the bottleneck is the Symbol SOM creation time: $T_H^{train} = O(C \cdot D \cdot (L^2 + L))$, where C is the number of learning cycles, D is the number of nodes, and L is the maximum length of an input string. At detection time $T_H^{det} = O(M \cdot D \cdot L^2)$.

T_H^{train} depends on both the number of training cycles, the BMU algorithm and node updating. The input is randomized at each training session and a constant amount of paths is used, thus the input size is $O(1)$. The BMU algorithm depends on both the SOM size and the distance computation, bounded by $L_{input} \cdot L_{node} = L^2$, where L_{input} and L_{node} are the *lengths* of the input string and the node string, respectively. More precisely, the distance between strings is performed by comparing all the vectors representing, respectively, each character of the input string and each character of the node string. The char-by-char comparison is performed in $O(1)$ because the size of each character vector is fixed. Thus, the distance computation is bounded by $L^2 \simeq L_{input} \cdot L_{node}$. The node updating algorithm depends on both the number of nodes D, the length of the node string L_{node} and the training cycles C, hence each cycle requires $O(D \cdot (L^2 + L))$, where L is the length of the longest string. The creation of the FSA is similar to the FSA-DF training, except for the computation of the relations between strings which time is no longer $O(N)$ but it is bounded by $M \cdot D \cdot L^2$ (i.e., the time required to find the Best Matching Unit for one string). Thus, according to *Proof 1*, this phase requires $O(S \cdot M + M \cdot D \cdot L^2) < O(C \cdot D \cdot (L^2 + L))$. The detection time T_H^{det} is bounded by the BMU algorithm, that is $O(M \cdot D \cdot L^2)$. ∎

The clustering phase of **S²A²DE** is $O(N^2)$ while with **SOM-S²A²DE** it grows to $O(N^2 L^2)$.

In the worst case, the clustering algorithm used in [3] is known to be $O(N^2)$, where N is the number of system calls: the distance function is $O(1)$ and the distance matrix is searched for the two closest clusters. In the case of SOM-S²A²DE, the distance function is instead $O(L^2)$ as it requires one run of the BMU algorithm. ∎

5   Related Work

Due to space limitations we focus on the subset of literature which uses unsupervised learning algorithms for anomaly detection over system calls. We refer the reader to [17] for a more comprehensive and taxonomic review.

The first mention of intrusion detection through the analysis of the sequence of syscalls from system processes is in [18], where "normal sequences" of system calls (similar to N-grams) are considered (ignoring the parameters of each invocation). Variants of [18] have been proposed in [19,7,1]; this type of techniques can also be used a reactive, IPS-like fashion [20]. The core assumption is that intrusions generate sequences of system calls that are unusual during normal application usage. Each sequence of system calls is tokenized in substrings using a sliding window of N elements. All the substrings seen in training are stored; during detection, any N-gram never seen before raises an alarm. The precision of this method depends on the value chosen for N. A low value of N tends to generate false negatives (the worst-case scenario, $N = 1$, only checks if a system call was already seen during training).

FSA have also been used to express the language of the system calls of a program, using either deterministic [21] or non-deterministic [22] automata. The issue when using FSA is how to define the states of the machine: at the highest level of detail, each state is linked to a specific instruction of the program, while transitions are usually identified with system calls. An FSA improves over the N-gram model with better efficiency and, in addition, it does not suffer from the choice of arbitrary parameter N.

A static analysis approach to extract a call graph was proposed in [23]. Giffin et al. [24] developed a different version of this approach, based on the analysis of the binaries, integrating the execution environment as a model constraint. However, static analysis approaches such as these follow all possible execution paths, therefore they are conservative and may include additional, extraneous control flows; they may also leave more way for mimicry attacks. On the other hand, automatically generating a compact FSA representation from system call traces is not an easy task. A similar method [25] uses pushdown automata to enrich the model with a "stack" structure, which is used to choose each next transition to take, and can be manipulated as part of the transition. In Section 2.1 we described more in depth an IDS based on this approach [2] which uses the program counter to define states and syscalls as transitions, but complements them with *dataflow* information. However, all these methods suffer from an inherent brittleness: if the training is insufficient, a number of false positives could be generated because the models are extremely narrow. The use of *Hidden Markov Models* (HMMs) has also been proposed to model sequences of system calls [9]. In [26] HMMs are compared with the models used in [19,20] and shown to perform considerably better, even if with an added computational overhead; unfortunately, the datasets used for the comparative evaluation are no longer available for comparison. Using Markov chains instead of hidden models decreases this overhead, as observed in [27]. In [28] HMMs are observed to perform considerably better than FSA and similar models. The main difference of these models stochastic part: the transitions are not deterministic but linked to a probability and this could allow a reduction of the FPR. In Section 2.2 we analyzed S^2A^2DE [3], a HIDS based on this approach, but which complements it with anomaly models built on syscall arguments.

The two systems analyzed in Section 2 also take into account the parameters of the system calls. Even if this is an inherently complex task, it has been already proven to yield a lot of potential. For instance, mimicry attacks [29] can evade the detection of syscall sequence anomalies, but it is much harder to devise ways to cheat both the analysis of sequence and arguments. Besides the ones we discuss in the following, two other recent research works focused on this problem. Another example is [30] in which a number of models are introduced to deal with the most common arguments, even if without caring for the sequence of system calls. In [31] the LERAD algorithm (Learning Rules for Anomaly Detection) is used to mine rules expressing "normal" values of arguments, normal sequences of system calls, or both. However, no relationship among the values of different arguments is learned; sequences and argument values are handled separately; the evaluation is quite poor however, and uses non-standard metrics.

6   Conclusions

We have presented two alternative, state-of-the-art approaches for anomaly detection over system call sequences and arguments: a deterministic IDS which builds an FSA model complemented by a network of dataflow relationships among the system call arguments (which we nicknamed FSA-DF), and a prototype named S^2A^2DE which builds a Markov chain of the system calls, complementing it with several models for detecting anomalies in the parameters and clustering system calls according to their content. We showed how the model for system call execution arguments implemented in S^2A^2DE can be improved by using better statistical models. We also proposed a new model for counting the frequency of traversal of edges on the FSA prototype, to make it able to detect denial-of-service attacks. Both systems needed an improved model for string (path) similarity. We adapted the Symbol SOM algorithm to make it suitable for computing a "distance" between two paths. We believe that this is the core contribution of the work.

We tested and compared the original prototypes with an hybrid solution where the Symbol SOM and the edge traversal models are applied to the FSA, and a version of S^2A^2DE enhanced with the Symbol SOM and the correction to the execution arguments model. Both the new prototypes have the *same* detection rates of the original ones, but significantly *lower* false positive rates. This is paid in terms of a non-negligible limit to detection speed, at least in our proof of concept implementation.

Future extensions of this work will re-engineer the prototypes to use an in-kernel system call interceptor, and generically improve their performance. We are studying how to speed up the Symbol SOM node search algorithm, in order to bring the throughput to a rate suitable for online use.

References

1. Hofmeyr, S.A., Forrest, S., Somayaji, A.: Intrusion detection using sequences of system calls. Journal of Computer Security 6(3), 151–180 (1998)
2. Bhatkar, S., Chaturvedi, A., Sekar, R.: Dataflow anomaly detection. In: IEEE Symposium on Security and Privacy, May 2006, pp. 15–62 (May 2006)
3. Maggi, F., Matteucci, M., Zanero, S.: Detecting intrusions through system call sequence and argument analysis. IEEE Transactions on Dependable and Secure Computing (accepted for publication)
4. Sharif, M.I., Singh, K., Giffin, J.T., Lee, W.: Understanding precision in host based intrusion detection. In: Kruegel, C., Lippmann, R., Clark, A. (eds.) RAID 2007. LNCS, vol. 4637, pp. 21–41. Springer, Heidelberg (2007)
5. Zanero, S.: Unsupervised Learning Algorithms for Intrusion Detection. PhD thesis, Politecnico di Milano T.U., Milano, Italy (May 2006)
6. Han, J., Kamber, M.: Data Mining: concepts and techniques. Morgan-Kauffman, San Francisco (2000)
7. Cabrera, J.B.D., Lewis, L., Mehara, R.: Detection and classification of intrusion and faults using sequences of system calls. ACM SIGMOD Record 30(4) (2001)

8. Casas-Garriga, G., Díaz, P., Balcázar, J.: ISSA: An integrated system for sequence analysis. Technical Report DELIS-TR-0103, Universitat Paderborn (2005)

9. Ourston, D., Matzner, S., Stump, W., Hopkins, B.: Applications of hidden markov models to detecting multi-stage network attacks. In: HICSS, p. 334 (2003)

10. Jha, S., Tan, K., Maxion, R.A.: Markov chains, classifiers, and intrusion detection. In: Proceedings of the 14th IEEE Workshop on Computer Security Foundations (CSFW 2001), Washington, DC, USA, June 2001, pp. 206–219. IEEE Computer Society Press, Los Alamitos (2001)

11. Joanes, D., Gill, C.: Comparing Measures of Sample Skewness and Kurtosis. The Statistician 47(1), 183–189 (1998)

12. Elmagarmid, A., Ipeirotis, P., Verykios, V.: Duplicate Record Detection: A Survey. IEEE Transactions on Knowledge and Data Engineering 19(1), 1–16 (2007)

13. Somervuo, P.J.: Online algorithm for the self-organizing map of symbol strings. Neural Netw. 17(8-9), 1231–1239 (2004)

14. Kohonen, T., Somervuo, P.: Self-organizing maps of symbol strings. Neurocomputing 21(1-3), 19–30 (1998)

15. Zanero, S.: Flaws and frauds in the evaluation of IDS/IPS technologies. In: Proc. of FIRST 2007 - Forum of Incident Response and Security Teams, Sevilla, Spain (June 2007)

16. Maggi, F., Zanero, S., Iozzo, V.: Seeing the invisible - forensic uses of anomaly detection and machine learning. ACM Operating Systems Review (April 2008)

17. Bace, R.G.: Intrusion detection. Macmillan Publishing Co., Inc., Indianapolis (2000)

18. Forrest, S., Hofmeyr, S.A., Somayaji, A., Longstaff, T.A.: A sense of self for Unix processes. In: Proceedings of the 1996 IEEE Symposium on Security and Privacy, Washington, DC, USA. IEEE Computer Society, Los Alamitos (1996)

19. Forrest, S., Perelson, A.S., Allen, L., Cherukuri, R.: Self-nonself discrimination in a computer. In: SP 1994: Proceedings of the 1994 IEEE Symposium on Security and Privacy, Washington, DC, USA, p. 202. IEEE Computer Society, Los Alamitos (1994)

20. Somayaji, A., Forrest, S.: Automated response using system–call delays. In: Proceedings of the 9th USENIX Security Symposium, Denver, CO (August 2000)

21. Michael, C.C., Ghosh, A.: Simple, state-based approaches to program-based anomaly detection. ACM Trans. Inf. Syst. Secur. 5(3), 203–237 (2002)

22. Sekar, R., Bendre, M., Dhurjati, D., Bollineni, P.: A fast automaton-based method for detecting anomalous program behaviors. In: Proceedings of the 2001 IEEE Symposium on Security and Privacy, Washington, DC, USA. IEEE Computer Society Press, Los Alamitos (2001)

23. Wagner, D., Dean, D.: Intrusion detection via static analysis. In: SP 2001: Proceedings of the 2001 IEEE Symposium on Security and Privacy, Washington, DC, USA, pp. 156–168. IEEE Computer Society Press, Los Alamitos (2001)

24. Giffin, J.T., Dagon, D., Jha, S., Lee, W., Miller, B.P.: Environment-sensitive intrusion detection. In: Valdes, A., Zamboni, D. (eds.) RAID 2005. LNCS, vol. 3858, pp. 185–206. Springer, Heidelberg (2006)

25. Feng, H., Kolesnikov, O., Fogla, P., Lee, W., Gong, W.: Anomaly detection using call stack information. In: Proceedings. 2003 Symposium on Security and Privacy, 2003, May 11-14, pp. 62–75 (2003)

26. Warrender, C., Forrest, S., Pearlmutter, B.A.: Detecting intrusions using system calls: Alternative data models. In: IEEE Symposium on Security and Privacy, pp. 133–145 (1999)

27. Jha, S., Tan, K., Maxion, R.A.: Markov chains, classifiers, and intrusion detection. In: CSFW 2001: Proceedings of the 14th IEEE Workshop on Computer Security Foundations, pp. 206–219. IEEE Computer Society, Washington (2001)

28. Yeung, D.Y., Ding, Y.: Host-based intrusion detection using dynamic and static behavioral models. Pattern Recognition 36, 229–243 (2003)

29. Wagner, D., Soto, P.: Mimicry attacks on host-based intrusion detection systems. In: CCS 2002: Proceedings of the 9th ACM conference on Computer and communications security, pp. 255–264. ACM, New York (2002)

30. Krügel, C., Mutz, D., Valeur, F., Vigna, G.: On the detection of anomalous system call arguments. In: Snekkenes, E., Gollmann, D. (eds.) ESORICS 2003. LNCS, vol. 2808, pp. 326–343. Springer, Heidelberg (2003)

31. Tandon, G., Chan, P.: Learning rules from system call arguments and sequences for anomaly detection. In: ICDM Workshop on Data Mining for Computer Security (DMSEC), pp. 20–29 (2003)

Author Index